International Claims:
Postwar French Practice

The Procedural Aspects of International Law Series

RICHARD B. LILLICH, *editor*

1. International Claims: Their Adjudication by
National Commissions
RICHARD B. LILLICH (1962)

2. International Claims: Their Preparation
and Presentation
RICHARD B. LILLICH and GORDON A. CHRISTENSON (1962)

3. The Role of Domestic Courts in the
International Legal Order
RICHARD A. FALK (1964)

4. The Use of Experts by International Tribunals
GILLIAN M. WHITE (1965)

5. The Protection of Foreign Investment:
Six Procedural Studies
RICHARD B. LILLICH (1965)

6. International Claims: Postwar British Practice
RICHARD B. LILLICH (1967)

7. Law-Making in the International
Civil Aviation Organization
THOMAS BUERGENTHAL (1969)

8. UN Protection of Civil and Political Rights
JOHN CAREY (1970)

International Claims: Postwar French Practice

BURNS H. WESTON

SYRACUSE UNIVERSITY PRESS

Standard Book Number 8156–2153–1

Library of Congress Catalog Card: 79–134507

Copyright © 1971 by the Procedural Aspects of
International Law Institute, Inc.
New York, New York

FIRST EDITION 1971

Manufactured in the United States of America

Editor's Foreword

This book, the ninth volume in the Procedural Aspects of International Law Series prepared by the Procedural Aspects of International Law Institute and published by Syracuse University Press, is the second of five studies which will be produced by the Institute's research project on "International Procedures to Protect Private Rights." This project, funded by a $160,000 grant from the Ford Foundation, has involved a four-year examination of a select number of procedural problems in three separate but interrelated areas: human rights; property rights; and, in a more limited sense, procedural rights (of aliens before national tribunals). The author of the present study, Professor Burns H. Weston of The University of Iowa College of Law, has spent the past three years working as a Research Fellow on this project in the property rights area. Having written several lengthy law review articles of note during this period, he now has produced his first full-length book, an important companion volume both to earlier studies in this Series, especially *International Claims: Postwar British Practice* (1967), and to subsequent studies such as Professor Isi Foighel's forthcoming *International Claims: Postwar Danish Practice*. These works, as the author remarks in his Preface, "when taken together, [will] begin to extrapolate a modern 'Law of International Claims' that has global significance" (p. xiii).

In view of the present sad state of international arbitration, the need for case studies of the postwar claims practice of leading countries should be self-evident. "Whereas *ad hoc* international claims commissions or mixed arbitral tribunals once provided a fairly frequent alternative to unilateral response," Professor Weston rightly observes that "today they perform a redressive role that is hardly significant, with the result that they are no longer the relatively rich source of norm articulation and clarification that they once were" (pp. 6–7). They have been replaced, in large measure, by the lump sum settlement-national claims commission device, whereby a claimant country accepts a lump sum from a respondent country in settlement of a large number of the claims of its nationals and then entrusts the distribution thereof to a commission established pursuant to its own domestic legislation. To date, save for the studies of American and British practice that have appeared in this Series, the decisions of the national commissions of other countries have received nothing like the attention they deserve. Surely this state of affairs is unfortunate. As the author indicates, "to overlook the practice of national claims commissions—to abstain from clarifying a normative synthesis from country to country—is to deny a growing edge of international law. Worse, it is to maintain a 'Law of International Claims' that has little more than historic interest and, so, small prospect of shaping the more stable world order that we all seek today" (p. 7).

This monograph, then, is a significant contribution toward the needed synthesis of the decisions of national claims commissions. It focuses, as its title implies, upon eight such commissions established by France since 1945 to distribute funds received by that country under settlement agreements with six East European countries plus Cuba and Egypt. The decisions of these commissions, like the minutes of adjudication of the British Foreign Compensation Commission, never have been published, and the French legal literature on their role in the international legal process is almost nonexistent. Two summers of painstaking research in France, during which Professor Weston examined and translated literally thousands of commission decisions and interviewed scores of government functionaries and private practitioners, were required before the author could begin to synthesize his findings and marshall his data to reach his general conclusion that "the decisions of the commissions ordinarily have been consistent with what is said to be customary international law, as well as with comparative American and British practice" (p. 189). The end product, obviously the result of prodigious effort by a meticulous scholar over a period of many months, is an exhaustively documented volume that should remain the "last word" on French international claims practice for many years to come.

The book, however, is no mere description of commission procedures and rulings. When the occasion warrants it, the author compares French with contemporary American and British practice as well as customary international law. Throughout the volume, but especially in Part IV, he criticizes French practice in a fair and impartial fashion. Moreover, he frequently steps back from the material at hand to offer, however tentatively at times, theoretical generalizations. Viewing national commissions as "decision-making agents of the international legal order" (p. 183), an international legal order "constituted mainly on a horizontal basis with minimal centralized or hierarchical command and enforcement structures" (p. 1), he rightly regards them "as an indispensable part of that vast process of claim and counterclaim through which our international legal order is maintained"(pp. 3–4). Hence, while scrutinizing the decisions of French national commissions in minute detail, he always evaluates their jurisprudential worth, and indeed the worth of the commission device itself, against the backdrop of the existing international legal order of which they are a part.

Finally, one unusual feature of this study requires special mention. As befits an international lawyer who, after receiving an A.B. from Oberlin College, took his LL.B. and J.S.D. at the Yale Law School, Professor Weston is a follower of the "policy-oriented" and "configurative" school of jurisprudence. Thus his frequent invocation of "meta-McDougal" phraseology, now understandable to most lawyers in the United States, may cause readers abroad, especially ones to whom English is a second language, some initial difficulties. Additionally, rejecting the standard organization of the "Law of International Claims" common since Borchard, the author has structured his monograph according to the dictates of the "policy-science" school, with the result that according to traditional lights many matters are taken up in a different place and frequently in a different context than one would expect. In most cases, however, a descriptive Table of Contents, coupled with an extensive Index, should guide the casual reader or the harried researcher directly to the topic that interests him. The possible hazards of specialized language and innovative organization, in any event, are a small price to pay for a book so rich in material and so rewarding in insights as is this volume.

RICHARD B. LILLICH

Charlottesville, Virginia
October, 1970

Preface

In the midst of mounting domestic and global crisis, a book about postwar French international claims practice can seem irrelevant. Indochina, the Arab-Israeli conflict, MIRVs in North Dakota, environmental pollution, racial discord, campus unrest—arguably these and other symptoms of fundamental disharmony are more deserving of attention, scholarly and otherwise. As implied, I have myself been deeply distracted by them. But there lies more behind the writing of this volume, I hasten to add, than first meets the eye: a long-standing concern for the development of the Third World and for the need, more pressing than generally is realized, to reconcile this development with the oftentimes conflicting priorities of the Industrialized World. The connection, I concede, is not immediately apparent.

For several years now, beginning as a student under the nimble and sage counsel of Professor Myres S. McDougal of the Yale Law School, I have been working to clarify how international law does and should regulate the nationalization and other taking of private foreign business and property (to be the subject of a treatise tentatively entitled *International Law and the Deprivation of Foreign Wealth*). The urgency of this inquiry lies in the fact that assaults upon private foreign wealth today enjoy their primary appeal, by no means wholly unwarranted, precisely in those regions of the globe where certain of the effects of such measures—*i.e.*, such growth-inhibiting consequences as deterrence of foreign investment, retaliatory aid and trade restrictions, even open hostilities (as in Suez and Cuba)—can least be afforded: the developing Third World. To be sure, there exists no universal one-to-one correlation between developmental retardation and the exercise of deprivative power. Still, a correlation there is, and if the ever-widening gap between the "haves" and the "have-nots" is ever significantly to be narrowed, since for political and other reasons there are not sufficient public funds to meet the needs of economic growth on a global scale, it is mandatory that conflicting demands for protection of private foreign investment, on the one hand, and for economic self-determination, on the other, be authoritatively and effectively restricted to the minimum that is reasonably necessary to secure common goals.

For the most part, however, international law scholarship has failed to contribute very much to this end. Over and over again, suggesting adherence to a highly restricted conception of international legal process, near-total reliance has been placed upon the decisions and decision-making institutions of a bygone era, and this, in turn, has tended to divert attention both from contemporary decision and policy and from evolving modes of norm prescription and application. Of course, past trends in decision and decision process are not without fundamental importance. History, like other conditioning factors, shapes present-day perspectives and for this reason alone requires always to be taken into account. Nevertheless, as I began my general inquiry into how international law regulates the taking of foreign property, it fast became clear that to avoid the pitfalls of past scholarship, or in any event to approach relevance to the problems posed by the deprivation-prone Third World, I would have to explore thoroughly the diplomatic and arbitral decisions that have resulted from that essentially post-1945 phenomenon we call the lump sum settlement–national claims commission device through which the vast majority of nationalization and related international claims have been resolved since World War II. Replacing in importance the contributions of the prewar *ad hoc* international claims commissions, the jurisprudence that emerges from these modern-day decisions reflects probably more accurately than anything else the norms of State responsibility that do now in fact prevail between investing and taking nations, including, of course, the developed and underdeveloped worlds. Manifestly, if present Third World demands are ever to be reconciled realistically with those of the Industrialized World, these prevailing norms, as realities of the contemporary scene which condition deprivative behavior and responses thereto, must be brought to light.

Hence this study of postwar French lump sum settlement–national claims commission practice. While obviously not an analysis of lump sum settlement–national claims commission practice world-wide (nor even of the entirety of French activity in this regard, being based on information available only up to August 1969), nonetheless it joins on the shelf of the Procedural Aspects of International Law Institute, my sponsor, several prior studies of equivalent American and British practice which, when taken together, begin to extrapolate a modern "Law of International Claims" that has global significance. Moreover, whenever possible, I have tried to highlight the principal comparisons that are to be drawn with the American and British approaches to the field. Two additional works to be published in this Series should expand the coverage markedly: *International Claims: Their Settlement by Lump Sum Agreements*, an analysis of the first half of the lump sum settlement–national claims commission device which I am co-authoring with Professor Richard B. Lillich of The University of Virginia; and *International Claims: Postwar Danish Practice*, a companion to this volume and to the others mentioned above.

Needless to say, this study, offshoots of which have appeared in 43 *Indiana Law Journal* 832 (1968) and 10 *Virginia Journal of International Law* 223 (1970), could not have been undertaken, let alone completed, without the encouragement and assistance of a great number of people. Special appreciation is extended to M. Pierre d'Huart and M. Léonce Calvy, respectively present and former directors of the *Service des Biens et Intérêts Privés, Ministère des Affaires Étrangères*, without whose official permission and gracious cooperation the study would have been impossible. Others who helped greatly were M. André Ernest-Picard, Director of the *Association Nationale des Porteurs Français de Valeurs Mobilières;* MM. Maurice Richard and Henri Glaser, respectively President and Secretary General of the *Association Pour la Sauvegarde et l'Expansion des Biens et Intérêts Français à l'Étranger;* M. Jacques Piguet, President and Director General of the *Office Juridique Français et International;* and M. Roger Branche, M. Charles Claudon, and Mlle. Jacqueline Drion, officials of the *Secrétariats des Commissions de Répartition des Indemnités de Nationalisation, Ministère des Affaires Étrangères*. Thanks are due also to Yale law professors Harold D. Lasswell, Leon Lipson, and Myres S. McDougal for their generous reading of the manuscript in its original

J.S.D. dissertation form and to my former research assistants, Mr. James K. Freeland, Miss Michelle F. Hopkins, and Mr. Roger P. Smith, who cheerfully withstood my constant harassments. Above all, however, I want to express my deep-felt thanks to three special people: M. Jean-François Dervieu, Deputy Director of the *Service des Biens et Intérêts Privés, Ministère des Affaires Étrangères,* for help and friendship that went far beyond what I had a right to expect; my good friend Professor Richard B. Lillich, Director of the Procedural Aspects of International Law Institute, for invaluable inspiration and ever wise and tactful guidance; and my wife, for steady expert criticism and loving support.

Also vital to the completion of this study was the financial support I received primarily from the Procedural Aspects of International Law Institute and secondarily from the College of Law and the Graduate College of The University of Iowa. Indispensable, too, were the office facilities and miscellaneous personal services that were freely extended by the *Centre Universitaire International* of the University of Paris where I made my headquarters during September 1967 and the summers of 1968 and 1969. For these contributions as well, I wish to record my wholehearted appreciation.

Of course, despite all the assistance that I have received, I alone bear full responsibility for the content of this volume, including all translations which, unless otherwise indicated, are mine.

BURNS H. WESTON

Iowa City, Iowa
July 1, 1970

Contents

xiii

International Claims:
Postwar French Practice

Part I

Introduction

The international legal order is today constituted, as in the past, mainly on a horizontal basis. Compared to domestic legal systems, it has minimal centralized or hierarchical command and enforcement structures. And where such structures do exist—judicial or parliamentary, global or regional, permanent or *ad hoc*—generally they are hampered by well-known limitations upon jurisdiction and access. In short, however much traditional notions about sovereignty and nationalism may be on the wane, the nation-state remains the primary repository of international legal authority and control, with most effective decisions being taken on a government-to-government plane among formally separate and equal bodies-politic.

Perhaps we need not remind ourselves of this basic horizontalism. It is, after all, easily observable (at least in terms of the foregoing crude approximation). But it merits recollection nevertheless because for many—most notably the "analytical" and "neo-realist" schools of jurisprudence—it simply bespeaks of no international legal order at all, or at best of a legal order that has only slight influence over the transnational affairs of man.[1] "Law" requires centralization of authority and control, so the popular wisdom runs, "morality" does not. The international system can boast little or none of this centralization. Therefore international law is but a euphemism for the morality that actually tempers the treacherous domain of international relations. If international law is to be more reality than illusion—that is, if we are to progress beyond mere wishful thinking—then centralized or hierarchical structures akin

---

[1] For "analytical" thinking, see *e.g.* H. HART, THE CONCEPT OF LAW 208–31 (1961). For "neo-realist" thinking, see *e.g.* G. KENNAN, AMERICAN DIPLOMACY 1900–1950, at 95–96 (1951); H. MORGENTHAU, POLITICS AMONG NATIONS 249–52 (2d ed. 1956). For an assessment of these and other "schools" from the standpoint of a "policy-oriented" and "configurative" jurisprudence, see McDougal, Lasswell, & Reisman, *Theories About International Law: Prologue to a Configurative Jurisprudence*, 8 VA. J. INT'L L. 188 (1968). *See also* McDougal, *Law and Power*, 46 AM. J. INT'L L. 102 (1952).

to those found in our vertical domestic orders must be established and developed. Or as Percy Corbett has put it, "the future of international law is one with the future of international organization. Concretely, this means that progress towards clarity and effectiveness in a supranational legal order will depend less upon the formulation and reformulation of general principles, or upon codification, than upon arrangements for the supranational administration of specific common interests."[2] In other words, to borrow from Richard Falk, "[m]ere *characteristics* of the domestic model are transformed into *prerequisites* for international order," and this "compels one to identify progress in the stabilization of international relations exclusively with centralizations of authority and power."[3] Ineluctably, with its correlative exaggeration of the role of force at the expense of authority in regulating human behavior, this centralist perspective generates a self-fulfilling cynicism about international law. Likewise, it raises doubts about the efforts of persons who, like this writer, would distill international legal significance from the practice of domestic decision-making institutions.

But surely these efforts are not in vain. For the trouble with the popular wisdom is that it fundamentally misconceives the nature of the international legal order, and in so doing erodes, if it does not deny altogether, the very real legitimacy that horizontal decision-making can and does have for the maintenance and growth of world public order.[4] A proper conception—one which neither despairs at, nor rejoices over, the existing horizontalism—would look upon international law in functional rather than structural terms, as a configurative *process* of authoritative and controlling decision whose many outcomes (what we call "law") evolve from, and in turn support, a medley of command and enforcement structures *both internal and external to nation-states*.[5] International law is not, as the "dual-

---

[2] P. CORBETT, LAW AND SOCIETY IN THE RELATIONS OF STATES 12–13 (1951).

[3] R. FALK, THE ROLE OF DOMESTIC COURTS IN THE INTERNATIONAL LEGAL ORDER 23 (1964).

[4] *See id.* for an incisive (and influential) discussion concerning this question, especially as regards the arguable limitations upon domestic courts in resolving world order controversies. For an indication of some of the difficulties that this writer has with some of Falk's views, see Weston, *Special Book Review—L'Affaire Sabbatino: A Wistful Review*, 55 KY. L. J. 844, 853–57 (1967), reviewing E. MOONEY, FOREIGN SEIZURES: SABBATINO AND THE ACT OF STATE DOCTRINE (1967).

[5] On how this world process of decision is constituted, see McDougal, Lasswell, &

ists" contend, a body of rules distinct and separate from domestic norms, the twain rarely meeting.[6] Nor is it, surely, a unitary system, as the "monists" would have us believe, with international law assuming a primary posture in relation to national law.[7] Rather, as Myres McDougal has insightfully observed, international law represents

> the reciprocal impact or interaction, in the world of operations as well as of words, of interpenetrating processes of international and national authority and control. The relevant hierarchies, if hierarchies are relevant, are not of rules but of entire social and power processes . . . of varying degrees of comprehension (global, hemispheric, regional, national, local), with the more comprehensive affecting "inward" or "downward" the less comprehensive, and the latter in turn affecting "outward" or "upward" the former. The metaphor of "nesting" tables or cups might be apt if such tables and cups could be conceived as being in process of constant interaction and change.[8]

Thus, hardly proof of world anarchy, the commonplace making of relatively unilateral world order decisions by national officials—not a wholly felicitous arrangement to be sure—may be seen as an indispensable part of that vast process of claim and counterclaim

Reisman, *The World Constitutive Process of Authoritative Decision*, in 1 THE FUTURE OF THE INTERNATIONAL LEGAL ORDER 73 (R. FALK & C. BLACK eds. 1969).

[6] A concise expression of the "dualist" conception is given by Lassa Oppenheim: "International Law and Municipal Law are in fact two totally and essentially different bodies of law which have nothing in common except that they are both branches—but separate branches—of the tree of law. Of course, it is possible for the Municipal Law of an individual state by custom or by statute to adopt rules of International Law as part of the law of the land, and then the respective rules of International Law become *ipso facto* rules of Municipal Law." Introduction to C. PICCIOTTO, RELATION OF INTERNATIONAL LAW TO THE LAW OF ENGLAND AND THE UNITED STATES 10 (1915).

[7] A concise expression of the "monist" conception is given by Josef Kunz: "The primacy of the Law of Nations means the supraordination of the international juridical order to the municipal juridical orders of the single States, means that the 'sovereign States' are delegated partial juridical orders of the international juridical order, means that the pyramid of the law does not end with the basic norm of the juridical order of a given single state, but at the top of the pyramid of law stands the international juridical order." *The "Vienna School" and International Law*, 11 N.Y.U.L.Q. REV. 370, 402 (1934). *See also* H. KELSEN, PRINCIPLES OF INTERNATIONAL LAW 551–88 (2d ed. R. Tucker 1966).

[8] McDougal, *The Impact of International Law Upon National Law: A Policy-Oriented Perspective*, in M. MCDOUGAL & ASSOCIATES, STUDIES IN WORLD PUBLIC ORDER at 157, 171 (1960).

through which our international legal order is maintained. From this perspective, one surely not lost upon students of "the conflict of laws" (or "private international law"),[9] clarification of the decisions of domestic institutions (insofar as they have world order relevance) is altogether justified—indeed, required! Placed side by side, as by definition horizontalism dictates, these decisions, from country to country, help form over time that synthesis which is in large measure what we today call international law.

This study, in keeping with the above perspective, is intended as a modest contribution towards this synthesis. It concerns primarily the practice of eight French claims commissions ("commissions spéciales de répartition") established by the French Government since World War II to distribute lump sums transferred to France (pursuant to agreement and in exchange for the release of outstanding claims) by Poland, Czechoslovakia, Hungary, Yugoslavia, Bulgaria, Romania, the United Arab Republic (Egypt), and most recently Cuba, for the purpose of compensating mainly French property interests damaged, destroyed or divested by nationalization and other deprivation measures taken in those countries.[10] As such,

[9] See Katzenbach, Conflicts on an Unruly Horse: Reciprocal Claims and Tolerances in Interstate and International Law, 65 YALE L. J. 1087 (1956).

[10] This is not to say that only eight distribution commissions have been established by France since World War II. Supplementing the eight whose practice is the subject of this study have been two others: (1) the now defunct Commission spéciale pour l'indemnisation des dommages de guerre français à l'étranger, which was constituted by Decree No. 55-1659 of December 20, 1955, [1955] J.O. 12484, to distribute sums to French nationals who had suffered war damage abroad; and (2) the continuing Commission spéciale des dommages de guerre français à l'étranger chargée de la répartition de la somme reçue de la République fédérale d'Allemagne au titre de l'accord franco-allemand du 27 juillet 1961 which, as its title indicates in part, is the above-noted war damage commission restructured (by Decree No. 63-359 of April 9, 1963, [1933] J.O. 3367) to distribute 11 million deutschmarks that West Germany has paid to France under an Exchange of Letters dated July 27, 1961, [1963] J.O. 3367, in final settlement of certain outstanding prewar debt claims held by French nationals against Germany.

Because the sums given for distribution to the first of these commissions were made available by French governmental appropriation rather than by international agreement, and because the second commission has been obliged to apply primarily West German domestic legislation rather than the Franco-German "treaty," the practice of both commissions may be held to be outside the scope of this particular study. Where appropriate, however, references to some of the rules that have regulated the practice of the second commission (hereinafter usually called "the 1961 German Commission" by virtue of the date and name of its controlling settlement agreement) will be noted. For details concerning the operations of the first commission, see Rapport sur les travaux de la commission spéciale pour l'indemnisation

it seeks to clarify the *combined* diplomatic-arbitral decisions that are explicitly and implicitly embodied in the rulings of these commissions and thereby to complement similar recent studies of the United States Foreign Claims Settlement Commission[11] and the British Foreign Compensation Commission,[12] as well as one other study now in progress concerning equivalent Danish practice.[13] In addition, in quest of horizontal synthesis, it recommends a technique through which "the Law of International Claims" can be rewardingly approached.

Of course, there are built-in limitations to any study which, like this one, has had to rely for information near-exclusively on officials charged with upholding governmental disclosure policies. One in particular stands out in this instance, however, and since potentially it threatens the accuracy of this survey as a contribution to horizontal synthesis it requires that it be recalled throughout. Simply, but regrettably, this work does not illuminate all the facts upon which the decisions of the eight French commissions have been premised—for example, the extent to which claimants have acted in good faith. Partly this is due to the decisions having been reported in the inimitable Spartan style that ordinarily characterizes civil law opinions. Also it is due to the near-total absence of scholarly discussion about the issues involved, doubtless a product of the French Government's unhappy refusal to publish the decisions.[14] On final anal-

---

des dommages de guerre français à l'étranger (unpublished mimeo., c. 1960), undersigned "Le Président de la Commission Spéciale, Guy Perier de Feral, Conseiller d'État." For details concerning some of the problems which the 1961 German Commission has been obliged to consider, see its *Procés-Verbal* of May 15, 1963 (unpublished mimeo.).

[11] *See* R. LILLICH, INTERNATIONAL CLAIMS: THEIR ADJUDICATION BY NATIONAL COMMISSIONS (1962) [hereinafter cited as "LILLICH (U.S.)"]; R. LILLICH & G. CHRISTENSON, INTERNATIONAL CLAIMS: THEIR PREPARATION AND PRESENTATION (1962) [hereinafter cited as "LILLICH & CHRISTENSON"]. Recent United States practice is to be the subject of a forthcoming treatise by Lillich tentatively entitled THE JURISPRUDENCE OF THE FOREIGN CLAIMS SETTLEMENT COMMISSION OF THE UNITED STATES.

[12] *See* R. LILLICH, INTERNATIONAL CLAIMS: POSTWAR BRITISH PRACTICE (1967) [hereinafter cited as "LILLICH (G.B.)"]. For a critique and synoptic account of this study, see Weston, *Book Review*, 19 SYRACUSE L. REV. 196 (1967).

[13] *See* I. FOIGHEL, INTERNATIONAL CLAIMS: POSTWAR DANISH PRACTICE, to be published by the Syracuse University Press. *See*, however, I. FOIGHEL, NATIONALIZATION AND COMPENSATION 284–87 (1964).

[14] Although French practice compares unfavorably with United States practice in this respect, it may be noted that the British Foreign Compensation Commission also has refused to publish its decisions. For criticisms of the British refusal, see LILLICH

ysis, however, it is due to a probably genuine (but in this writer's view excessive) concern for claimant privacy, the practical effect of which has been to deny access to a number of probative documents that are to be found in each claimant "dossier" on file with the French Foreign Ministry.[15] Whether or not this concern is fully justified is of course a matter about which reasonable men may differ. According to persons who have had occasion to deal with the French commissions from outside of government, the concern is not wholly genuine. Some attribute the commissions' non-disclosures less to the possibility that claimant privacy may be unduly invaded than to a bureaucratic mentality that prefers anonymity and therefore fears responsibility for individual discretion.[16] Whatever the proper interpretation, however, in fact this concern has been a limiting force. Naturally, one hopes to have caught sufficiently the spirit of French commission practice to prevent its being a major one.

Despite this and other possible limitations, however, the study still is required. Whereas *ad hoc* international claims commissions or mixed arbitral tribunals once provided a fairly frequent alternative to unilateral response, today they perform a redressive role that

---

(G.B.) 15–16, 142. For criticisms of the French refusal, see text at Part IV, notes 3–6.

[15] Reference is made, in particular, to (1) the "rapport" of the *rapporteur* (appointed by each commission to make a "preliminary examination" of each claim), (2) the "conclusions" of the *commissaire du gouvernement* (an official of the French Foreign Ministry whose principal function is to act in an adversarial capacity on behalf of *all* claimants), and (3) the "procés-verbal," or minutes, of the proceedings of each commission.

[16] In his recent fascinating survey of postwar France, British journalist John Ardagh observes this phenomenon: "In their attempts to simplify bureaucratic procedures, the [social] reformers are inhibited, too, by the hostility of the *petits fonctionnaires* themselves. . . . The real issue is the French concept of authority as something absolute, monarchic, and anonymous, and this colours relations within organisations as much as it does those with the public. In almost any office or firm, clearly defined areas of responsibility are laid down for the different grades, and the links between them are strictly formal. Michel Crozier suggests [in LE PHÉNOMÈNE BUREAUCRATIQUE (1963)] that one of the most characteristic of French traits is the fear of informal relations between subordinates and superiors; work routines and chains of command are therefore codified and formalized, in order to avoid favouritism and conflict. And so it becomes difficult for anyone in a junior position to act officially on his own initiative, for this means breaking the codes. Crozier points out that the desire to avoid awkward face-to-face confrontations is a common facet of French society, noticeable in all work relations. . . . It is one reason why the bold technocratic zeal of [the] post-war years has not always achieved its aims." THE NEW FRENCH REVOLUTION 442–43 (1968).

is hardly significant, with the result that they are no longer the relatively rich source of norm articulation and clarification that they once were. In their stead, for reasons to be noted, has emerged the lump sum settlement–national claims commission device, with the decisions of national (sometimes called "domestic" or "municipal") commissions constituting "at least 95 per cent of postwar [international] claims practice."[17] It is not that the mixed commissions have fallen into complete desuetude. Rather, they are not now as common as before, owing partly to what Richard Lillich has described as their "inherent defects and repeated failures"[18] and partly to the severe strains that would have been placed upon them from the plethora of claims that have been spawned by World War II, postwar revolutionary ideology, and the coming of the Third World. Accordingly, to overlook the practice of national claims commissions—to abstain from clarifying a normative synthesis from country to country—is to deny a growing edge of international law. Worse, it is to maintain a "Law of International Claims" that has little more than historic interest and, so, small prospect of shaping the more stable world order that we all seek today.

[17] LILLICH (G.B.) xi.
[18] LILLICH (U.S.) 10.

Part II

The Context of Claim

A realistic appreciation of any process of claim—in particular the decisions that evolve from and, in turn, help to shape it—cannot be had without a conscious understanding of the real-world variables from which it gains its lifeblood. To quote Montaigne, "[w]e are all framed of flaps and patches and of so shapeless and diverse a contexture that every piece and every moment playeth his part."[1] These variables, to be sure, affecting both the interactions out of which claims arise and the arenas within which claims are finally resolved, can be many and different. In postwar French practice, for example, they have included such diverse conditions as the territorial-political organization of the world community, the increasing interdependence of peoples and governments, the accelerating "revolution of rising expectations," the notions of economic order to which France has herself been committed, the over-all economic enlightenment of French officials, the traditions of civil law experience, and so forth. Of course, incomplete information as well as the needs of economy prevent our accounting for all these "flaps and patches." Still, the essentials of the social-legal context which has surrounded postwar French practice are discernible and manageable, and because we cannot expect fully to understand, or to approach understanding, who has gotten what and why without them, it is necessary that they at least be taken into account. They divide, conveniently, into three frames of reference.

1. THE HISTORICAL CONTEXT

Before World War II, belief in private property enjoyed astonishing universality. True, there were notable exceptions; but, by and large, recognition of private wealth as the *sine qua non* of the social

---

[1] M. MONTAIGNE, *Of the Inconstancy of Our Actions*, in W. KAISER ed., SELECTED ESSAYS OF MONTAIGNE 24, 30 (J. Florio transl. 1964).

fabric scarcely wavered. It is thus unsurprising that, in 1926, during an International Law Association discussion concerning "the inviolability of private property in international relations," the Soviet Union should have been condemned for its "attack upon this international agreement as to the sacredness of private property" and for its failure to "agree with the common conscience of all other civilized nations upon this most fundamental question of morals and ethics" and, so, judged "exclude[d] and excommunicate[d] . . . from the society of civilized nations."[2]

The war of course helped to change all this. Where once collectivist ideologies were mainly responsible for the erosion of laissez-faire values, now the unprecedented depradation of whole economies (and attendant fears of foreign economic domination) combined with them to place the State at stage-center of economic ownership and control. Never before, as in the years immediately following World War II—save for the Mexican, Soviet, and minor "Succession State" experiments of the interwar period—had the State become so extensively involved in the economic enterprise. Little by little over the years, but now overwhelmingly by comparison, direct and indirect interference with private wealth (domestic and foreign), on major and minor scale, became a fundamental strategy —a "determined system"[3]—of national policy, most notably in Eastern Europe where was undertaken what is now recognized as one of the most sweeping economic reformations of all time. In Czechoslovakia (1945–48), Poland (1945–48), Hungary (1945–49), Yugoslavia (1946–47), Bulgaria (1946–49), and Romania (1946–50)—progenitors of things to come again there and elsewhere (*e.g.,* the United Arab Republic and Cuba)—was the tale thus writ large.

For French foreign investors (direct and portfolio), as for their counterparts from abroad (particularly from Great Britain, Switzerland, and the United States), these postwar Eastern European developments augured ill. To be sure, the French, during and soon after World War I, had suffered extraordinary financial losses, losses in excess of $4 billion "or nearly half the French investments outstanding at the beginning of the war."[4] Furthermore, French foreign

---

[2] INT'L L. ASS'N, REPORT OF THE THIRTY-FOURTH CONFERENCE 259 (Vienna, 1926).
[3] K. KATZAROV, THE THEORY OF NATIONALISATION 75 (1964).
[4] U.N. DEP'T OF ECONOMIC AFFAIRS, INTERNATIONAL CAPITAL MOVEMENTS DURING

investments newly made during the interwar period never surpassed in the aggregate the losses sustained: "[b]y 1938, the total of French foreign investments amounted to roughly 3.9 billion dollars, against which there were obligations of about 560 millions, leaving net investments of about 3.3 billions."[5] In sum, France—at least until World War I long second only to Great Britain among the world's creditor nations—was by World War II only fourth among the major creditor powers (behind Great Britain, the United States, and the Netherlands, in that order).[6] Yet for all these setbacks and despite World War II losses, French foreign investors still were to suffer major economic hardships in Eastern Europe following the Axis surrender. As of 1938, apparently the last pre-deprivation year for which figures are available, French long-term investments ranked foremost among all foreign long-term investments in Poland, Yugoslavia, and Czechoslovakia, second in Bulgaria, and fourth in both Romania and Hungary, as indicated in the following table:[7]

(All Figures in Millions of Dollars)

	Bulg.	Czech.	Hung.	Pol.	Rom.	Yugo.
Benelux	10.8	—	2.7	42.1	12.0	5.3
France	22.5	39.4	32.6	165.2	69.7	101.6
Germany	1.5	1.6	46.0	70.5	75.0	2.8
Italy	4.8	—	8.0	18.9	16.0	11.3
Neth.	.3	3.3	6.0	18.1	83.3	1.8
Sweden	—	1.0	2.8	53.9	45.0	3.0
Switz.	9.2	31.0	14.2	24.6	12.2	23.0
U.K.	48.9	35.9	86.6	66.5	215.0	25.5
U.S.	7.9	15.9	57.0	79.2	52.5	38.3

Significantly, the total of these French investments ($431.1 million) represented about 43 percent, or nearly half, of the aggregate French long-term investments outstanding in Europe generally in

---

THE INTER-WAR PERIOD 4 (U.N. Pub. Sales No. 1949, II.D.2). These losses were due not only to the war itself, but also (1) to the 1918 Soviet repudiation of governmental, industrial, and war debt obligations of predecessor Russian governments, (2) to the virtual repudiation of Turkish and Austro-Hungarian bonds by "Successor State" regimes, (3) to the liquidation of high-grade securities, and (4) to the depreciation of the French franc. *See* C. LEWIS, DEBTOR AND CREDITOR COUNTRIES: 1938, 1944, at 10 (1945).

[5] C. LEWIS, *supra* note 4, at 10. "This compares with some 7.6 billions net in 1914." *Id.*

[6] *Id.* at 2–11.

[7] The table is drawn from C. LEWIS, *supra* note 4, at 54–99.

1938 ($998.2 million); and this total, in turn, represented roughly 26 percent of French long-term investments worldwide.[8] Add that few French interests in Eastern Europe (least of all the major ones) wholly escaped the Popular Democratic reach and that they usually were given little or no compensation for their losses,[9] and it is little wonder that the French should have greeted postwar Eastern European wealth deprivations[10] with some consternation (however much they may have themselves domestically accepted public ownership of the means of production).[11]

[8] *Id.*

[9] These facts have been abundantly although not exhaustively treated elsewhere. *See* G. Vienot, Nationalisations Étrangères et Intérêts Français 19–87 (1953) [hereinafter cited as "Vienot"]. *See also* I. Foighel, Nationalization and Compensation 77–106 (1964); G. Fouilloux, La Nationalisation et le Droit International Public 90–104 (1962); S. Friedman, Expropriation in International Law 29–50 (1953); K. Katzarov, *supra* note 3, at 53–64; Les Nationalisations en France et à l'Étranger: Les Nationalisations à l'Étranger *passim* (H. Puget ed. 1958); S. Sharp, Nationalization of Key Industries in Eastern Europe *passim* (1946); G. White, Nationalisation of Foreign Property 183–93 (1961); B. Wortley, Expropriation in Public International Law 66–70 (1959); Doman, *Postwar Nationalization of Foreign Property in Europe*, 48 Colum. L. Rev. 1125 (1948); Herman, *War Damage and Nationalization in Eastern Europe*, 16 Law & Contemp. Prob. 498 (1951).

[10] The term "wealth deprivation" and such derivatives as "deprivation measure" and "deprivation claim" are used principally to avoid the simultaneous and, hence, ambiguous reference to both facts and legal consequences which so often characterizes the more popular "expropriation," "confiscation," "condemnation," "taking," "forfeiture," and the like. It is therefore conceived as a neutral expression which describes the public or publicly sanctioned imposition of a wealth loss (or blocking of a wealth gain)—at whatever time, by whatever means, with whatever intensity, and for whatever claimed purpose—which in the absence of some further act on the part of the depriving party would involve the denial of a *quid pro quo* to the party who sustains the deprivation (the component "wealth" usually being preferred to the more popular "property" because it refers to all the relevant values of goods, services, and income without sharing the latter's common emphasis upon physical attributes nor the civil law's stress on "ownership"). Depending on a multitude of factual variables, a wealth deprivation may be found lawful or unlawful. As implied and as thus defined, however, the term is superior in ways other than its descriptive neutrality. By stressing more the results than the implementing procedures of the institution, it underscores the ultimate gravamen to which all claims arising out of any social interaction are addressed: value change. At the same time, but without straint of legal-technical language, it affords a broad mantle under which a variety of procedures may take shelter, whether the archetypal "direct taking" or its many "indirect" functional equivalents. Finally, it more readily admits that there can be a loss by one party without there being a one-for-one gain by another.

[11] For a perceptive account of French approaches and reactions to State *dirigisme* of the French industrial economy since World War II, see J. Ardagh, The New French Revolution 12–66 (1968). *See also* F. Bloch-Lainé, Pour une Réforme de l'Entreprise (1963); S. Cohen, Modern Capitalist Planning: The French

How have the French reacted to, and coped with, these and later deprivation measures in Eastern Europe and elsewhere (*e.g.*, the United Arab Republic and Cuba)? How have French wealth owners been able, if at all, to obtain compensation for postwar foreign governmental assaults upon their property?

Since 1945, as before, consistent with customary international practice and in keeping with the orthodox theory that "whoever ill-treats a citizen indirectly injures the state,"[12] French nationals with claims against foreign governments ordinarily have had to seek redress by convincing the Quai d'Orsay to espouse their claims for them.[13] As Georges Berlia has succinctly remarked, "[i]f the State does not intervene, there is no method for claim within the international system and the individual is left without recourse against the decisions of internal law, jurisdictional or others, which can have given him grief."[14] Of course, this procedure presupposes that the French claims are contested by the foreign government. Like most governments, the French will not intervene—at least not in principle—when, for example, the foreign government undertakes to indemnify satisfactorily the French nationals it has damaged (as when French interests, deprived by postwar British nationalization measures, accepted virtually without discussion the indemnity proposed by London).[15] Nor usually will it intervene when the foreign government provides realistic opportunities for redress through its own internal processes of decision.[16] Assuming

MODEL (1970); M. EINAUDI, M. BYÉ, & E. ROSSI, NATIONALIZATION IN FRANCE AND ITALY (1955); J. GUYARD, LE MIRACLE FRANÇAIS (1965); LES NATIONALISATIONS EN FRANCE ET À L'ÉTRANGER: LES NATIONALISATIONS EN FRANCE (Julliot de la Morandière & M. Byé eds. 1948).

12 E. DE VATTEL, LE DROIT DES GENS, *liv.* 2, § 71 (1758).

13 *See* VIENOT 38.

14 Berlia, *Contribution à l'Étude de la Nature de la Protection Diplomatique,* ANNUAIRE FRANÇAIS DE DROIT INTERNATIONAL 63 (1957).

15 Interview with Jean-François Dervieu, Deputy Director of the *Service des Biens et Intérêts Privés, Ministère des Affaires Étrangères,* in Paris, July 1, 1968. Interviews with Monsieur Dervieu, of which there have been many, will hereinafter be referred to as "Interview with Dervieu."

16 *Id.* This belief is confirmed in correspondence dated December 5, 1967, from Henri Glaser, *"Secrétaire Général"* of the *Association Pour la Sauvegarde et l'Expansion des Biens et Intérêts Français à l'Étranger* (374, Rue Saint-Honoré, Paris I) [hereinafter cited as "Glaser Correspondence—12/67"]. As may be inferred from its name, one of the many functions of this private association has been to serve an intermediary role between French foreign investors and the French Foreign Ministry in connection with the promotion of these interests at home and abroad.

appropriate conditions, however, generally it is understood—*i.e.*, not required—that the *Ministère des Affaires Étrangères* will intervene on behalf of the international claims raised,[17] although without liability for potential mishandling[18] and sometimes with the negotiating assistance of non-governmental agencies.[19]

Historically, it has done so in ways that parallel closely the experience of the British Foreign Office and the United States Department of State: principally through individual diplomatic espousal, mixed claims commission or other international arbitral adjudication, and "lump sum," "en bloc," or "global" settlement followed by national administrative distribution or national claims commission adjudication.[20] Each of these techniques has been em-

[17] Formerly this intervention was undertaken by the Foreign Ministry's *Direction Économique et Financière;* today it is done by its *Direction des Conventions Administratives et des Affaires Consulaires.* Interview with Dervieu, in Paris, July 1, 1968. It deserves mention, however, that while the French Foreign Ministry has been the usual governmental advocate of such claims, it has not been the only one. Sometimes the French Ministry of Finance has assumed this role. This is inferred in VIENOT 229, and is explicitly confirmed in correspondence dated November 13, 1967, from André Ernest-Picard, "Directeur" of the *Association Nationale des Porteurs Français de Valeurs Mobilières* (22, Boulevard de Courcelles, Paris XVII) [hereinafter cited as "Ernest-Picard Correspondence—11/67"]. For details about the *Association Nationale,* see note 19 *infra.*

[18] See *In re* Taurin and Mérienne, [1955] D. S. Jur. 361, decided by the *Conseil d'État* on October 29, 1954, in which it was held that French courts must decline to entertain claims of French nationals that arise out of alleged negligence of the French Government in conducting negotiations with foreign governments. As recounted in 21 I.L.R. at 16, "[t]he Court said that the owners of a ship . . . taken by the British authorities in exercise of the right of angary during the Second World War . . . were not entitled to sue the French Government for damages for alleged negligence in failing to obtain on their behalf sufficient compensation from the British Government." See also Bénoit, *Note,* [1955] D. S. Jur. 362. Interestingly enough, this point was touched upon by one of the commissions which are the subject of this study. Thus, in *Décision Juridictionelle* No. 261, dated December 7, 1956, the *Commission spéciale de répartition de l'indemnité polonais,* in rejecting a claimant's plea for special treatment, noted that "the action of the Government, when it concludes an agreement in the name and for the benefit of its nationals, is not that of a simple agent beholden to the rules of agency as they are defined by private law."

[19] Among the more conspicuous of these agencies has been the *Association Nationale des Porteurs Français de Valeurs Mobilières* (22, Boulevard de Courcelles, Paris XVII). The *Association,* a quasi-public utility created in 1898 by the *Chambre Syndicale des Agents de Change de Paris* at the request of the then French Minister of Finance, has as its main functions the enlightenment and assistance of French bondholders and stockholders, especially those with interests abroad. As such, it is similar to, but more diversified than, the Council of Foreign Bondholders in Great Britain. See ASSOCIATION NATIONALE DES PORTEURS FRANÇAIS DE VALEURS MOBILIÈRES, RAPPORT PRÉSENTÉ À L'ASSEMBLÉE GÉNÉRALE POUR L'ANNÉE 1967, at 50 (June 3, 1968). For related remarks, see note 21 *infra.*

[20] As to British practice, see LILLICH (G.B.) 1–3. As to United States practice, see

ployed by France since 1945. The negotiations between France and the United Arab Republic securing compensation in 1958 for French interests divested by Cairo's nationalization of the *Compagnie Universale du Canal Maritime de Suez*, for example, is perhaps the best known recent illustration of the venerable practice of individual diplomatic espousal.[21] Further, mixed arbitral tribunals were constituted following World War II (as after World War I) mainly to resolve war damage and related debt claims.[22] The last principal alternative, the lump sum settlement followed by national administrative distribution or national claims commission adjudication, appears to have been first resorted to by France in direct response to the widespread wealth deprivations inflicted in Eastern Europe.

Like the United Kingdom, the United States, and others, France has negotiated numerous lump sum settlements over the years,[23]

Department of State Memorandum, *Nationalization, Intervention or Other Taking of Property of American Nationals (March 1, 1961)*, in 56 Am. J. Int'l L. 166 (1962), quoted in Lillich (G.B.) 1 n.3. For further details on United States practice, see Lillich (U.S.) 5–15.

[21] The text of the agreement is reprinted in 14 Rev. Egyptienne de Droit Int'l 338 (1958) and 54 Am. J. Int'l L. 493 (1960). Sharing substantially in the negotiation of this agreement, in addition to the Egyptian and French governments, was the Suez Canal Company itself, a practice that has recurred often in French international claims practice whenever a substantial business interest has been involved. Sometimes, indeed, the principal negotiating responsibility is delegated to the injured French party or its representative with the French Foreign Ministry merely cooperating through its "good offices." Interview with Dervieu, in Paris, June 6, 1969. *See, e.g.,* notes 56 & 118 *infra.*

[22] *See, e.g.,* the Agreement with Italy, November 19, 1947 (Decree No. 48–1934 of December 22, 1948), [1948] J.O. 12436, establishing the Franco-Italian Mixed Commission in accordance with the Treaty of Peace of February 10, 1947. This statement is not to mean that France has used the mixed commission device to resolve *only* war damage and related claims. *See, e.g.,* La Réparation des Dommages Causés aux Étrangers par des Mouvements Révolutionnaires—Jurisprudence de la Commission Franco-Méxicaine des Réclamations (1924–1932), 5 U.N.R.I.A.A. 325–560. However, it appears that the French Government does not often resort to this device today. If employed at all, as apparently it has been with Cuba, Guinea, and Tunisia, its functions have been limited mainly to a preliminary determination of valid claims in anticipation of global settlement. Interview with Dervieu, in Paris, June 6, 1969. The only known recent instance in which it has been used in a more traditional manner has been in connection with Title II of the Agreement with the United Arab Republic of July 28, 1966 (Decree No. 67–874 of October 4, 1967), [1967] J.O. 9939, which called for a mixed commission to apply the agreement generally, but particularly as regards post-1958 deprivation claims against Egypt. *See* note 57 *infra.* Yet even these limited uses have not been looked upon with much enthusiasm by the French Government. According to one informed official, the mixed commission makes for "negotiative and adjudicative non-maneuverability." Interview with Dervieu, in Paris, June 6, 1969. *Accord,* note 29 *infra.*

[23] A useful working definition of "lump sum settlement" has been given by a former

16   INTERNATIONAL CLAIMS

many of them followed by national administrative distribution. However, only the United States appears to have utilized national claims commissions to any significant degree for post-settlement adjudication before 1945.[24] At any rate, there is no known evidence to indicate that France ever used the combined settlement-commission device before the Second World War. Why not? Partly, no doubt, because of "juri-political" perspectives and traditions special to France in the prewar era. But mainly, it seems, because there was little before 1945 to challenge severely the more traditional methods of international claims settlement and distribution. The number of claims requiring resolution at any one time seldom exceeded in amount or kind what individual diplomatic espousal (or private negotiation) and administrative distribution could accommodate. And when they did, in which case specially constituted mixed tribunals were usually found helpful,[25] typically the context of resolution was one in which widely shared notions of laissez-faire justice and fair dealing were easily transmuted into broad patterns of acceptable international behavior. Quite simply, the need for bold alternatives did not exist.

The years immediately following World War II, on the other hand, seem ineluctably to have compelled the lump sum settlement–national claims commission approach (for other States as well as

---

chairman of the United States Foreign Claims Settlement Commission: "[A] 'lump sum,' 'en bloc' or 'global' settlement involves an agreement, arrived at by diplomatic negotiation between governments, to settle outstanding international claims by the payment of a given sum without resorting to international adjudication. Such a settlement permits the state receiving the lump sum to distribute the fund thus acquired among claimants who may be entitled thereto pursuant to domestic procedure." Re, *Domestic Adjudication and Lump-Sum Settlement as an Enforcement Technique*, 58 PROCEEDINGS OF THE AMERICAN SOCIETY OF INTERNATIONAL LAW 39, 40 (1964). *Compare* M. LITMANS, THE INTERNATIONAL LUMP-SUM SETTLEMENTS OF THE UNITED STATES 1–2 (1962). For additional discussion concerning the worldwide use of lump sum settlements in recent years, see I. FOIGHEL, *supra* note 9, at 106–11, 207–14; G. FOUILLOUX, *supra* note 9, at 444–48; LILLICH (U.S.) and LILLICH (G.B.); LILLICH & CHRISTENSON; G. WHITE, *supra* note 9, at 205–26, 230–31; Bindschedler, *La Protection de la Propriété Privée en Droit International Public* (Hague Academy of International Law), 90 RECEUIL DES COURS 173, 278–95 (1956–II). A study of the lump sum settlement process is a current major project of this writer and Richard B. Lillich of the University of Virginia, undertaken under the auspices of the Procedural Aspects of International Law Institute. The final product, to be published soon, will be a treatise entitled INTERNATIONAL CLAIMS: THEIR SETTLEMENT BY LUMP SUM AGREEMENTS.

[24] *See* LILLICH (G.B.) 3.
[25] *See* note 22 *supra*.

for France)—at least as concerns claims relating to foreign-wealth deprivations. The magnitude and importance of the claims that arose, as well as the new revolutionary context within which international diplomacy was required to function, served to highlight both the inherent and circumstantial weaknesses of traditional French strategies and so to render impractical, if not always impossible, all other means of settlement and distribution. Gilles Vienot, to date author of the only other extended (but now incomplete) inquiry into postwar French international claims practice,[26] has detailed the point at some length.[27] Against the backdrop of multiple claims and revolutionary politics, he traces the factors which, derived from this setting, necessitated innovation. *Compelling the lump sum settlement* ("le réglement global et forfaitaire"), he notes, were the following principal needs: (1) from the French point of view, a need for real and collective bargaining power—thus militating against private mediation by "un groupement de défense" or diplomatic negotiation via "un accord sur les principes de l'indemnisation," or such other devices as would likely dilute or otherwise limit satisfactory recovery;[28] and (2) from the Eastern European point of view, a need for safeguarding socialist conceptions about sovereign authority and control over the economic process—thus preventing resort to mixed arbitral devices where relatively independent decision might create compromising or otherwise undesirable precedent.[29] And *compelling the national claims*

---

[26] *Supra* note 9. Vienot is presently affiliated with the *Association Pour la Sauvegarde et l'Expansion des Biens et Intérêts Français à l'Étranger* (as to which see note 16 *supra*). Among his colleagues is Maurice Richard, "Président" of the *Association* and the first director of the *Service des Biens et Intérêts Privés* of the French *Ministère des Affairés Étrangères*, the governmental office to which most private French international claims are required to be brought if diplomatic protection is to be expected. While more will be detailed about the *Service* below (*see, e.g.*, notes 148 & 176 *infra*), it is important here to recognize that Vienot's link with Richard doubtless lends considerable authority to his study.

[27] VIENOT 73–87, 223–29.

[28] *Accord*, Interview with Dervieu, in Paris, June 6, 1969.

[29] *Accord, id. See also* Sarraute & Tager, *Les éffets en France des nationalisations étrangères*, 79 J. DROIT INT'L 1138, 1171 (1952). According to Vienot, France and Yugoslavia agreed in 1945 to the establishment of a mixed claims commission. VIENOT 167. However, because of disenchantment on both sides and because of later measures taken by the Yugoslav Government against French nationals, this agreement (if ever formally signed) was never acted upon. *Id.* at 77 n.1. "It is probable," writes Vienot, "that nationalizing governments [including the Yugoslav Government] have estimated that such an institution would be judged inconsistent with the prin-

commission ("la commission spéciale de répartition"), he continues, were the following key factors: (1) the aforementioned Eastern European refusal to consider the establishment of mixed claims tribunals and the consequent settlement provision that "la répartition de l'indemnité globale forfaitaire entre les intéressés relève de la seule compétence du Gouvernement français";[30] and (2) a clear— but, Vienot insists, not altogether justified—"répugnance" on the part of concerned French interests for the quasi-discretionary and political character of "la répartition administrative" in contrast to their complementary preference for more rigorously institutionalized impartiality and professionalism. As one informed observer has confirmed, the French Government "wished to create a system that would be secure from the encroachment of executive power. This consideration conformed to the principle of the separation of powers [and] tended to assure claimants that they were to be equitably judged."[31] In sum, relatively unprecedented circumstances called for relatively unprecedented solutions.

As might be expected, however, the lump sum settlement–

---

ciple of national sovereignty; it is certain that they wanted above all to avoid the risk of decisions rendered by independent proceedings, preferring to reserve the opportunity to refuse all indemnification should the French Government be too exacting. It is not very surprising that the latter did not, of its own, propose this solution which, advantageous though it might have seemed since it was the claimant, must have constituted, in its eyes, an undesirable precedent for the settlement of nationalization indemnities of which it was itself debtor toward foreign nationals". *Id.* at 77. Later Vienot writes: "the experience of the analogous commissions constituted between Belgium, Sweden, Czechoslovakia and Switzerland on the one hand, and Yugoslavia on the other, caused the French authorities to conclude that mixed commissions were without power by reason of the excessive limitation on their competence, the absence of a third-party arbiter and the low rank ("sujétion") of the Yugoslav delegation. Thus restricted, such an organism could not arrive at any positive result." *Id.* at 167–68. For related discussion, see text following note 77 *infra*. For discussion indicating that like factors have been at work in equivalent American and British practice, see LILLICH (G.B.) 3.

[30] This quotation is drawn from Article 5 of the Agreement with Poland of March 19, 1948 (Decree No. 51–1288 of November 7, 1951), [1951] J.O. 11190, the first lump sum agreement negotiated by France after World War II. For discussion and reference to similar language in later French lump sum agreements, see text at notes 135–36 *infra*.

[31] *Accord,* Interview with Dervieu, in Paris, June 6, 1969. Glaser Correspondence —12/67, *supra* note 16. It also should be added that because of the amount and complexity of the known claims involved it was assumed that the regular French civil tribunals could not assume the task of distribution. Interview with Dervieu, in Paris, June 6, 1969.

national claims commission solution that was ultimately to prevail was initially never so apparent as the foregoing would have one believe, at least not as concerns deprivation claims against Eastern Europe. Historical reconstructions have a way of making events seem more rationally conceived than they actually are, of causing us to forget that solutions are the product of human and therefore fallible perceptions. A case in point, strikingly so when we note the *concurrent* negotiation and *prior* conclusion of the 1948 lump sum agreement between France and Poland,[32] is the Franco-Czech Accord of August 6, 1948, relating to the compensation of French interests divested by Czech nationalization decrees of October 24, 1945.[33]

The only postwar settlement agreement between France and Eastern Europe that was *not* a lump sum accord,[34] it registers not only how little is to be gained when mutuality of expectation is absent between negotiating parties, but also the uncertain plight in which French investors found themselves when trying to assess the meaning of post-1945 Eastern Europe. The product of their too sanguine assumption, explicitly rejected by the Quai d'Orsay, that the nationalization decrees in question were only provisional in character and that Czechoslovakia would soon return to the fold of Western economic and political liberalism,[35] it amounted to little more than a statement of "indemnisation en principe." Czechoslo-

---

[32] See note 30 *supra*.

[33] Agreement with Czechoslovakia of August 6, 1948, reprinted (in French) in VIENOT 147–48 (hereinafter referred to as the "Czech Accord of 1948" or the "1948 Czech Accord"). The agreement (including its companion Special Accord, Additional Protocol, and two "lettres-annexes" of the same date, also reproduced by VIENOT 149–54) was never officially published in the *Journal Officiel de la République Française*. The reason, Vienot notes at 131–32, is that the French Government, displeased with the arrangement reached and concerned about additional (post-1948) Czech deprivation measures, never submitted the Accord for ratification by the French Parliament. *Cf.* note 77 *infra*.

[34] *Cf.* the General Agreement with the United Arab Republic, August 22, 1958 (Decree No. 58–760 of August 22, 1958), [1958] J.O. 7919, signed in Zurich and providing for the settlement of outstanding French claims (accrued against Egypt in 1956) by requiring recourse to Egyptian processes of decision. Together with its attached 3 protocols, 12 "lettres-annexes," and an Agreement on Transfers (including 5 "lettres-annexes"), this agreement is hereinafter usually referred to as the "1958 Zurich Accord." For further discussion of this accord, see text at notes 86–96 *infra*. For other non-Eastern European postwar agreements that do not appear to have been lump sum settlements, see note 22 *supra*.

[35] See VIENOT 123–25.

vakia agreed to pay directly, but in its discretion, "une indemnité adéquate et éffective"[36] to French claimants who, by direct and individual appeal to appropriate Czech authorities[37] under a "most-favored-nation" régime,[38] could prove the legitimacy of their claims. Considering the large authority and discretion thus left to Prague, not surprisingly this venture proved far from conclusive.[39] As Vienot has written, "[i]n the silence of the convention, each interested party [saw] himself as obliged to undertake discussions with the Czechoslovak authorities on his own; that is, that he [would] be limited to accepting, or refusing, proposals that he [would] be unable effectively to debate since, most of the time, he [did] not have at his disposal any of the resources ("contreparties") which permit, in contrast, on the occasion of intergovernmental negotiation, opposition to adverse claims deemed excessive."[40] Of course, in fairness to the French we should acknowledge that earlier, similar and, so, presumably exemplary (but also ultimately unsuccessful) experiments with Czechoslovakia were undertaken by the linguistically related Swiss and Belgian governments, among others.[41] Yet the fact remains: Czechoslovakia persistently challenged both the legitimacy of the French claims presented and the amount of compensation sought.[42] And when she did not—apparently a rare occurrence—still she allowed only for a complex, if not onerous, system of indemnification: part in Czech crowns to be used only in Czechoslovakia and part in public bonds whose amortized portion could be transferred abroad only by a reduction in the Czech share in the balance of payments between the two countries.[43] The need

---

[36] Czech Accord of 1948, art. 1, para. 1.

[37] Id. art. 2.

[38] Id. art. 6. The provision continues: "They [French nationals] will not be, in any case, less well treated than Czech nationals."

[39] For details, see VIENOT 123–25.

[40] Id. at 130.

[41] See G. WHITE, supra note 9, at 199–201. According to White, one such agreement, the Agreement Between the Netherlands and Czechoslovakia of November 4, 1949, "was not superseded by a lump-sum compensation agreement, so that it may perhaps be assumed that the individual procedure proved workable in this case." Id. at 199. It has to be noted, however, that White was writing in 1961, before the negotiation of the later and superseding lump sum Agreement Between the Netherlands and Czechoslovakia of June 11, 1964. See 556 U.N.T.S. 89.

[42] See VIENOT 130.

[43] See 2 AFFAIRES ÉTRANGÈRES 12–14 (October 1950). This journal is a publication of the Association Pour la Sauvegarde et l'Expansion des Biens et Intérêts Français à l'Étranger (as to which see note 16 supra).

for an alternate solution was thus made vividly—and painfully—clear.[44]

The predominant solution, at least as concerns nationalization and other wealth deprivation claims, has been the lump sum settlement–national claims commission device[45]—as indicated, commonplace in international claims practice since World War II.[46] In the case of non-deprivation claims (*i.e.*, "ordinary" commercial and bondholder debt claims), the predominant solution—to the extent that these claims have been resolved through "en bloc" negotiations at all—has been the lump sum settlement followed by individual distribution via "la répartition administrative."[47] Differing markedly from British practice which requires "ordinary" debt claims to be adjudicated by the Foreign Compensation Commission,[48] apparently the repartition of these claims has been found to be less complex than the repartition of wealth deprivation claims and therefore not

[44] This statement is not to mean that agreements for "indemnisation en principe" (like the 1948 Czech Accord) were never again to be entertained by the French Government. Obviously, decisions about the wisdom of entering into these or any other kinds of compensation agreements necessarily have had to be based upon assessments that account for a wide variety of conditioning variables, including of course the identifications, demands, and expectations of the other High Contracting Party. Consider, thus, the Agreement with Morocco of July 24, 1964 (concerning the indemnification of French interests divested by Moroccan agrarian reform laws) which, although not yet officially published, appears to embody a Moroccan acceptance of the principle of compensation. For a brief exposé, see 68 REV. GÉNÉRALE DU DROIT INT'L PUB. 941 (1964).

[45] In the case of Czechoslovakia: (1) the Agreement of June 2, 1950 (Decree No. 51–1286 of November 7, 1951), [1951] J.O. 11188, hastened by relative success in equivalent Franco-Polish negotiations in 1948 and by a French refusal to renew remunerative commercial agreements except upon achievement of a satisfactory claims settlement; and (2) the later established *Commission spéciale de répartition de l'indemnité tchécoslovaque,* constituted by Law No. 51–671 of August 4, 1952), [1952] J.O. 8428. For individual and comparative details, see Sections 2–3 *infra.* Together with the contemporaneous orchestration of like Polish and Hungarian claims programs, this arrangement represented for France the beginning of an extended resort to the combined device.

[46] In addition to Great Britain, France, and the United States, the combined device has been used by Denmark (*see* text at Part I, note 13) and by Belgium, The Netherlands, and Switzerland among other States. See "Technical Discussion on Claims Problems," a record of an informal meeting held in London on September 20–22, 1967, at the initiative of the British Government, among officials from Australia, Belgium, Canada, Denmark, France, The Netherlands, New Zealand, Norway, Sweden, Switzerland, and the United Kingdom (unpublished mimeo.).

[47] A minor exception to this pattern may be seen in connection with the distribution of the lump sum paid under the Agreement with Yugoslavia of July 12, 1963 (Decree No. 64–239 of March 13, 1964), [1964] J.O. 2525. *See* text at note 157 *infra* and at Part III, note 417.

[48] *See* LILLICH (G.B.) 76–104.

requiring commission adjudication.[49] At any rate, it is the lump sum settlement–national claims commission device as used by France since World War II that is the primary concern of this study. Accordingly, to its principal structural details the next two sections are devoted.

2. THE SETTLEMENT CONTEXT

Since World War II, except for war reparation or related agreements[50] and agreements pursuant to which France has paid other States for outstanding French "obligations,"[51] the French Government has been party to fifteen known lump sum agreements, all but four with Eastern European countries. Alphabetically by country, they are as follows:

Bulgaria

A.   Agreement of July 28, 1955[52]

Cuba

B.   Agreement of March 16, 1967[53]

Czechoslovakia

C.   Agreement of June 2, 1950[54]

D.   Protocol of January 16, 1964[55]

---

[49] *See* Ernest-Picard Correspondence—11/67, *supra* note 17.

[50] *See, e.g.,* the Agreement with the Federal Republic of Germany, July 15, 1960 (Decree No. 61–945 of August 24, 1961), [1961] J.O. 8020, concerning the indemnification of French nationals affected by "National-Socialist measures of persecution"; the Agreement with Italy, *supra* note 22. The author is advised, in addition, of a still classified agreement between France and Austria, dated July 18, 1949, by which, in exchange for lump sum payment by Austria, France waived all French claims concerning French property in Austria which had been taken by Germany. He is indebted for this information to Professor Ignaz Seidl-Hohenveldern of the University of Köln.

[51] *See, e.g.,* the Agreement with France and Switzerland, November 21, 1949, [1949] 7 ANNUAIRE SUISSE 136.

[52] Decree No. 59–361 of February 27, 1959, [1959] J.O. 2742. Together with its attached "Protocole d'Application" and three "lettres-annexes," this agreement is hereinafter usually referred to as "the 1955 Bulgarian Accord."

[53] Decree No. 67–853 of September 20, 1967, [1967] J.O. 9761 (hereinafter usually referred to as "the 1967 Cuban Accord").

[54] Decree No. 51–1286 of November 7, 1951, [1951] J.O. 11188. Together with its two attached "protocoles additionnels" and two "lettres-annexes," this agreement is hereinafter usually referred to as "the 1950 Czech Accord." The two "lettres-annexes," it should be noted, were published nearly 12 years later, under Decree No. 63–735 of July 10, 1963, [1963] J.O. 6811. As to the consequence of this fact, see Part III, note 26 and accompanying text.

[55] Decree No. 64–149 of February 15, 1964, [1964] J.O. 1755 (hereinafter usually referred to as "the 1964 Czech Protocol"). For details, see text at notes 70–71 *infra*.

Egypt

E. Agreement of November 5, 1964[56]

F. Agreement of July 28, 1966[57]

West Germany

G. Agreement of July 27, 1961[58]

Hungary

H. Agreement of June 12, 1950[59]

I. Agreement of May 14, 1965[60]

Poland

J. Agreement of March 19, 1948[61]

K. Agreement of September 7, 1951[62]

Romania

L. Agreement of February 8, 1959[63]

---

[56] Decree No. 64–1233 of December 11, 1964, [1964] J.O. 11149. Together with its attached "Annexe I," this agreement, negotiated between representatives of the *Association Nationale des Porteurs Français de Valeurs Mobilières* (as to which see note 19 *supra*) and the U.A.R. and later formalized by an exchange of letters between the French and Egyptian governments, is hereinafter usually referred to as "the 1964 Egyptian Accord." For background discussion, see text at notes 86–96 *infra. See also* text following note 71 *infra.*

[57] Decree No. 67–874 of October 4, 1967, [1967] J.O. 9939. Together with its attached Protocol and two "lettres-annexes," this agreement, in particular Title I thereof, is hereinafter usually referred to as "the 1966 Egyptian Accord." Title I settled pre-1958 wealth-deprivation claims by lump sum payment. Title II settled post-1958 deprivation claims by providing for mixed commission determination in lieu of lump sum payment. For background discussion, see note 22 *supra* and text at notes 86–96 *infra.*

[58] Decree No. 63–538 of April 9, 1963, [1963] J.O. 3367. This agreement, in the form of an exchange of letters and discussed in Part I, note 10, is hereinafter usually referred to as "the 1961 German Accord."

[59] Decree No. 52–1079 of September 23, 1952, [1952] J.O. 9260. Together with its three attached "lettres-annexes," this agreement is hereinafter usually referred to as "the 1950 Hungarian Accord."

[60] Decree No. 65–589 of July 15, 1965, [1965] J.O. 6308 [hereinafter usually referred to as "the 1965 Hungarian Accord"].

[61] Decree No. 51–1288 of November 7, 1951, [1951] J.O. 11190. Together with its attached "Annexe" and its later negotiated "Protocole d'Application" of September 7, 1951 (Decree No. 57–892 of July 26, 1957, [1957] J.O. 7779, at 7780—hereinafter usually called "the 1951 Polish Protocol"), this agreement is hereinafter usually referred to as "the 1948 Polish Accord." For pertinent discussion, see text at notes 115–119 *infra.*

[62] Decree No. 57–892 of July 26, 1957, [1957] J.O. 7779. Together with its attached "Protocole d'Application" and four "lettres-annexes," this agreement is hereinafter usually referred to as "the 1951 Polish Accord." For details, see text at note 67 *infra.*

[63] Decree No. 59–439 of March 11, 1959, [1959] J.O. 3287. Together with its attached two "protocoles d'application" and three "échanges de lettres," this agreement is hereinafter usually referred to as the "1959 Romanian Accord."

Yugoslavia

M. Agreement of April 14, 1951[64]

N. Agreement of August 2, 1958[65]

O. Agreement of July 12, 1963[66]

Four of these agreements may be seen to have represented mostly non-deprivative debt claims settlements (mainly bondholder claims settlements) whose negotiated sums have been distributed through other than claims commission adjudication. Thus, in the case of the 1951 Polish Accord (K above), which agreement was designed to improve "les relations économiques réciproques" by payment of 4.2 billion French francs as final compensation for French creditor claims against (a) the Polish Government and (b) Polish State enterprises and private juridical persons which (1) matured before 1939, (2) resulted from agreements concluded during World War II, or (3) were founded on named titles issued before September 1, 1939, distributive responsibility was assigned to the *Association Nationale des Porteurs Français de Valeurs Mobilières*[67] (a quasi-public utility not unlike the British Council of Foreign Bond-holders).[68] The *Association Nationale* was delegated the same responsibility again in connection with the lump sum transferred under the 1958 Yugoslav Accord (N above),[69] *i.e.,* the equivalent in French francs of U.S. $10,250,000 for the "repurchase" of certain prewar Serbian and Yugoslav public loans. In the case of the 1964

---

[64] Decree No. 53–653 of July 24, 1953, [1953] J.O. 6723. Together with its attached "Protocole Additionnel" and a "Tableau Annexe," as well as a "Protocole Financier," a "Procès-Verbal," and three special agreements all relating to the settlement of certain debt claims against the Yugoslav Government (these latter five documents being reprinted in VIENOT at 202-207), this agreement is hereinafter usually referred to as "the 1951 Yugoslav Accord." For background discussion, see text at notes 78–85 *infra* and *see also* note 106 *infra.*

[65] Decree No. 59–654 of May 5, 1959, [1959] J.O. 5244. Together with its attached "tableaux," three "lettres-annexes," and "Avenant," this agreement is hereinafter usually referred to as "the 1958 Yugoslav Accord." It may be noted that this agreement, in addition to providing for a lump sum payment to cover certain Yugoslav public debts, modified the terms by which a balance due under the 1951 Yugoslav Accord would be paid. For background discussion, see text at notes 78–85 *infra* and *see also* note 106 *infra.*

[66] Decree No. 64–239 of March 13, 1964, [1964] J.O. 2525 [hereinafter usually referred to as "the 1963 Yugoslav Accord"]. For background discussion, see text at notes 78–85 *infra* and *see also* note 106 *infra.*

[67] *See* the *Association's* COMMUNICATION No. 434 (October 15, 1960).

[68] For further details about the *Association Nationale,* see note 19 *supra.*

[69] *See* "Avis" relating to "Emprunts Serbes et Yougoslaves," [1959] J.O. 5039.

Czech Protocol (D above), whose aim was to settle "toutes les questions financières encore en suspens entre les deux pays" by calling for a "redemption" of all French claims accruing from a 1930 long-term 6 percent "equipment loan" issued by the since nationalized *Société des Anciens Établissements Skoda* (now known as the "Usines V.I. Lénine") up to an amount, "brut et forfaitaire," equal to 61 percent of the "nominal value" of the loan certificates,[70] responsibility for lump sum distribution was charged to five Parisian banks.[71] And, finally, in the case of the 1964 Egyptian Accord (E above), providing for indemnification of several thousand French stockholders of major companies "sequestered" in 1956, this responsibility was assigned, per the 1964 Accord itself, to both Egyptian and French banks. In other words, distribution under 4 of the 15 lump sum agreements negotiated by France since World War II has proceeded via "la répartition administrative." Accordingly, except for occasional reference, none of these agreements will be further considered herein.[72] For reasons already mentioned, neither will much be said about the earlier cited 1961 German Accord (G above).[73]

The remaining 10 agreements, however, all of them having been charged in whole or in part to claims commission administration, are central to our inquiry and therefore command our attention (these agreements being hereinafter usually referred to as "the Settlement Agreements"). Obviously the worth of the lump sum settlement–national claims commission device, at least from the perspective of a French commission claimant, is bound to depend substantially upon the nature of the gains won by the French Government in the process of diplomatic protection. At any rate, considering the special relevance that each of these Settlement Agreements may be seen to have had for French lump sum distribution, failure to account for the settlement context would risk presenting a distorted picture of the role of the French commissions later to be

[70] The 1964 Protocol was anticipated in a "protocole financier" of July 11, 1963 (mimeo. available at the French Foreign Ministry).
[71] *See* "Avis relatif au remboursement des obligations . . . Skoda," [1964] J.O. 5697.
[72] For some demonstration of how these agreements have had particular impact upon the rulings of the French commissions later to be described, see text at Part III, notes 336–344.
[73] *See* Part I, note 10.

discussed. On the other hand, because presignature indices of party expectation—*e.g.*, the *travaux préparatoires*—as well as other helpful data have been held outside the limits of permissible investigation,[74] because the many textual details of the Settlement Agreements are treated in subsequent discussion,[75] and because, in any event, at least the principal texts of the Settlement Agreements are reproduced in the Appendix to this volume,[76] meticulous examination of each provision would serve little useful purpose at this juncture. We need consider now only the broad contours.

At the outset, it needs emphasis that few if any of the Settlement Agreements—each providing for "indemnization globale et forfaitaire" or "une solution définitive" of the claims covered—have been easy to come by, requiring as they have usually intermittent exchanges ranging from 2 to 10-plus years. Hence, for example, the above-mentioned difficulties encountered by France in her dealings with Czechoslovakia[77]—difficulties, it should be added, that were common to many of France's Eastern European negotiations.

The history of the Franco-Yugoslav settlement is a particularly vivid case in point. Following the liberation of Yugoslavia in 1944, Vienot recounts, "French property and interests [in Yugoslavia] found themselves the targets of the confiscation of property disguised as German or Italian, of prosecutions for collaboration with the enemy, [and] of fiscal arrangements resulting in the sequestration and liquidation of war earnings and illicit profits."[78] These measures, he charges, "constituted no more than a series of pre-

---

[74] According to the "Secrétaire" of the French commissions constituted to distribute funds received under the Bulgarian, Hungarian, and Yugoslav accords, the French Foreign Ministry never has communicated *travaux préparatoires* even to the commissions charged with applying the accords, preferring instead to be consulted for interpretative advice as the need might from time to time arise. Interview with Roger Branche, in Paris, July 10, 1969. [Interviews with Monsieur Branche are hereinafter referred to as "Interview with Branche."]

[75] *See generally,* but in particular, Part III.

[76] Hereinafter, all notations concerning these lump sum agreements will assume reference to the Appendix.

[77] *See* text at notes 34–44 *supra*. It must be added that the 1948 Czech Accord was not completely abortive. Although it never was ratified by France, Czechoslovakia did make some tentative transfers in 1948–1949 in consideration of claims that Prague had considered legitimate. *See* VIENOT 137. *See also* note 98(2) *infra*. Of course, the 1950 Czech Accord did represent a formal annulment of its predecessor. *See* 1950 Czech Accord, Additional Protocol No. II, art. 3.

[78] VIENOT 167.

texts to permit the Yugoslav Government to seize private property and interests."[79] One can of course debate the historical accuracy of this sweeping indictment. What matters, however, is that the French Government, apprised of the situation generally, protested a number of these measures and in 1945 secured agreement from Yugoslavia (as did Belgium, Sweden, Switzerland, and, interestingly, Czechoslovakia for like reasons) to establish a mixed commission to settle the existing grievances.[80] However, soon faced with the Yugoslav nationalization law of December 5, 1946, this procedure came to naught,[81] and France began to seek alternative means of settlement. But the Yugoslavs were in no mood, without special inducement, to negotiate a settlement that would in any way compromise their socialist principles or further burden their already fractured economy. Not until more than two years later, with Yugoslavia under increased pressure to trade with the West (due mainly to her rupture with the Soviet Union and other Cominform countries), was any progress possible.[82] On May 21, 1949, after both sides had diligently clarified their positions, the two countries concluded two protocols and a commercial agreement. The first called for negotiations by no later than October 1, 1950 (1) to settle the question of "French property, rights, and interests affected by Yugoslav nationalization laws and by other restrictive measures," (2) to rule on private commercial and financial debts owing to French nationals, (3) to set conditions and time limits for settlement of the Yugoslav public debt, and (4) to conclude a long-term "accord d'équipement."[83] The second protocol provided for a deposit into a special Yugoslav account in the Bank of France of a sum in French francs equal to U.S. $1.6 million to be transferred to France for nationalization and similar claims against Yugoslavia as part of a global indemnity eventually to be fixed.[84] In this setting, following continued but alternatingly friendly and stormy negotiations, the two governments at last agreed to the first of three lump sum settlements that were finally to be concluded

[79] *Id.*
[80] *Id.*
[81] *Id.* at 167–68. For related discussion, see note 29 and accompanying text *supra*.
[82] *Id.* at 168–69.
[83] *See id.* at 194 for the text to this agreement.
[84] *See id.* at 194–95 for the text to this agreement.

between them, the 1951, 1958, and 1963 accords. Only the first and last of these, it will be recalled, were ultimately assigned to a French claims commission.[85]

Lest it be assumed, however, that East-West rivalries have alone been responsible for these straits, consider further the tensions surrounding the protracted Franco-Egyptian settlement. Following Cairo's "seizure" of the *Compagnie Universale du Canal Maritime de Suez* in 1956—a "delict" which then French Premier Guy Mollet, in "anti-Munich reflex,"[86] dubbed the act of an apprentice dictator whose *The Philosophy of the Revolution* should better have been called *Mein Kampf*[87]—the French and the British (with help from the Israelis) mounted their now infamous Egyptian invasion.[88] This action, in turn, under a declared "state of siege," provoked a storm of "sequestration," "liquidation," and other "Egyptianization" measures that was not to subside, and then only temporarily, until late 1957 to early 1958.[89] Predictably, concerned French interests sought the energetic intervention of the Quai d'Orsay. The result, after "long and laborious" negotiations whose "many interruptions" required finally the mediation of the World Bank,[90] was the so-called Zurich Accord of August 22, 1958.[91] Following by about one month the agreement reached between the U.A.R. and the Suez Canal Company,[92] it called for, *inter alia*, a lifting of all "sequestrations" imposed by both countries, a mutual release of claims, an extension of French industrial credits, and compensation within certain agreed limits obtainable in Egypt pursuant to special procedures.

The friendlier relations thus won, however, were not to be long-lived. Although shortly thereafter President Nasser "desequestered" French assets seized at the time of Suez, the U.A.R.'s formal recognition and firm support of breakaway Algeria (with whom France

---

[85] *See* text at note 69 *supra*. For further discussion, see note 106 *infra*.

[86] *Quoted in* H. Thomas, Suez 48 (1967).

[87] Keesing's Contemporary Archives, July 28–August 4, 1956, at 15003, col. 1.

[88] See the above-cited volume by Professor Thomas for a brilliant "contemporary history" of these events.

[89] For details, see 56 Affaires Étrangères A1–A3 (3rd trim., 1964). For further details, see Keesing's Contemporary Archives, May 18–25, 1957, at 15555A, and June 15–22, 1957, at 15608E.

[90] Affaires Étrangères, *supra* note 89, at A3. *See also* Keesing's Contemporary Archives, June 13–20, 1959, at 16856, col. 1.

[91] *See* note 34 *supra*.

[92] *See* note 21 and accompanying text *supra*.

was at war), coupled with her continued efforts to rid herself of foreign economic "influence" through "Egyptianization," put an end to the cooperation that was needed to give full effect to the 1958 Zurich Accord.[93] In other words, it was not until after the 1962 Evian cease-fire and the U.A.R.'s subsequent release of French political prisoners arrested since 1958 that Franco-Egyptian relations could even begin to resume normality.[94] Happily, they did; but not, be it noted, without more hard bargaining. For now it was not just the fulfillment of 1958 expectations that had to be broached, but the resolution of the many wealth deprivation and related claims that had accrued since that time as well. In short, however much French claimants have come to feel dissatisfied with the 1964 and 1966 accords that were finally to be realized,[95] it must be remembered that these settlements were cast in that same rich-poor–colonial-postcolonial matrix that has in recent years so influenced lump sum negotiation and therefore the possibilities for subsequent distribution. About these agreements, and particularly the 1966 Egyptian Accord,[96] more will be said later.

Granted, then, that France's lump sum negotiations have been difficult and usually protracted (whether because of East-West rivalries, Third World xenophobia, or a combination of these and other factors), what about the settlements themselves? Limiting ourselves, as indicated, to the agreements that have been charged in whole or in part to French commission administration, a number of general observations, each bearing heavily if not always directly upon the ultimate French commission distributions, need to be made.[97]

[93] AFFAIRES ÉTRANGÈRES, *supra* note 89, at A3–A4.

[94] *Id.*

[95] *Supra* notes 56 & 57.

[96] Title I of the 1966 Accord, it will be recalled, is the only part of the Egyptian settlement that has been given to French commission administration. *See* Decree No. 68–103 of January 30, 1968, [1968] J.O. 1228, pursuant to which has been established the *Commission spéciale de répartition de l'indemnité égyptienne* (officially known as the *Commission de priorité de transferts et de répartition de l'indemnité égyptienne*) to distribute funds transferred under Article 4 of the 1966 Egyptian Accord. *See also* notes 56 & 57 *supra*, and text following note 71 *supra*.

[97] For details concerning most of these and related agreements, see Weston, *Postwar French Foreign Claims Practice: Adjudication By National Commissions—An Introductory Note*, 43 IND. L.J. 832, 840–866 (1968), from which much of the following discussion is drawn.

First, none of the settlements appear to have approached what might be called "full compensation."[98] For example, the best that could be won under the 1948 Polish Accord seems to have ranged in the neighborhood of 24 percent of the "intrinsic value" of the claims at issue,[99] this figure to be reduced substantially by the later amendatory but not additionally remunerative 1951 Polish Protocol.[100] Similarly, recoupments under the 1950 Czech and 1951 Yugoslav settlements appear to have been limited to no more than 50 and 25 percent, respectively, of the claims accrued.[101] While doubtless due to the inaccessibility of relevant data and to a desire to avoid the hard and potentially disruptive bargaining that line-by-line evaluation necessarily entails, surely this state of affairs was also attrib-

---

[98] The actual lump sums agreed to under the Settlement Agreements were as follows:

1. *1948 Polish Accord* (and 1951 Polish Protocol), art. 6 = 3.8 million tons of high-grade coal (as to which see text at notes 107–111 *infra*), this amount representing in value about U.S. $60 million [VIENOT 98];

2. *1950 Czech Accord,* art. 1 = 4.2 billion French francs, including (per Additional Protocol No. II) 550 million French francs already transferred under the 1948 Czech Accord (as to which see note 77 *supra*), the payment terms on the gross amount being later adjusted pursuant to a 1956 "Avenant" to the 1950 Accord (Decree No. 59–668 of May 5, 1959, [1959] J.O. 5379);

3. *1950 Hungarian Accord,* arts. 1 and 2 = the equivalent in French francs of U.S. $914,285 (320 million francs) and 2 million Hungarian forints (59,600,000 francs), the equivalent franc figures being taken from O. MOREAU-NÉRET, VALEURS ÉTRANGÈRES, MOUVEMENTS DE CAPITAUX ENTRE LA FRANCE ET L'ÉTRANGER DEPUIS 1940, at 173 (1956), who writes that the smallness of the 1950 Hungarian lump sum was due to French entrepreneurs having alienated practically all their Hungarian assets before nationalization;

4. *1951 Yugoslav Accord,* art. 1 = the equivalent in French francs of U.S. $15 million (as to which see note 106 and accompanying text *infra*);

5. *1955 Bulgarian Accord,* art. 1 = 1.5 billion French francs ("on the basis of 350 francs per United States dollar") supplemented as needed (per Article 2) by "a 7% levy on bank payments made by French purchasers of merchandise of Bulgarian origin");

6. *1959 Romanian Accord,* art. 1 = the equivalent in French francs of U.S. $21 million, including (per Article 5) proceeds equivalent to U.S. $2,853,598 derived from percentages levied under a 1954 Franco-Romanian financial protocol;

7. *1963 Yugoslav Accord,* art. 1 = the equivalent in French francs of U.S. $200,000;

8. *1965 Hungarian Accord,* art. 2 = 1,150,000 French francs;

9. *1966 Egyptian Accord,* art. 4 = 300,000 Egyptian pounds; and

10. *1967 Cuban Accord,* art. 1 = 10,861,532 New French francs.

[99] *See* VIENOT 98: "The initial French asking amounted to about 400 million U.S. dollars. It is reasonable to expect that it allowed an appreciable margin for maneuver for the [French] negotiators. We believe, nevertheless, that the intrinsic value of the interests in question was more than $250 million. Anyway, the indemnity obtained affected no more than $60 million."

[100] *See* text at notes 115–119 *infra.*

[101] *See* VIENOT 137 (Czechoslovakia), 177 (Yugoslavia).

utable to the financial crises and monumental economic reforms that obviously must have curbed the ability to pay. Otherwise, unless for ideological reasons, it is difficult to explain the total absence of interest-bearing payments. To avoid distortion, however, it has to be added that most all the settlements have included, implicitly if not explicitly, the release of the outstanding debts owed by the "interested parties," including taxes due at the time of claim accrual. At least in the case of Czechoslovakia this factor appears to have been not insubstantial.[102]

Second, the time of payment has not always lived up to what doctrinally has been understood by "prompt compensation." Except for the 1959 Romanian Accord (which, thanks to Romanian accounts blocked in France, prescribed near-total payment of the lump sum upon its entry into force)[103] and the 1966 Egyptian Accord (which called for total payment of only 300,000 Egyptian pounds "within six months from the date of entry into force of this Agreement"),[104] all the Settlement Agreements have called for non-interest-bearing installments to be paid over periods ranging from 14 months to more than 15 years from the date of signature, entry into force or other functional equivalent.[105] Indeed, the 10-year

[102] Vienot observes that, at the time, Czech taxes on foreign property, rights, and interests often amounted to as much as 30 percent of the value of the property. VIENOT 137.

[103] See 1959 Romanian Accord, art. 7. Per Article 15, the agreement entered into force on the date of its signature, February 9, 1959.

[104] 1966 Egyptian Accord, art. 4. The agreement entered into force on September 1, 1967, about 13 months after its signature. See [1967] J.O. 9939 n.1.

[105] The schedules agreed to under the other Settlement Agreements were as follows:

1. *1948 Polish Accord*, art. 6 = delivery of 3.8 million tons of high-grade coal, the first 2 million tons over the 15-year period 1951–65, the remaining 1.8 million tons according to schedules later to be fixed (although to speed up lump sum distribution, derivable from French sales of the coal, Poland agreed—per Article 7—to issue non-interest-bearing bonds made out for the delivery amounts designated, with these to be given to whatever "organisme" France would designate and to be restored to Poland when the counterpart deliveries shall have been made) [for further details see text at notes 107–111 *infra*];

2. *1950 Czech Accord*, Additional Protocol No. II, art. 1 = 20 biannual installments commencing December 31, 1950, and ending June 30, 1960;

3. *1950 Hungarian Accord*, art. 2 = French franc payment in five annual installments commencing within three months after the date of signature, Hungarian forint payment upon the date of signature;

4. *1951 Yugoslav Accord*, art. 1 = within 10 years of the date of signature according to a schedule fixed in the Additional Protocol (as to which see note 106 and accompanying text *infra*);

5. *1955 Bulgarian Accord*, art. 2 = unspecified time limits, but according to a detailed transfer arrangement;

schedule agreed to under the 1951 Yugoslav Accord had later to be revised upward.[106]

Third, although in most instances France has been able to secure "effective compensation" (*i.e.*, French franc or alternate "hard currency"), this goal has not always been realized.[107] As already mentioned, the 1966 Egyptian Accord provided for payment in Egyptian pounds. Under the 1948 Polish Accord, however, it was not even a matter of money. In lieu of monetary compensation, the medium of payment in every other case, the French and Polish governments chose to fix compensation (subject to France simultaneously extending financial credits equal to 50 percent of the value thereof) in 3.8 million tons of high-grade coal ("charbon flambant") to be delivered,

---

6. *1963 Yugoslav Accord*, art. 1 = two annual installments, on July 15, 1963, and July 15, 1964;

7. *1965 Hungarian Accord*, art. 2 = 3 installments over 14 months commencing 2 months after the date of signature; and

8. *1967 Cuban Accord*, art. 2 = 12 installments commencing June 3, 1967, and ending June 3, 1972.

106 The lump sum payment required by the 1951 Accord was to be drawn in part from levies upon Yugoslav exports to France. Risky though this may seem in theory, it must not have been thought injudicious at the time. As of 1951, according to one report, France ranked about sixth in importance in Yugoslavia's external trade. *See La commerce franco-yougoslave à la lumière des statistiques de commerce exterieure yougoslave*, 7 AFFAIRES ÉTRANGÈRES C.1, C.5 (January 1952). Of course, no future could be guaranteed. Soon after the settlement, owing to a series of bad harvests, Yugoslavia suffered a severe economic crisis, and this inevitably had negative impact upon her ability to export. By April 14, 1954, when payments derived from export proceeds were due to end, monies advanced to France amounted to only about 25 percent of that required by the 1951 schedule. *See* Response by the Minister of Foreign Affairs to the written question of M. André Armengaud of March 8, 1955, [1955] J.O. 630 (*Débats Parlementaires, Conseil de la République*).

Naturally the French were concerned, and in late May 1954 the two countries resumed negotiations with a view to concluding new financial arrangements. This step led, first, to the Protocol of July 27, 1955 (covering the period April 15, 1954, to April 14, 1957) [typewritten copy available on request at the French Foreign Ministry] and, second, after further protracted negotiations strongly influenced by disagreement over the treatment to be accorded French public bondholder claims, to the 1958 Yugoslav Accord, *supra* note 65. Taking past payment difficulties into account, the Accord modified the terms by which the balance due on the 1951 lump sum would be paid. For related background discussion, see text at notes 78–85 *supra*. *See also* Jaudon, *Rapport Moral*, 28 AFFAIRES ÉTRANGÈRES B.10–B.11 (2nd Trim. 1957); Jaudon, *Rapport Moral*, 32 AFFAIRES ÉTRANGÈRES B.1, B.11 (2nd Trim. 1958).

107 One example is to be seen under the 1950 Hungarian Accord which, per articles 1 and 2, called for payment partly in Hungarian forints. *See* note 98(3) *supra*. It appears, however, that this technique cannot be considered to have been entirely an "ineffective" payment. According to one report, these forints were destined principally to French claimants living in Hungary. O. MOREAU-NÉRET, *supra* note 98(3), at 173.

f.o.b. Polish ports, over a period of more than 15 years.[108] To the negotiators this means of payment not only obviated having to debate perhaps irreconcilable issues of legal and monetary policy, it also allowed for the rapid reopening of commercial relations.[109] True, only about U.S. $60 million (or 24 percent) of an estimated $250 million of losses were covered by the settlement.[110] True, also, France was obliged to bear the risk of a fall in coal prices over the delivery years.[111] But Poland, ravaged by war, scarcely could grant more, and France, anxious to stabilize her own economy and to avert the kinds of wholesale losses that she sustained at the hands of the Soviet Union three decades earlier, could ill afford to chance less.

Finally, inadequate as they have seemed to the French, probably none of the settlements could have been won without France accepting, still further, what may be called "value-tying" arrangements.[112] Without going into details, none of the Settlement Agreements, except possibly the second Yugoslav and Hungarian Accords and the 1967 Cuban Accord, have been concluded without the promise of French commercial, financial, or industrial credits or the negotiation of an immediate or future trade agreement.[113] Sometimes, indeed, a restoration of productive economic relations has been expressly acknowledged as one of the basic reasons for settlement.[114] In other words, it seems that the payor countries have deemed "value-tying" to be essential to their economic growth. Without these arrangements, the agreements reached, to say nothing of the indemnities obtained, would likely have proved impossible, at least for a long time.

[108] 1948 Polish Accord, arts. 3 and 6.

[109] Vienot writes that coal was chosen as the medium of payment partly to avoid French monetary instability. VIENOT 98. To this comment may be added Ardagh's observation that "French coal is mainly poor quality, and because it is hard to extract it also works out as more expensive than American or Polish coal. Therefore, though it is not plentiful . . . , France soon [after the war] found herself having to limit production as the coal era in Europe began to wane." *Supra* note 11, at 49.

[110] *See* note 99 *supra.*

[111] *See* Bindschedler, *supra* note 23, at 263.

[112] These "value-tying" arrangements are not unique to France. For comparative indication, see I. FOIGHEL, *supra* note 9, at 111–19.

[113] *See, e.g.,* 1950 Czech Accord, art. 6 and Additional Protocol No. II, art. 2. For details, see VIENOT 132.

[114] *See, e.g.,* 1959 Romanian Accord, preamble.

In sum, all the settlements have had to be responsive to the economic and other vicissitudes of the world social process within which they have been made, a fact which seems to have been at least tacitly acknowledged even by French politicians. With one exception, there appears to have been no serious debate in the French Parliament concerning either the adequacy of the indemnities obtained or the "value-tying" concessions given. Only in connection with the 1951 Polish Protocol do tempers appear to have been aroused. This "Protocole d'Application," it will be recalled, was intended to expand the coverage authorized under the 1948 Polish Accord.[115] No longer was the 1948 lump sum to be restricted to compensating "French interests affected by the Polish law of 3 January 1946 on nationalizations."[116] Now it was to be shared also by "French interests" which, as of the signature of the 1948 Accord, had sustained deprivation because of (1) "agrarian and forestry reform," (2) "the municipalization of Warsaw terrains," and (3) "all other measures restrictive of the right of property."[117] It is not apparent why this dilution of the 1948 indemnity, already small, was deemed necessary. Certainly it was not apparent to the "Président et Rapporteur" of the *Commission des Affaires Économiques, des Douanes et des Conventions Commerciales*, Monsieur Rochereau, who, at the time of the Protocol's presentation for ratification to the *Conseil de la République*, had the following to say:

> At the time [of the negotiation of the 1948 Accord] our negotiators let themselves be carried away to the extent of a considerable renunciation [of claims]. They justified them then by the difficult situation in Poland. . . . The 1948 Accord affects a large number of small shareholders in French enterprises doing business in Poland and industrial groups still active there. These shareholders and industrialists who, as a result of the delay in enforcing the Accord, having not yet received even the smallest portion of these reduced indemnities, now see curtailed once again the meager indemnities they had every right to hope would be definite. This curtailment is moreover subject to the highest criticism juridically, since it would alter legislative provisions adopted in 1948 by the two governments, and

115 *See* note 61 and text at notes 99–100 *supra.*
116 *1948 Polish Accord*, preamble.
117 1951 Polish Protocol.

which constituted solemn engagements on behalf of those concerned. These latter can therefore legitimately request that the French Government take into consideration, in the payment of the nationalization indemnities, the new hardship that is imposed upon them. This can be accomplished either by refusing to ratify the protocol, which is practically impossible and is not recommended by the Commission [des Affaires Économiques], or by an equitable fixing of the price at which France takes Polish coal and for which the Treasury currently declares a reduction to a level as low as it is unjustified.[118]

But the fact remains: like all the other Settlement Agreements the 1951 Protocol was ratified with little or no parliamentary opposition.[119] One is therefore led to conclude either an extraordinary sophistication or tolerance on the part of French officialdom or, alternatively, the absence of at least any perceived high stakes in the domestic political arena.

At any rate, like it or not, French commission claimants have had to be content with only percentage compensation. The French commissions, without benefit of supplementary French appropriations, have been able to do no more.[120] Before looking to the decisional context within which these distributions have been determined, however, three further observations about the settlement context are in order.

First, looking to the Settlement Agreements as a whole, we find three distinct kinds of international grievances covered: (1) "peacetime" deprivation claims; (2) "wartime" deprivation claims; and (3) "ordinary" (i.e., non-deprivative) commercial and bondholder debt claims. Proceeding seriatim, all of the Settlement Agreements have provided for the first of these sets of claims. Initially under the 1948 Polish Accord and at all times under the 1966 Egyptian

---

[118] [1952] J.O. 1361 (Débats Parlementaires, Conseil de la République). Recounting the negotiation, Vienot defends the 1948 French negotiators (among them representatives from the Association Pour la Sauvegarde et l'Expansion des Biens et Intérêts Français à l'Étranger, as to which see note 16 supra): "The French took a realistic position. Considering an agreement on the principle [of compensation] impossible, they indicated their desire to devote discussion to the fixing of a lump sum indemnity. The Polish seem to have wanted to reserve this question for a further negotiation, but they finally accepted the French proposal because they sensed the French resolve not to conclude any financial and commercial agreements then in preparation until after the nationalization negotiations had ended." VIENOT 92–93.

[119] See note 61 supra.

[120] See Part III, notes 443–444 and accompanying text.

Accord these claims have had to arise from a specified deprivation measure.[121] Under all the other agreements, however, they can have arisen from any one of a number of such measures; to wit, "from . . . measures of nationalization, expropriation and other measures of similar restrictive character,"[122] language obviously pregnant with interpretative possibility. "Wartime" deprivation claims, on the other hand, have been covered by only three of the Settlement Agreements. Owing obviously to World War II alliances, the 1950 Hungarian, 1955 Bulgarian, and 1959 Romanian Accords thus provided for "war damages" for which Hungary, Bulgaria, and Romania, as former Axis Powers, had been made responsible by their respective Peace Treaties of 1947.[123] Like "wartime" deprivation claims, finally, "ordinary" debt claims have been covered by only a minority of the Settlement Agreements: the 1951 and 1963 Yugoslav accords,[124] the 1955 Bulgarian Accord,[125] and the 1959 Romanian Accord.[126] Apparently the silence of the other Settlement Agreements in this respect was due principally to the presence or prospect

---

[121] *See* 1948 Polish Accord, preamble and arts. 2 and 3, which authorize compensation only for interests damaged or divested by "the Polish Law of 3 January 1946 on nationalizations"; 1966 Egyptian Accord, Title I, which authorizes compensation only for interests "sequestered" under "[Egyptian] Proclamation No. 5 of 1 November 1956." It will be recalled that the 1951 Polish Protocol later eliminated the single law restriction of the 1948 Polish Accord. *See* text at notes 115–119 *supra*.

[122] *See* 1950 Czech Accord, art. 1; 1950 Hungarian Accord, preamble; 1951 Yugoslav Accord, preamble and art. 1; 1951 Polish Protocol, subparas. 1–3; 1955 Bulgarian Accord, art. 1(a); 1959 Romanian Accord, art. 1(a); 1963 Yugoslav Accord, art. 2. Somewhat differently, Article 1 of the 1967 Cuban Accord authorizes compensation for interests "affected by the laws and measures promulgated by the Revolutionary Government of the Republic of Cuba since 1 January 1959." Under the 1959 Romanian Accord, "peacetime" deprivation claims have been eligible to share in the lump sum authorized, together with "wartime" deprivation claims, only to the extent of 37 percent. *See id.*, art. 11. *See also* note 126 *infra*.

[123] *See* Treaty of Peace with Bulgaria, February 10, 1947, arts. 22 and 23, [1949] 41 U.N.T.S. 21 (in English at 50); Treaty of Peace with Hungary, February 10, 1947, arts. 24 and 26, [1949] 41 U.N.T.S. 135 (in English at 168); Treaty of Peace with Romania, February 10, 1947, arts. 23 and 24, [1949] 42 U.N.T.S. 3 (in English at 34). Under the 1959 Romanian Accord, "wartime" deprivation claims have been eligible to share in the lump sum authorized, together with "peacetime" deprivation claims, only to the extent of 37 percent. *See id.* art. 11. *See also* note 126 *infra*.

[124] *See* 1951 Yugoslav Accord, "Protocole Financier," art. 4; 1963 Yugoslav Accord, art. 2.

[125] *See* art. 1(c).

[126] *See* art. 1(c). "Ordinary" debt claims have been eligible to share in the lump sum authorized to the extent of 63 percent. *See* art. 11. *See also* notes 122 & 123 *supra*.

of separate debt claims settlements.[127] Accuracy compels noting, however, that more or less separate debt claims settlements were similarly achieved *within* the 1951 Yugoslav and 1955 Bulgarian accords. Under the first, all "ordinary" debt claims payments were to be deducted not from the lump sum authorized for payment of deprivation claims but from proceeds derived from a percentage to be levied upon Yugoslav exports to France.[128] Under the second, these payments were to be charged both against the principal lump sum indemnity and against export levies.[129]

Second, although all the Settlement Agreements left the matter of final distribution exclusively within the jurisdiction of the French Government,[130] not all of them have been equally unconcerned about the discretion that France might exercise in this connection. At one extreme is the 1948 Polish Accord (and by later amendment the 1951 Polish Protocol) which, unlike any of the other Settlement Agreements, actually set forth the "interested parties" to be covered.[131] At the other extreme are the two Hungarian accords and the 1955 Bulgarian, 1959 Romanian, 1963 Yugoslav, and 1967 Cuban accords—all of them variously adverting, generally, to "French nationals," "French interests," "natural and juridical French persons," or to a combination of these categories.[132] Partaking of both extremes, finally, are the 1950 Czech, 1951 Yugoslav, and 1966 Egyptian accords. While alluding to "French nationals," "French interests," or "natural and juridical French persons," each of these agreements

---

[127] Interview with Dervieu, in Paris, June 6, 1969. For example, debt claims based on certain issues of the *Crédit Foncier* of Hungary had been settled before the 1950 Hungarian Accord through agreements made in 1949. *See* COMMUNICATION No. 425 of the *Association Nationale des Porteurs Français de Valeurs Mobilières* (August 10, 1950). *See also, e.g.,* agreements cited *supra* notes 55, 62, & 65.

[128] *See* the "Protocole Financier" cited at note 64 *supra.*

[129] 1955 Bulgarian Accord, art. 2.

[130] *See* note 136 and accompanying text *infra.*

[131] *See* art. 4. The Accord even specifies many of the intended beneficiaries by name and industrial category. *See id.* art. 4 and "Annexe." It must be added, however, that the beneficiaries mentioned in the "Annexe" were listed "à titre indicatif et sauf justifications contraires."

[132] *See* 1950 Hungarian Accord, preamble and art. 3; 1955 Bulgarian Accord, preamble and art. 5; 1959 Romanian Accord, arts. 1, 3, and 11; 1963 Yugoslav Accord, preamble and art 2; 1967 Cuban Accord, preamble and arts. 1–4, 6. Both the 1955 Bulgarian Accord (at art. 5) and the 1959 Romanian Accord (at art. 3) stipulated as covered: "French natural or juridical persons . . . , as proprietor, shareholder, creditor, etc."

has also placed restrictions upon certain kinds of potential claimants, mainly creditor claimants.[133] In manifesting this spread, the Settlement Agreements have reflected what is characteristic worldwide.[134]

Finally, all of the agreements with which we are primarily concerned, as well as all the other lump sum agreements to which France has been party, may be seen to have constituted formal and permanent releases by France of all claims against the payor countries and their nationals bearing upon the grievances covered within the settlement terms.[135] This discharge is, after all, the essence of "un réglement global et forfaitaire." Accordingly, any "interested party" who has wanted to make good on his international claim has had no legal standing (upon entry into force of the relevant Settlement Agreement) to seek recourse other than against the French Government, an option clearly invited by almost all the Settlement Agreements in their express stipulation that lump sum distribution should fall "within the sole competence of the French Government" (or equivalent language).[136] Of course, whether or not an "interested party" would succeed in the end is another matter, one fundamentally conditioned not only by the merits of his claim but also by the nature of the decisional context within which his claim might be brought. To an examination of this context, therefore, it is now appropriate to turn.

---

[133] See 1950 Czech Accord, Additional Protocol No. I, paras. 1(a) and 1(b); 1951 Yugoslav Accord, art. 5; 1966 Egyptian Accord, arts. 4 and 5.

[134] See Lillich, *Eligible Claimants Under Lump Sum Agreements*, 43 IND. L. J. 816 (1968). *See also* 2 R. LILLICH & B. WESTON, INTERNATIONAL CLAIMS: THEIR SETTLEMENT BY LUMP SUM AGREEMENTS, soon to be published by the Syracuse University Press.

[135] See 1948 Polish Accord, art. 3; 1950 Czech Accord, art. 3; 1950 Hungarian Accord, art. 4; 1951 Yugoslav Accord, art. 3; 1955 Bulgarian Accord, art. 4; 1959 Romanian Accord, arts. 2 and 4; 1963 Yugoslav Accord art. 3; 1965 Hungarian Accord, art. 3; 1966 Egyptian Accord, art. 18; 1967 Cuban Accord, art. 4.

[136] See 1948 Polish Accord, art. 5; 1950 Czech Accord, art. 7; 1950 Hungarian Accord, art. 7; 1951 Yugoslav Accord, art. 6; 1959 Romanian Accord, art. 11; 1963 Yugoslav Accord, art. 4 (incorporating *mutatis mutandis* articles 3–9 of the 1951 Yugoslav Accord); 1965 Hungarian Accord, art. 4; 1966 Egyptian Accord, art. 4; 1967 Cuban Accord, art. 6. Only the 1955 Bulgarian Accord lacks this explicit statement, presumably because of oversight. That final distribution was expected to rest exclusively within the jurisdiction of the French Government is clearly implied, however, throughout the text and in particular in Article 2(a).

3. THE DECISIONAL CONTEXT

The development of the "Law of International Claims" and the "Law of State Responsibility," it still may be insisted, is only going to be retarded—or at least little advanced—by municipal distribution decisions. Possibly there is some justification for this contention in some cases—as in Great Britain, *arguendo*, where domestic Orders in Council assume a major prerogative role.[137] In the case of France, however, as in the case of the United States where the Foreign Claims Settlement Commission is required to apply "provisions of the applicable claims agreement" and "the applicable principles of international law, justice and equity,"[138] the argument is less persuasive, at least as concerns the eight *commissions spéciales* that are at the focus of the present inquiry. Except in the case of the commission charged to distribute the 1966 Egyptian indemnity, and except for prescriptions we are wont to call "procedural," neither the legislation establishing the French commissions nor their self-adopted rules of procedure have stipulated any "substantive" norms—national, foreign, or international—to which the commissions should refer for decisional guidance. That is, the Settlement Agreements themselves, in addition to voicing some "procedural" guidelines of their own, have stood almost alone, albeit by way of validating domestic legislation,[139] in prescribing "substantive" standards upon which the decisions of the French commissions could be premised. As Rudolf Bindschedler has said of postwar French practice, "[neither French] law nor the enabling decrees give any indication of the applicable law; one can assume that it is international law, in the first instance the agreements."[140] In other words, the

---

[137] *See* LILLICH (G.B.) 141–42. As Lillich is careful to point out, however, the Orders in Council "reflect norms of international law and hence enable the [Foreign Compensation Commission] to apply international law by reference." *Id.* at 142.

[138] International Claims Settlement Act of 1949, § 4(a), 22 U.S.C. § 1623 (1964). For details, see LILLICH (U.S.) 71–75.

[139] *See* notes 52–66 *supra*. In this connection, see THE FRENCH CONSTITUTION OF 1958, art. 55: "Treaties or agreements duly ratified or approved shall, upon their publication, have an authority superior to that of laws, subject, for each agreement or treaty, to its application by the other party" (French Embassy transl.). *See also* Decree No. 53-192 of March 14, 1953, relative to the ratification and publication of international commitments ("engagements") signed by France, [1953] J.O. 2436.

[140] Bindschedler, *supra* note 23, at 293. To similar effect, see Berlia, *supra* note 14,

decisions of these domestic institutions—essentially treaty interpretations—may be seen generally as international legal reference points of first instance, rather like those of the more venerable mixed arbitral tribunals. For present jurisprudential purposes, it is a matter of mere formality that the Settlement Agreements have been made "internal law" by parliamentary enactment.

Of course, the distinction drawn between "procedural" and "substantive" guidelines, normatively ambiguous conceptions whose utility is seldom more than organizational and whose putative distinctiveness is on final analysis immaterial to persons on the receiving end of decision (win or lose), should not obscure the fact that value change—the ultimate gravamen to which all legal claims are addressed—results from the prescription and application of any norm, however characterized. Thus, while the Settlement Agreements have been mainly responsible for the so-called substantive decisions of the French commissions (and as well for some we may call "procedural"), they have been by no means the only "source" upon which the commissions have had to rely to effect value change, least of all in the case of the commission constituted to apply the 1966 Egyptian Accord. The enabling legislation establishing the commissions (hereinafter usually called the "Statutory Instruments") and the commissions' *réglements de procédure* (hereinafter usually called the "Commission Rules"), each having mainly "procedural" attributes, have likewise determined outcomes. For that matter, so also have French and foreign law, although neither have been expressly invoked in the Settlement Agreements, the Statutory Instruments or the Commission Rules (two or more of these three sources being hereinafter called the "Controlling Texts").

In short, to understand properly the decisional context within which French commission claimants have had to operate, it is necessary to account not only for the Settlement Agreements but, as well, for the other Controlling Texts that have circumscribed French commission practice. Before doing so, however, it is helpful to make four historical observations.

---

at 69: "French practice . . . shows that it has never been a question of applying French law, no more than Yugoslav, Czechoslovak or Hungarian law. It has amounted to an elaboration of an international law doubtless different from customary international law but certainly foreign to national laws."

First, and perhaps most important to comparativists, France has not followed the same institutional pattern that has prevailed in the United Kingdom and the United States. Unlike those countries, each of which has created but one commission to dispose of all lump sum transfers—in the United States, the International Claims Commission of 1950 and its successor, the existing Foreign Claims Settlement Commission of 1954;[141] in Great Britain, the Foreign Compensation Commission of 1950[142]—France has elected, as indicated at the outset, to establish a number of *commissions spéciales de répartition*. Why this path was chosen is not altogether clear. Two reasons, neither entirely persuasive, have been given by one informed observer:[143] first, the textual differences that have distinguished the separate Settlement Agreements; and second, the multiplicity of claims involved and the consequent concern to simplify their processing. There is no doubt that these considerations were present at the beginning;[144] but a more satisfying answer, since both the United States and Great Britain had opted for a single commission before even the first French commissions had been constituted in 1951,[145] is that the French experience has simply grown like Topsy, responding *ad hoc* (although not illogically) to events as they have arisen.[146] As will be discussed in Part IV, however, while this multiple approach has allowed for some administrative inefficiency, it has not made for much if any decisional inconsistency.[147] A number of elements in the institutional environment within which the commissions have had to function, most notably the French Foreign Ministry's *Sérvice des Biens et Intérêts Privés*[148]

---

[141] *See generally* LILLICH (U.S.) ; LILLICH & CHRISTENSON.

[142] *See generally* LILLICH (G.B.).

[143] *See* Glaser Correspondence—12/67, *supra* note 16.

[144] *Accord,* Interview with Dervieu, in Paris, June 11, 1969; Interview with Branche, in Paris, July 10, 1969.

[145] *See* note 162 *infra.*

[146] For illustration, see VIENOT 229–30.

[147] *Accord,* Ernest-Picard Correspondence—11/67, *supra* note 17.

[148] The *Service des Biens et Intérêts Privés,* under the jurisdiction of the French Foreign Ministry's *Direction des Conventions Administratives des Affaires Consulaires,* has as its principal function the safekeeping and defense of private French interests abroad. With headquarters in Paris (31, Rue Dumont d'Urville, Paris XVI), branch offices in Nantes and Strasbourg, and a total staff of about 35 persons, it performs a role not dissimilar to the Assistant Legal Adviser for International Claims of the United States Department of State and the Claims Department of the British Foreign Office. Additionally, the Director of the *Service,* currently Monsieur Pierre d'Huart,

and the office of *commissaire du gouvernement*,[149] plainly have supplied a considerable degree of harmonization. Still, the multiple approach has not escaped some French criticism.[150]

Next, while separate commissions have been established to distribute lump sums transferred from each payor country (*i.e.*, Bulgaria, Cuba, Czechoslovakia, Egypt, Hungary, Poland, Romania, and Yugoslavia), the French have not created separate commissions to handle each Settlement Agreement. The Hungarian and Yugoslav settlements, it will be recalled, entailed two lump sum agreements each. Accepting *arguendo* the rationale given for resort to multiple commissions, it is of course somewhat illogical that France did not constitute different commissions to administer separately the 1950 and 1965 Hungarian accords and the 1951 and 1963 Yugoslav accords. Wisely, however, doubtless for reasons of administrative efficiency, the French Government determined against this kind of consistency. Demonstrating faith in the separate Hungarian and Yugoslav claims programs already underway, it simply delegated responsibility for the 1965 Hungarian and 1963 Yugoslav accords to the commissions earlier constituted to apply the 1950 Hungarian and 1951 Yugoslav accords.[151] Similarly, "because it was easier to change the name than to change the structure," responsibility for the 1967 Cuban Accord has been given to the all-but-defunct commission charged to apply the 1948 Polish Accord.[152] To avoid confusion between these claims programs, however, it is nevertheless helpful hereinafter usually to speak of "the Cuban Commission," "the 1950 Hungarian Commission," "the 1965 Hungarian Commission," "the Polish Commission," "the 1951 Yugoslav Commission," and "the 1963 Yugoslav Commission."[153]

---

has administrative responsibility for the French commissions. Interview with Dervieu, in Paris, June 11, 1969. For further details, see note 176 *infra*.

[149] *See* note 178 *infra*.

[150] *See* O. MOREAU-NÉRET, *supra* note 98(3), at 165; VIENOT 229–30; La Pradelle, *Jurisdiction Administrative et Droit International,* 1962 ÉTUDES ET DOCUMENTS (*Conseil d'État*) 13, 39.

[151] *See* Decree No. 64–709 of July 7, 1964, [1964] J.O. 6246 (assigning responsibility for the 1963 Yugoslav Accord); Decree No. 66–102 of February 18, 1966, [1966] J.O. 1549 (assigning responsibility for the 1965 Hungarian Accord). For the initial legislation establishing the already constituted commissions, see note 162 *infra*.

[152] Interview with Dervieu, in Paris, June 11, 1969. For the law assigning this responsibility, see Decree No. 67–854 of September 20, 1967, [1967] J.O. 9762.

[153] These designations of course refer to the signature years of, and the payors

THE CONTEXT OF CLAIM 43

Third, just as the French Government has exercised its prerogative by relegating four of its postwar lump sum "ordinary" debt claims agreements to "la répartition administrative,"[154] so also has it removed from commission jurisdiction "ordinary" debt claims provisions that are to be found, as earlier recounted,[155] in the 1955 Bulgarian, 1959 Romanian, and 1951 Yugoslav accords.[156] The only "ordinary" debt claims that have been admitted to commission adjudication have been those covered under the 1963 Yugoslav Accord.[157] Accordingly, but for this minor exception, it is fair to say that the postwar French commissions have been constituted exclusively to adjudicate "peacetime" and "wartime" deprivation claims (as earlier mentioned, the only other kinds of grievances covered by the Settlement Agreements).[158]

Finally, as already implied, all the commissions (including the 1961 German Commission)[159] have been constituted purely on a temporary and, insofar as concerns the commission members, a part-time basis. As originally conceived, all were to be liquidated upon completion of their work. Since their founding first with the Czech, 1950 Hungarian, and Polish claims programs in 1951, however, only

---

under, the controlling Settlement Agreements. The years are not to be confused with the dates upon which the commissions were originally established. Using the same logic, the other commissions will hereinafter usually be referred to as "the Bulgarian Commission," "the Czech Commission," "the Egyptian Commission," and "the Romanian Commission."

154 *See* text at notes 66–73 *supra.* For related comment concerning British practice, see text at note 48 *supra.*

155 *See* text at notes 124–129 *supra.*

156 The reference is to (1) Article 1(c) of the 1955 Bulgarian Accord, (2) the "Protocole Financier" of the 1951 Yugoslav Accord (see note 64 *supra*), and (3) Article 1(c) and (d) of the 1959 Romanian Accord.

Distribution under the 1951 "Protocol Financier" was assigned to the *Association Nationale des Porteurs Français de Valeurs Mobilières.* Letter from Jean-François Dervieu, Deputy Director of the *Service des Biens et Intérêts Privés,* January 22, 1970.

Distribution under Article 1(c) of the 1955 Bulgarian Accord was charged to seven French banks. *See* "Avis relatif à l'accord franco-bulgare sur le réglement des créances financiers françaises sur la Bulgarie," [1959] J.O. 9211.

Distribution under Article 1(c) and (d) of the 1959 Romanian Accord was assigned by simple letter from the Minister of Finance to the *Association Nationale des Porteurs Français de Valeurs Mobilières. See* "Avis-Emprunts Roumains," [1959] J.O. 4190. *See also* the *Association Nationale's* COMMUNICATION No. 450 (April 15, 1959).

157 *See* art. 2.

158 *See* text at notes 121–129 *supra.*

159 *See* Part I, note 10.

the Bulgarian and Czech commissions have "actually disappeared" as of this writing.[160] On the other hand, it has also to be noted that, but for some minor technicalities, the 1950 Hungarian, Polish, and 1951 Yugoslav claims programs—as distinct from the commissions constituted to administer them—have likewise been terminated.[161] Thus, still actively in operation, in addition to the recently constituted Cuban and Egyptian commissions, are the 1965 Hungarian, Romanian, and 1963 Yugoslav commissions.

Summarizing, the following chart should be helpful:

Commission	Claims Assigned	Current Status
Bulgarian	1955 Bulgarian Accord, art. 1(a) and (b)—*i.e.*, only deprivation claims.	Terminated
Cuban	1967 Cuban Accord—*i.e.*, only deprivation claims.	In Operation
Czech	1950 Czech Accord—*i.e.*, only deprivation claims.	Terminated
Egyptian	1966 Egyptian Accord, Title I in particular—*i.e.*, only individual deprivation claims.	In Operation
Hungarian	1950 Hungarian Accord—*i.e.* only deprivation claims.	Virtually Terminated
	1965 Hungarian Accord—*i.e.*, only deprivation claims.	In Operation
Polish	1948 Polish Accord, including 1951 Polish Protocol—*i.e.*, only deprivation claims.	Virtually Terminated
Romanian	1959 Romanian Accord, art. 1(a) and (b)—*i.e.*, only deprivation claims.	In Operation
Yugoslav	1951 Yugoslav Accord, excluding "Protocol Financier"—*i.e.*, only deprivation claims.	Virtually Terminated
	1963 Yugoslav Accord—*i.e.*, both deprivation and "ordinary" debt claims.	In Operation

160 *See* "Avis relatif à la clôture des travaux de la commission spéciale de répartition de l'indemnité bulgare," [1968] J.O. 12075 (as to the Bulgarian Commission); letter from Jean-François Dervieu, Deputy Director of the *Service des Biens et Intérêts Privés*, January 22, 1970 (as to the Czech Commission).

161 *Id. Also*, Interview with Charles Claudon, "Secrétaire" of the Polish Commission, in Paris, July 1, 1969; Interview with Branche, "Secrétaire" of the Bulgarian, 1950 Hungarian, and 1951 Yugoslav commissions, in Paris, July 10, 1969.

Now, with these preliminaries in mind, it is appropriate to examine the other Controlling Texts that have circumscribed French commission practice, to wit, the Statutory Instruments and the Commission Rules.

A. *The Statutory Instruments*

The Czech, 1950 Hungarian, and Polish commissions, the first French commissions, were created at virtually the same time. For this reason, their Statutory Instruments (*i.e.*, their "constitutive" *and* "applicative" laws) were nearly word for word the same.[162] More importantly, their Statutory Instruments may be seen to have served as the model not only for their own successors, the Cuban and 1965 Hungarian claims programs, but for nearly all the commissions established later as well. Accordingly, they merit detailed treatment. Using as a guide the instruments establishing the Czech Commission (they were unencumbered by the special coal transfer provisions of the equivalent Polish Commission legislation), we can later note the major and minor variations on the basic theme.

The Basic Theme

The Czech Commission Constitutive Law is representative, concise and straightforward. Accordingly, for clarity and economy, this dictates quoting its key features in full,[163] making appropriate notes along the way.

> Art. 2—In view of the execution [of the 1950] Accord . . . and by application of its Article 7 [*i.e.*, the provisions placing sole responsibility for final distribution in the hands of the French Government], there is established *une commission spéciale* composed as follows:[164]

---

[162] *See* Law No. 51–671 of May 24, 1951 (constituting the Czech Commission), [1951] J.O. 5787, and Application of Law No. 51–671 (Aug. 4, 1952), [1952] J.O. 8428; Law No. 51–673 of May 24, 1951 (constituting the Polish Commission), [1951] J.O. 5788, and Application of Law No. 51–673 (May 13, 1952), [1952] J.O. 4862; Law No. 51–674 of May 24, 1951 (constituting the 1950 Hungarian Commission), [1951] J.O. 5789, and Application of Law No. 51–674 (Aug. 4, 1952), [1952] J.O. 8428. These laws and the laws establishing the other commissions are hereinafter usually referred to as the "Constitutive Laws" and the "Application Laws."

[163] Emphases added in the following translation.

[164] Commission members always have been appointed, sometimes to more than

A *président de chambre* at the *cour de cassation,* President, and a *conseiller* at the *cour de cassation,* both designated by the First President of the *cour de cassation;*

A *conseiller d'État,* active or honorary, designated by the *garde des sceaux* [*i.e.,* the Minister of Justice];

A *conseiller maître* at the *cour des comptes,* active or honorary, designated by the Minister of Finance;

An official designated by the Minister of Foreign Affairs.[165]

Art. 3—The claimants . . . shall, at risk of forfeiture and no later than three months after the promulgation of the present law, except in case of *force majeur,* present their claims to the *commission spéciale* established at Article 2 above.[166]

Equally admissible are:[167]

(a) Claims presented by associations constituted or capable of being constituted . . . to represent natural or juridical French persons having participation, even minority participation, in companies that are neither French nor under French control;

(b) Claims drawn up on behalf and in place of a company by the

---

one commission, with terms extending for the life of each commission. These appointees, whose names are published in the *Journal Officiel,* have been uniformly nominated by the governmental agency where they are otherwise employed full-time. When members have later retired from their full-time work, as has happened several times, they nonetheless have usually continued as commission members. Interview with Dervieu, in Paris, June 16, 1969. As a result, the commissions generally have been composed of erstwhile—sometimes elderly—governmental officials.

165 Vienot has commented upon the composition of the commissions as follows: "By the quality of their members and by the variety of the Agencies to which the members belong, the Commissions constitute *collèges* perfectly adapted to the tasks which are theirs. The multiple problems of the juridical, administrative, diplomatic and financial orders are easily solved by these highly competent personalities." VIENOT 230. It must be added, however, that the commission members, although expert in their full-time fields and usually trained in French law, never have been required to have any *special* training to qualify for commission membership (except insofar as they have been required to be chosen from among the agencies designated). To avoid conflict of interest, however, they cannot have been, simultaneously, practicing professionals and commission members. Interview with Dervieu, in Paris, June 16, 1969.

166 This provision was replaced of course by equivalent—and as it happens nearly identical—language in the laws constituting the successor Cuban and 1965 Hungarian claims programs. *See* Decree No. 67–854, art. 2, *supra* note 152 (Cuban); Decree No. 66–102, art. 2, *supra* note 151 (Hungarian). Similarly, claimants eligible under the 1951 Polish Protocol were given a later filing deadline than those eligible for relief under the 1948 Polish Accord. *See* "Arrête" of March 28, 1958, [1958] J.O. 3301. For relevant discussion, see text at Part III, notes 311–335.

167 As shall be seen, the following two subparagraphs have had substantial influence upon the decisions of the French commissions. Accordingly, they will be referred to frequently.

shareholders of French companies or of companies under French control, if they are presented within the time allowed above and if the company is not itself appealing.

Art. 4—Transfers of assets by natural or juridical persons to the German State or to its nationals remain annulled by virtue of Ordinance No. 1224 of 9 June 1945. Amounts received for these transfers shall be turned over to the *Trésor*.

To apply this provision, the *Trésor* is admitted in the place of the transferors to compete in the lump sum distribution to the extent of the transfer price, and can, in the case where the nationalization indemnity is less than the transfer price, demand the balance directly from the transferors or their beneficiaries.

In the case where the transferors shall not have presented their claims according to the conditions fixed in the present article, the *Trésor* is admitted to compete in the lump sum distribution in their place and can, if the nationalization indemnity is less than the transfer price, demand the balance directly from the transferors or their beneficiaries.[168]

Art. 5—The *commission spéciale* shall:

Draw up a definitive list of distributees;

Rule *souverainement* on the merits of the claims and on the value of the debts or the nationalized property that belonged to the distributees;[169]

Determine the distributees' share of the [lump sum] indemnity.

The *commission spéciale*, judging in equity,[170] shall charge to the distributions allowed a deduction which takes into account the use

---

[168] This provision and its related clauses throughout the law (*see* art. 5) were designed to penalize persons who, through property transfers, profited from the Germans during the German occupations of World War II. Since there was no mention of this item in the relevant accords, the provision is illustrative of the prerogative role of the French Government in the distribution process. For details concerning this anti-collaboration provision, see Sarraute & Tager, *supra* note 29, at 1173–77; VIENOT 241–43. The provision was repeated neither in the law constituting the successor 1965 Hungarian claims program (presumably because by that time the problem of German cessions had become moot), *supra* note 151, nor in the law constituting the successor Cuban claims program (for obvious reasons), *supra* note 152. For relevant discussion, see text at Part III, notes 345–351.

[169] The thrust of this provision was to deny judicial review. *But see* text at notes 185–191 *infra*. In this connection, it may be noted that the word "souverainement" was not included in the Hungarian law. But as Sarraute & Tager have remarked (*supra* note 29, at 1177), "this is probably a mere oversight."

[170] It should be noted that the direction to judge in equity related only to the valuation of the claims of persons who, by constraint or otherwise, transferred property to the German authorities during World War II.

value of the amounts collected by property owners who transferred their property to the [German] State or to German nationals; it must equally take into account the revalorization of investments made by the transferors with the amounts collected.[171]

The *commission* shall establish these charges by taking into account the situation of proprietors who transferred their property following a measure of sequestration, a measure of effective liquidation or the naming of an administrator of their property or any other equivalent measure. The *commission* may in these various cases withhold any charge.

The claimants who have transferred their assets without constraint shall receive nothing beyond the value of the transfer price already received; the surplus which they would have been able to receive shall be repartitioned among the other distributees.

Art. 6—The administrative costs of the *commission spéciale* and its secretariat shall be charged to the sum total of the *indemnité globale forfaitaire*.[172]

Art. 7—The *commission* shall terminate the examination of claims and render the decisions relative thereto within eighteen months of the promulgation of the present law.[173]

Art. 8—Appropriate measures to assure the execution of the Accord . . . and of the present law will be taken by joint decision of the Minister of Foreign Affairs and the Minister of Finance and Economic Affairs.

The Czech Application Law is equally concise and to the point. Again, subject to appropriate passing notations, the key language bears quotation in full.[174]

Art. 1—The *commission spéciale* [previously constituted] shall undertake all measures relative to its functioning. It shall regulate its own procedure. It may select *rapporteurs* and seek expert advice.[175]

---

[171] For the significance of this provision and its two paragraphs following, see note 168 *supra*.

[172] *See* notes 180–181 and accompanying text *infra*.

[173] This provision reappears in the laws constituting the successor Cuban and 1965 Hungarian claims programs, *supra* notes 151 & 152. The time requirement, however, proved impossibly short for the Czech, 1950 Hungarian, and Polish commissions. Accordingly, the French Parliament subsequently granted two 18-month extensions. *See* Law No. 54–282 of March 15, 1954, [1954] J.O. 2541; Law No. 55–994 of July 29, 1955, [1955] J.O. 7627.

[174] Emphases added in the following translation.

[175] *See Société anonyme de l'industrie textile*, [1964] Rec. Cons. d'Ét. 360, wherein

Its secretariat shall be guaranteed by the *office des biens et intérêts privés* where it has its headquarters.[176]

It shall report periodically on the state of its work to the Ministry of Foreign Affairs, *direction générale des affaires économiques et financières*,[177] and to the Minister of Finance, *direction des finances exterieures*.

Art. 2—The director of the *office des biens et intérêts privés* or his representative shall function as *commissaire du gouvernement* to the *commission*.[178]

---

the *Conseil d'État* held that it was material error for the Polish Commission to base a valuation decision on erroneous expert advice.

[176] The *Office des Biens et Intérêts Privés*, a bureau of the French Foreign Ministry founded in 1919 to attend to French foreign interests damaged by World War I and thereafter preoccupied with the protection and defense of French foreign interests generally, was replaced in 1954–1955 by the *Service des Biens et Intérêts Privés* which today performs many of the same functions as its predecessor. For a brief official history of the *Office*, see MINISTÈRE DES AFFAIRES ÉTRANGÈRES, OFFICE DES BIENS ET INTÉRÊTS PRIVÉS, 1919–1953 (c. 1954). Contrary to an earlier understanding (*see* Weston, *supra* note 97, at 871 n.202a), the change in name from *Office* to *Service* has meant somewhat of a demotion for this bureau. As an *Office* the bureau had virtual financial autonomy. As a *Service* it is subject to the financial control of the French Ministry of Finance, a control sought by the Finance Ministry on the grounds that financial autonomy was "potentially dangerous." Interview with Dervieu, in Paris, June 23, 1969. For further details concerning the *Service*, *see* note 148 *supra*.

[177] Now to the Foreign Ministry's *Direction des Conventions Administratives et des Affaires Consulaires*.

[178] From the founding of the first French Commissions in 1951, there have been three directors ("Chefs") of the *Office* [or *Service*] *des Biens et Intérêts Privés* who have served simultaneously as *commissaires du gouvernement* to the commissions: Maurice Richard, Léonce Calvy, and currently, Pierre d'Huart. All three directors have had at least some legal training and all three have been "hautes fonctionnaires" within the French Foreign Ministry. Interview with Dervieu, in Paris, June 21, 1969. Since his retirement as "Chef du Service" in early 1958, however, Monsieur Calvy, mainly for practical reasons, has continued as *commissaire* to the Eastern European and Cuban commissions. For the law making this arrangement possible, see Decree No. 68–512 of May 29, 1968, [1968] J.O. 5393. Accordingly, with Monsieur d'Huart presently serving as *commissaire* to the Egyptian Commission, there are now two *commissaires*. Interview with Dervieu, in Paris, June 21, 1969.

The principal role of the *commissaire du gouvernement* has been to act in an adversarial capacity on behalf of *all* claimants. In this way, he has performed an important integrative, or harmonizing, function among the commissions. *See* Glaser Correspondence—12/67, *supra* note 16. The *commissaire* is not a mere agent of the French Government, however; he is both "prosecution" and "defense," concerned to protect the lump sum against all improper claims whether made by the Government (through the "rapporteur") or by the claimant. As such the *commissaire* enjoys a status about equal to the president of each commission. Interview with Dervieu, in Paris, June 21, 1969. For further details, see text at notes 242–256 *infra*. It should also be noted that the role of *commissaire du gouvernement* has been several times considered by the *Conseil d'État*. See, e.g., *Commissaire du gouvernement près de la Commission de répartition de l'indemnité des nationalisations tchécoslovaques*, [1959]

Art. 3—Responsibility for the payments made by the Czechoslovak Government pursuant to the Accord shall be assumed by the *agent comptable* of the foreign assets of the *Trésor*.[179]

Art. 4—The *commission spéciale* shall notify the *agent comptable* of the foreign assets of the *Trésor* of its distribution decisions.

The *commission spéciale*, according to the progress of its work, may decide to grant [repartition] instalments before determining definitively the distribution due all distributees.

Art. 5— ... [T]he sums necessary to the functioning of the *commission* shall be charged against the sum total of the *indemnité globale forfaitaire* by the *agent comptable* of the foreign assets of the *Trésor* in accordance with the decisions of the *commission* and the conditions stipulated by its president.

Specifically included in the operating costs shall be the salaries of the members of the *commission*,[180] the sum total of which shall be fixed by decision of the Minister of Foreign Affairs, the Minister of Finance and the minister in charge of the budget, and the fees of the *rapporteurs* and the experts, the sum total of which shall be fixed by the president of the *commission* upon approval of the minister in charge of the budget.[181]

Rec. Cons. d'Ét. 674, wherein the *Conseil* stated that the *commissaire* "ought to be regarded as having for his mission a watchdog function, in the interest of all the claimants . . . who could not be called upon in each particular instance [and who otherwise] would be wholly deprived of recourse in respect to the rules posed by the law. . . ." As to the similar roles of the Legal Officer of the British Foreign Compensation Commission and the erstwhile Solicitor of the United States Foreign Claims Settlement Commission, see LILLICH (G.B.) 13–14; Lillich, *International Claims: A Comparative Study of American and British Postwar Practice*, 39 IND. L. J. 465, 473–74 (1964).

[179] As in Great Britain [*see* LILLICH (G.B.) 5], the French Government receives the lump sum funds in its own name and theoretically has complete discretion over their disposition. As a matter of custom, however, with the funds deposited in a "compte spéciale" in the *Trésor* in the name of the potential distributees, it is understood that these monies will not be used for other purposes. Ernest-Picard Correspondence—11/67, *supra* note 17. *Accord*, Interview with Dervieu, in Paris, June 11, 1969. It may be added that, even though the *Trésor* has invested these funds, at no time has interest been paid to successful claimants. *Id.* For contrasting British practice in this connection, see LILLICH (G.B.) 130–32. For further relevant commentary, concerning especially American practice, see Part IV, notes 10–11 and accompanying text.

[180] The commission members, it will be recalled, have always served on a part-time basis. Accordingly, their "salaries" have been more in the nature of "honoraria," reportedly in the amount of about 300 francs (now about U.S. $50) per month. No "salaries" are paid to Egyptian Commission members, however, owing mainly to the small lump sum received under the 1966 Egyptian Accord. Interview with Dervieu, June 16, 1969. *Cf.* note 220 *infra*.

[181] Judging from the financial statements maintained by each commission, total

Thus the basic theme. Before turning to its later variations, however, thoroughness and accuracy compel noting how it came to be formulated and in what manner it has itself been significantly modified.

In the first place, it was by no means self-evident in the beginning, at least not as regards deprivation claims, exactly what form the French distribution program should take. That it should be neither strictly "judicial" nor strictly "administrative" in character, i.e., that it should partake in some way of "la notion d'arbitrage,"[182] was generally accepted. Yet it cannot be overlooked that it was not until May 1951, nearly three full years after the first Settlement Agreement (the 1948 Polish Accord) received French ratification that the first three commissions were founded.[183] Add to this fact that two other lump sum agreements (the 1950 Czech and 1950 Hungarian accords) were negotiated in the interim and it must be apparent that, at the start, the French had no firm views about how distribution should proceed. Indeed, it is not even necessary to look to this sequence of events. Referring to the 1948 Polish Accord (already more than 18 months old), a French Foreign Ministry Decree of August 31, 1950, established a three-man "commission administrative d'études" to consider the arrangements necessary for indemnifying eligible claimants.[184]

The result of these efforts was the basic theme just noted. It remained, on the whole, remarkably constant, even taking into account its later variations. One major revision, however, one which took place before the establishment of the other later commissions— although after and arising out of the 1951 Yugoslav Commission, the fourth created—concerned the question of judicial review.

The basic theme, it will be recalled, expressly stipulated that the *commissions spéciales* should rule "souverainement" on the merits and worth of the claims presented.[185] Practically speaking, this provision was understood to mean that commission decisions would not

---

operating costs—*i.e.*, commission member salaries, expert fees, personnel wages, materiel—generally have ranged in the neighborhood of 1 to 6 percent of total disbursements.

182 VIENOT 229.

183 *See* note 162 *supra.*

184 *See* Decree of August 31, 1950, [1950] J.O. 10088.

185 *See* text at note 169 *supra.*

be subject to judicial review. As Sarraute and Tager (*avocats* at the *Cour d'Appel* of Paris) wrote in 1952, "[t]he organism . . . created [i.e., the commission] appears to be one for arbitration, without any administrative powers, and one whose decisions do not seem to be subject to review by the *Conseil d'État*."[186] In any case, what was considered likely in 1952 was made unequivocally clear in 1955 when the *Conseil d'État* itself, in a case arising out of a 1951 Yugoslav Commission decision, had occasion to affirm the point.[187] The ruling, however, caused not a little stir,[188] and in December of 1956 the French Parliament passed a law of "un caractère interprétatif" which, in effect, reversed the *Conseil d'État*.[189] Henceforth, the decisions of the Czech, 1950 Hungarian, Polish, and 1951 Yugoslav commissions were "susceptible to no means of redress other than redress *en cassation* before the *Conseil d'État*."[190] The effect of this

---

[186] *Supra* note 29, at 1179. *Cf.* Duez, *Les actes de gouvernement*, 1953 J. Droit Int'l 54, 66–67. For evidence that this was a correct conclusion, see the 1951 Yugoslav Commission's *Décision Juridictionelle* No. 311 (1956) wherein the commission noted that it was judging without being subject to appeal.

[187] *Epoux Deltel*, [1956] D.S. Jr. 44.

[188] *See*, *e.g.*, Rousseau, *Notes de Jurisprudence*, 1956 Rev. Droit Pub. Sci. 150; Sialelli, *Chronique de Jurisprudence*, 1956 J. Droit Int'l 674.

[189] Law No. 56–1251 of December 11, 1956, [1956] J.O. 11871.

[190] *Id.* art. 1. By Article 2, the *Conseil d'État* was given a six-month period for rehearings. The *Deltel* case was subsequently reconsidered on the merits. *See Dame veuve Deltel*, [1957] Rec. Cons. d'Ét. 512. Law No. 56–1251 was later interpreted by the *Conseil d'État*, in a case arising out of the Polish Commission, as having no retroactive effect. *Banque des Pays de l'Europe Centrale*, [1960] Rec. Cons. d'Ét. 32. In a case arising out of the Czech Commission, it was interpreted to preclude a claimant's requesting a revision or reversal of an adverse decision by the Czech Commission itself. *Société financière et industrielle des pétroles et commissaire du gouvernement près de la Commission de répartition de l'indemnité tchécoslovaque*, [1964] Rec. Cons. d'Ét. 233. *See also Société Financière*, note 191 *infra*. The ruling has been accepted throughout French commission practice whenever the requested revision has been major in kind. Where minor, however, the commissions have been flexible. As for the *Conseil d'État* itself, the following quotation from F. Lawson, A. Anton, & L. Brown, Amos and Walton's Introduction to French Law 2 (3d ed. 1967) is helpful: "French law is made up of many parts, each of which constitutes a separate discipline and, as often as not, falls under the jurisdiction of a separate set of courts. The most fundamental distinction is between public and private law. Questions relating to government and public administration are in general withdrawn from the courts which administer justice between private persons or corporations, and committed to separate administrative courts headed by the *Conseil d'État*, which exercise, *inter alia*, the sort of control over administrative authorities and tribunals exercised in England by the ordinary courts." It will be noted, however, that in this instance the *Conseil d'État* was expected to rule "en cassation," a procedure manifestly familiar to the *Cour de Cassation*, the court in France having supreme jurisdiction over questions of "private law."

law was to be seen not only in the heightened involvement of the *Conseil* thereafter,[191] but also in the legislation by which the later commissions were established.

The Minor Variations

THE YUGOSLAV COMMISSION

The Yugoslav Commission Constitutive Law was passed by the French Parliament in July 1952.[192] Its companion Application Law was decreed three months later in October 1952.[193] The latter, ex-

---

In this connection, given that the *Conseil* has approached the review of French commission decisions in the same manner that the *Cour de Cassation* reviews lower civil court decisions (Interview with Dervieu, in Paris, June 23, 1969), the following additional Lawson-Anton-Brown commentary is pertinent: "The Court of Cassation is not a court of appeal. It only *reviews* findings of law—not of fact, though sometimes it treats as law what might at first sight seem to be fact—brought before it by *pourvoi*. It can only quash a decision of which it disapproves and send the case back to a neighboring court of the same rank . . . . It cannot in any case substitute its own decision for the one of which it disapproves." *Id.* at 8.

Accordingly, when a French commission decision has been annulled by the *Conseil d'État*, ordinarily for *excès de pouvoir*, the latter uniformly has sent the case back to the commission from whence it arose, with a direction to apply the law as "found." For a case demonstrating the ostensible distinction between "law" and "fact" as applied to postwar French practice, see *Sieur Faller*, [1962] Cons. d'Ét., Section du Contentieux, No. 57,839 (unpublished mimeo.), on appeal from a decision of the Romanian Commission. The *Conseil d'État* refused to annul the Commission's rulings relative to the valuation of the claimant's losses on the grounds that the claimant's grievances concerned disagreement with the Commission's factual findings, not an abuse of Commission authority. For a classic study of the *Conseil d'État* from a comparative point of view, see C. HAMSON, EXECUTIVE DISCRETION AND JUDICIAL CONTROL (1954).

191 Since being granted the right of judicial review, the *Conseil d'État* has inquired into many aspects of French Commission practice, most of its decisions concerning allegations of "excès de pouvoir" on the part of the commissions. Although technically the commissions have not been obliged to execute the *Conseil's* decisions, in fact they have done so, with the result that the *Conseil's* judgments have played an important role in setting guidelines for commission rulings. As of this writing, the *Conseil* has been involved in about 50 separate litigations arising out of French commission practice. Several of the decisions are *à propos* at this juncture. See *Société financière et industrielle des pétroles*, [1961] Rec. Cons. d'Ét. 314, wherein the *Conseil*, in a case arising out of the Czech Commission, affirmed a decision of the *Tribunal administratif de Paris* which rejected a petition on the grounds that review of a French commission decision could be had only by the *Conseil d'État*; *Sieur Treger*, [1963] Cons. d'Ét., Section du Contentieux, No. 59,418 (unpublished mimeo.), wherein the *Conseil*, in a case arising out of the Romanian Commission, rejected a "recours" because the claimant, in making his appeal, failed to obtain the signature of an "avocat" at the *Conseil d'État*, as required by law. See *also* the cases cited *supra* note 190.

192 Law No. 52–861 of July 21, 1952, [1952] J.O. 7362.

193 Application of Law No. 52–861 (October 29, 1952), [1952] J.O. 11158.

cept for obvious necessary changes, was identical to its Czech, Hungarian, and Polish predecessors. The former, however, though rhetorically close to its precursors, evinced several noteworthy revisions (applicable of course to the Yugoslav Commission only).

First: Composition.[194] While before only a president of a *chambre* at the *Cour de Cassation* could be commission president, now either this person *or* a president of a *section* at the *Conseil d'État* might fill that chair. Also, whereas before the Commission President and a *conseiller* at the *Cour de Cassation* were named by the First President of the *Cour de Cassation,* now these members were to be designated by the *garde des sceaux* (*i.e.,* the Minister of Justice). Further, all five members of the Commission, rather than only two as before, now could be chosen from the active and inactive ranks of *magistrats* and *fonctionnaires.*

Second: Due Date for Filing Claims.[195] Previously, claimants were allowed three months from the promulgation of the Constitutive Law to file their claims with the commissions. Now, subject to the same reservation of *force majeur,* they were given three months from the publication of the later Application Law.[196]

Third: "Receivable" Claims.[197] The following additional claims were deemed admissible: "claims presented in the name of the [French] State when it has exercised its rights of assignment within the conditions set forth in Article 3 of the Ordinance of 9 June 1945."[198]

Fourth: Duties of the Commission.[199] The functions were here

[194] *Supra* note 192, art. 2. This provision of course was replaced by equivalent— and as it happens nearly identical—language in the 1963 Yugoslav Commission Constitutive Law. *See* Decree No. 64–709 art. 2, *supra* note 151. By its Article 3, this decree made applicable to the 1963 Yugoslav claims program all provisions and rules prescribed for the 1951 Yugoslav claims program.

[195] *Id.* art. 3.

[196] Probably this change was a reflection of the difficulties that resulted from the promulgation of the earlier Application Laws more than three months after the promulgation of their companion Constitutive Laws.

[197] *Supra* note 192, art. 3.

[198] This provision was not contained in the original draft of this law. Because the earlier Czech, 1950 Hungarian, and Polish Commission Constitutive Laws had dealt with the German cession problem, however, it finally was added, although not without some rancorous and sometimes humorous debate in the *Assemblée Nationale. See* [1952] J.O. 3470–72, 3488–90. As to the significance of the provision, see note 168 *supra.* Presumably because the problem was moot, it was not included in the law constituting the successor 1963 Yugoslav claims program, *supra* note 151.

[199] *Supra* note 192, art. 5.

stated to be the same as before except that the Commission was now to "pronounce itself" rather than "rule souverainement" on the claims presented. In light of the foregoing discussion,[200] this change at first seems a major one. However, an additional provision was added which had the same general effect as before: the commission was now to "fix its own procedure and rule *souverainement*."[201]

Fifth: Due Date for Rendering Decisions.[202] As before, the Commission was required to render decisions within 18 months. However, that period was now to commence as of the publication of the Application Law rather than as of the promulgation of the Constitutive Law. Obviously, this change was to coincide with the new due date required for the filing of claims.[203]

THE BULGARIAN AND ROMANIAN COMMISSIONS

Although the Bulgarian and Romanian settlements were more than four years apart, the Bulgarian and Romanian commissions were created at the same time. For this reason, and probably also because the two settlements were similar, their Statutory Instruments were—with insignificant though necessary exception—almost identical in all respects.[204] It is therefore convenient to treat them together.

Consider, initially, their Constitutive Laws.[205] Significantly, they

---

200 *See* text at notes at 185–191 *supra*.

201 Perhaps, indeed, it was because this item was singled out for special separate mention that it became a major issue for the spouses Deltel. *See* text accompanying notes 185–191 *supra*. It also may be noted that the direction here to the Commission to "fix its own procedure" was new, even though it was repeated in the Yugoslav Application Law. The same language is to be found in the laws constituting the successor Cuban and 1965 Hungarian claims programs, *supra* notes 151 & 152.

202 *Supra* note 192, art. 6.

203 This provision likewise was recreated in the law constituting the 1963 Yugoslav claims program, *supra* note 152. Also, as in the case of the Czech and 1950 Hungarian claims programs, it was subject to 18-month extension, although only one such extension in this instance.

204 One curious exception which is unexplained, however, is the inclusion of a "German transfer" provision in the Romanian Commission Application Law but its complete omission in the Bulgarian Commission Statutory Instruments. As it happens, however, the difference has been of little importance, neither of these commissions apparently having had to deal with the problem to date. *See* text at Part III, notes 345–351. *See* Law No. 55–994 of July 29, 1955, [1955] J.O. 7627.

205 Decree No. 59–1116 of September 19, 1959 (constituting the Bulgarian Commission), [1959] J.O. 9348; Decree No. 59–1117 of September 19, 1959 (constituting the Romanian Commission), [1959] J.O. 9348; Decree No. 60–522 of May 1, 1960 (amending Decree No. 59–1117), [1960] J.O. 5312.

differed only slightly from their Yugoslav equivalent. First, all but two of the variations introduced in the Yugoslav Commission Constitutive Law were incorporated here. The two exceptions concerned the due dates for filing claims and for rendering decisions. Whereas the Yugoslav Commission dates were keyed to the publication of the Application Law, in the case of the Bulgarian and Romanian commissions they were keyed, once again, to the promulgation of the Constitutive Law.[206] This departure was, of course, a reversion to the basic theme, a retreat which is perplexing considering the difficulties that had arisen previously.[207] Ultimately, indeed, extensions did prove necessary.[208] Second, in adding two provisions not found in the Yugoslav Commission Constitutive Law, the Bulgarian and Romanian equivalents only made express what by now was already present in practice in the Yugoslav (and other) claims programs. The first, requiring that the director of the *Service des Biens et Intérêts Privés* or his representative be the *commissaire du gouvernement* to the commissions,[209] had been decreed previously in the Application Laws. The second, providing that Bulgarian and Romanian commission decisions be "susceptible to no means of redress other than redress *en cassation* before the *Conseil d'État*,"[210] had been required earlier, as explained, by special enactment of the French Parliament.

The Bulgarian and Romanian commission Application Laws, lastly, differed only inconsequentially from their prior counterparts.[211] Mainly the variations were formalistic, reflecting more the

---

206 *Id.* arts. 2 and 5 (in both decrees).

207 *See* notes 173, 196, & 203 *supra.*

208 *See* Decree No. 60–488 of May 4, 1960, [1960] J.O. 4867; Decree No. 61–539 of May 29, 1961, [1961] J.O. 4973; Decree No. 61–540 of May 29, 1961, [1961] J.O. 4973; Decree No. 62–1360 of November 19, 1962, [1962] J.O. 11307.

209 *Supra* note 205, art. 1 (in both decrees). In the case of the Romanian Commission Constitutive Law, this provision was amended to authorize the *commissaire* to appear before the *Conseil d'État. See* Decree No. 60–552, *supra* note 205. Why this was done in this instance but not in the case of the Bulgarian Commission Constitutive Law is unclear.

210 *Id.* art. 3 (in both decrees).

211 *See* Decree of March 10, 1960 (applying Bulgarian Commission Constitutive Decree No. 59–1116), [1960] J.O. 2808; Decree of March 10, 1960 (applying Romanian Commission Constitutive Decree No. 59–1117), [1960] J.O. 2809.

212 For example, these decrees contained no direction to the commissions to fix their own procedures. Nor did they provide for a *commissaire du gouvernement*, both of these matters having been dealt with in the Constitutive Laws.

need for consistency with the companion Constitutive Laws (and to lesser extent Fifth Republic institutional changes) than anything else.[212]

The Major Variation

THE EGYPTIAN COMMISSION

As seen, the Eastern European and Cuban claims programs (or commissions) were each fashioned in the same basic mold, one that was also to shape a number of the key features of the Egyptian Commission. In several important respects, however, the Egyptian Commission Constitutive Law, coming only four months after the entry into force of the 1966 Egyptian Accord,[213] may be seen to have differed markedly from its Eastern European and Cuban commission counterparts.[214] Unlike the other Statutory Instruments, the Egyptian Commission Constitutive Law embodied—or, more accurately, recast—a goodly portion of the terms, relevant to the Commission's functioning, that had been set forth in the 1966 Accord.[215] Hence, if there is anywhere to be seen in French practice a close systemic resemblance to British practice, where intervening Orders in Council have had the effect of "cutting the [Foreign Compensation Commission] off from international law as a reference point of first instance,"[216] it is here. In turn, this development suggests that the decisions of the Egyptian Commission have been, as Lillich says of the decisions of the British Commission, "a much more accurate reflection of its government's position than are the decisions of the [U.S. Foreign Claims Settlement Commission]."[217] Accordingly, so also have they probably been a better reflection of French governmental policy than the decisions of the other French commissions.

All of the incorporated treaty provisions to which we have just alluded will of necessity be dealt with when, in Part III, the French commission decisions are examined. Thus it would be only redun-

---

[213] This rapid movement tends to confirm the uncertain state of French thinking when France first debated about how to distribute the lump sums promised under her early Settlement Agreements. *See* text at notes 182–184 *supra*.

[214] *See* Decree No. 68–103 of January 30, 1968, [1968] J.O. 1228.

[215] *See id.* art. 5.

[216] LILLICH (G.B.) 141.

[217] *Id.*

dant to recount them here. It remains to consider, however, in what manner and to what degree the basic theme earlier outlined has otherwise continued to prevail. As may be seen, even without accounting for certain non-distributive functions that were assigned to it (none of which are relevant to this study),[218] the Egyptian Commission was constituted with a number of significant variations, its mission, of course, remaining basically the same.

First: Composition.[219] The Egyptian Commission was given a membership different from the other commissions. First, it was constituted with seven rather than five members. Second, although the members were to be appointed as earlier described,[220] their otherwise full-time affiliations have been somewhat different, to wit: a *conseiller maître* at the *Cour des Comptes* designated by the Minister of Economy and Finance, President; two officials designated by the Minister of Foreign Affairs; an official designated by the Minister of Economy and Finance; a representative of the Bank of France designated by the Minister of Economy and Finance on nomination of the governor of the Bank of France; and a *maître des requêtes*[221] at the *Conseil d'État* and a *magistrat de l'ordre judiciaire*,[222] each designated by the *garde des sceaux* (*i.e.*, the Minister of Justice). In addition, echoing the basic theme, the director of the *Service des Biens et Intérêts Privés* or his representative was again to assume the functions of *commissaire du gouvernement*.[223] The additional members—*i.e.*, the *maître des requêtes* and the *magistrat*—are reported to have been holdovers from an earlier non-distributive commission organized to give effect to the 1958 Zurich Accord.[224] As elsewhere, the operation of the Commission's *secré-*

---

[218] The Commission, in addition to being assigned responsibility for the distribution of funds received under Article 4 of the 1966 Egyptian Accord, was charged to give its opinion on the priority of miscellaneous transfers due from Egypt pursuant to the 1958 and 1966 accords. *See supra* note 214, art. 2.

[219] *Id.* art. 4.

[220] *See* note 164 *supra*. It may be recalled, however, that Egyptian Commission members have received no "salaries" for their part-time labors (*see* note 180 *supra*), apparently, in part, because their work has been regarded as "a service to France." Interview with Dervieu, in Paris, June 16, 1969. *Cf.* note 180 *supra*.

[221] *I.e.*, a judicial officer lower in rank than a *conseiller* at the *Conseil d'État*.

[222] *I.e.*, a judicial officer lower in rank than a judge at the *Cours de Cassation*.

[223] *See* note 178 *supra*. It will be recalled that the present director of the *Service des Biens et Intérêts Privés* himself serves today as *commissaire du gouvernement* to the Egyptian Commission. *Id.*

[224] Interview with Dervieu, in Paris, July 16, 1969.

tariat was to be "assured" by the *Service des Biens et Intérêts Privés.*[225]

Second: Due Date for Filing Claims.[226] As in the case of the Yugoslav Commission, claimants were allowed three months from the publication of the Constitutive Law to file their claims, except in case of *force majeure.*

Third: "Receivable" Claims.[227] Owing mainly to treaty stipulations, the Commission was authorized to receive claims only from natural persons having French nationality as of both the signature of the 1958 Zurich Accord and the entry into force of the 1966 Accord (September 1, 1967); or, should French nationality not have been acquired until after 1958, from natural persons having both French nationality and French residence as of September 1, 1967.[228]

Fourth: Duties of the Commission.[229] Like all the other commissions, the Egyptian Commission was charged to "pronounce itself" on the claims presented, to evaluate the losses sustained, to draw up a definitive list of distributees, to fix the means of lump sum distribution, to determine the distributees' share of the indemnity, and to fix its own rules of procedure. Notably absent was any authorization to "rule *souverainement*," doubtless reflecting a preceding stipulation that the Commission's decisions should have the authority of "la chose jugée" subject to review, "en cassation," only by the *Conseil d'État.*[230]

Fifth: Due Date for Rendering Decisions. In contrast to the Statutory Instruments of the other French commissions, the Egyptian Commission Constitutive Law was silent on this point. This omission may be interpreted to reflect an awareness on the part of the French Government of the repeated extensions that were required earlier to cope with operational delays.[231] It cannot be inter-

---

225 *Supra* note 214, art. 8.

226 *Id.* art. 6.

227 *Id.* art. 5(a).

228 As to the significance of the French residency requirement and the manner in which it has been handled by the Egyptian Commission, see text at Part III, notes 65–70.

229 *Supra* note 214, art. 7.

230 *Id.* art. 4.

231 Interview with Dervieu, in Paris, June 25, 1969.

preted to mean that the Egyptian Commission was deemed to be a permanent, rather than a temporary fixture on the French scene.[232]

B. *The Rules of Procedure*

As seen, all the French commissions were instructed to formulate their own rules of internal procedure. They all did so, twice in the case of the Hungarian and Yugoslav commissions and once again in the case of the successor Cuban Commission.[233] Significantly, all these *réglements de procédure* have been very much alike—if not always to the letter, at least in spirit. The Czech and Polish commission Rules, for example, are nearly identical. So too are the Rules of the Bulgarian and Romanian commissions. In sum, the variations that are to be found—mainly in the Egyptian Commission Rules— have been by and large minor in character, compelling one, when finding differences, to avoid exalting form over substance.

All the separate Rules have been divided into three main Titles ("Titres"): *présentation de la demande, instruction de la demande,* and *examen de la demande* (in the Rules of the Czech, Polish, and and two Yugoslav commissions, and also in the 1950 Hungarian Commission Rules) or *jugement de la demande* (in the Rules of the Bulgarian, Cuban, Egyptian, and Romanian commissions, and also in the 1965 Hungarian Commission Rules). It is convenient

---

[232] *Id.*

[233] *See* Bulgarian Commission Rules, "Avis" of December 20, 1959, [1959] J.O. 12158; Cuban Commission Rules (unpublished mimeo., copies available at *Le Secrétariat de la Commission spéciale de répartition de l'indemnité cubaine,* 80, Rue de Lille, Paris VII); Czech Commission Rules, 12 AFFAIRES ÉTRANGÈRES F.I. (2d Trim., 1953); Egyptian Commission Rules (unpublished mimeo., copies available at *Le Secrétariat de la Commission de priorité de transferts et de répartition de l'indemnité égyptienne,* 31, Rue Dumont d'Urville, Paris XVI); 1950 and 1965 Hungarian Commission Rules (unpublished mimeo., copies available at *Le Secrétariat de la Commission spéciale de répartition de l'indemnité hongroise,* 80, Rue de Lille, Paris VII); Polish Commission Rules, 9 AFFAIRES ÉTRANGÈRES E.I. (July 1952); Romanian Commission Rules, "Avis" of December 19, 1959, [1959] J.O. 12110; 1951 and 1963 Yugoslav Commission Rules (unpublished mimeo., copies available at *Le Secrétariat de la Commission spéciale de la répartition de l'indemnité yougoslave,* 80, Rue de Lille, Paris VII). Unlike as in Great Britain, where the rules adopted by the Foreign Compensation Commission are subject to the approval of the Lord Chancellor [*see* LILLICH (G.B.) 9], the French Commission Rules, in accordance with the Statutory Instruments, have been entirely of the commissions' making. Interview with Dervieu, in Paris, June 23, 1969.

to review them summarily in that order, pointing out the principal differences and other pertinent matters along the way.

Presentation of the Claim[234]

All claims have had to be filed by the claimant, his legal representative or an authorized proxy at the main offices of the commissions within the time limits set forth in the relevant Statutory Instruments.[235] Persons living abroad with claims to present to the Bulgarian, Cuban, Hungarian, and Romanian commissions also have been entitled to file, optionally, with a French consulate, legation, or embassy in the country where they are residing.[236] While the Rules have required no special forms, nevertheless all the petitions have had to be reasoned ("motivée"), dated, and signed, stating the facts that arguably justify indemnification and the specific amount of damage sustained.[237] If a natural person, the claimant has had

---

[234] See Czech, Polish, and 1951 Yugoslav Commission Rules, supra note 233, arts. 1–11; 1950 Hungarian Commission Rules, supra note 233, arts. 1–10; 1963 Yugoslav Commission Rules, supra note 233, arts. 1–8; Bulgarian, Cuban, Egyptian, 1965 Hungarian, and Romanian Commission Rules, supra note 233, arts. 1–5.

[235] It should be noted that it is at this juncture that the French Government for the first time becomes completely aware of the number and amount of claims actually involved in its claims programs, a fact which surely must affect its lump sum bargaining. However, although France has not made pre-settlement registration of claims a condition precedent to distributive relief, it has usually undertaken through press publicity, official notices and the like to secure reasonably close estimates of the actual numbers and amounts at stake. See testimony of J. E. Girodet of the Service des Biens et Intérêts Privés in "Technical Discussion on Claims Problems," supra note 46. On the other hand, notwithstanding that claimants may have filed claims with the Quai d'Orsay at the pre-settlement stage, they have still been required, at risk of forfeiture, to file with the French commissions. Interview with Dervieu, in Paris, June 23, 1969. As might be expected, early filing has been encouraged. Id. For discussion concerning the potential profitability of "preadjudicating" international claims, see R. LILLICH, THE PROTECTION OF FOREIGN INVESTMENT 167–205 (1965). See also Re, The Presettlement Adjudication of International Claims, in INTERNATIONAL ARBITRATION—LIBER AMICORUM FOR MARTIN DOMKE at 214 (P. Sanders ed. 1967).

[236] That this option was not expressed in the other Commission Rules is said to have been of little consequence. "The commissions have uniformly taken into account the intention and situation of the claimant." Interview with Dervieu, in Paris, June 23, 1969.

[237] The Cuban and Egyptian Commission Rules, in stating that claims can be filed "by simple letter" [supra note 233, art. 2 (in both sets of Rules)], make explicit what has always been implicit among the French commissions in practice. This informal procedure, it may be noted, contrasts sharply with equivalent American and British practice. See LILLICH & CHRISTENSON 106; LILLICH (G.B.) 9. It is appro-

also to state his name, profession (except before the Bulgarian, Cuban, Egyptian, 1965 Hungarian, and Romanian commissions), domicile, and nationality, and, if a juridical person, the name of the firm, its "siège," nationality, and legal representative.[238] Further, all petitions have had to be supported by annexed documents, written in French and prepared in duplicate, each establishing (1) the claimant's French nationality on the date or dates specified in the relevant accord, and (2) the merits of the claim itself. Before the Czech, Polish, and two Yugoslav commissions, supporting individual testimony has had to be in the form of a written declaration, dated and bearing the legal signature of the witness or declarant. Upon deposit, all these materials, constituting the "dossier," have had to be "registered" by the *secrétaire* of each commission who, in turn, has had to deliver a receipt therefor to the claimant together with the duplicate set of supporting documents previously prepared and submitted by the claimant.[239] Although not stated in any of the Commission Rules, it has been understood that additional documentation, not originally filed, will be accepted for deposit, provided, of course, that a decision has not already been rendered or that the supplementary data do not represent, in effect, a "novation" (or new claim) outside the time limits authorized for initial filing.[240]

priate to mention here also that the Cuban Commission Rules have uniquely provided that stockholder claimants whose certificates are held by fiduciaries need not claim in their own name except when their fiduciaries do not claim on their behalf. *Supra* note 233, art. 3. While this stipulation has not been stated explicitly in the other Commission Rules, doubtless it has been implied—except in the case of the Egyptian Commission, stockholder claims against Egypt having been required to be handled by "la répartition administrative" in accordance with the 1964 Egyptian Accord. *See* note 56 and text following note 71 *supra*.

[238] Because the Egyptian Commission was not authorized to receive "company" claims, this requirement was not included in the Egyptian Commission Rules. For relevant discussion, see text at Part III, notes 71–76.

[239] Each of the French commissions has had a *secrétariat* headed by an official— "le secrétaire"—who has been appointed by the *Service des Biens et Intérêts Privés* on a non-contractual, full-time basis and paid by the commissions from their lump sum funds (*see* note 181 and accompanying text *supra*). Frequently, one *secrétaire* has been responsible for more than one *secrétariat*. Responsible for the registration of claims, the recording of the *procès-verbal* (or minutes) of the commission sessions, the verification of documents, and like matters, it has been necessary neither that the *secrétaires* be "fonctionnaires" in the French civil service system nor that they be legally trained. Interview with Dervieu, in Paris, June 21, 1969. All the same, given their functions and the fact that frequently one of them has performed the same duties simultaneously for more than one commission, it is clear that the "secrétaires" have played a significant harmonizing role among the different claims programs.

[240] Interview with Dervieu, in Paris, June 23, 1969; Interview with Branche, in

Preliminary Examination of the Claim[241]

When the preliminary examination is to begin and end is not stated in the Rules. Apparently the commissions have operated in their own discretion, subject of course to the 18-month limitations specified in their Statutory Instruments.[242] At any rate, upon commencement the President of each commission has had to name for each "affaire" (or series of "affaires" of like nature) a *rapporteur* taken from among the members of the commissions or from a list established by the commissions.[243] Once designated, the *rapporteur* has been required to proceed to a preliminary examination of the claim or claims involved. To this end he has been free to require the claimant to produce, at risk of ultimate claim forfeiture, all manner of information and supporting documentation that may be deemed necessary. Likewise, he has been authorized to seek such independent research and verification as may be needed.[244] If in his judgment it is necessary to have expert testimony, he has had so to inform the commission which, in turn, would proceed to obtain it.[245] Once finished with his preliminary examination, the *rapporteur*

Paris, July 10, 1969. *Accord, Banque Franco-Serbe,* [1964] Cons. d'Ét., Section du Contentieux, No. 61,055 (unpublished mimeo.).

241 *See* Czech, Polish, and 1951 Yugoslav Commission Rules, *supra* note 233, arts. 12–14; 1950 Hungarian Commission Rules, *supra* note 233, arts. 11–13; 1963 Yugoslav Commission Rules, *supra* note 233, arts. 9–11; Bulgarian, Cuban, Egyptian, 1965 Hungarian, and Romanian Commission Rules, *supra* note 233, arts. 6–8.

242 The time needed for the "instruction de la demande" (*i.e.,* the preparation of each *dossier*) has averaged two to three months, of course conditioned by the nature and complexity of the claim. The *Service des Biens et Intérêts Privés* has assisted the commissions actively at this stage in the proceedings. Interview with Dervieu, in Paris, June 25, 1969.

243 In practice, the *rapporteurs* usually have been picked from among the members of the commissions, partly because of the members' familiarity with commission proceedings, partly because in such event no additional remunerations have had to be paid (as a matter of custom). When they have not been chosen from among the commission members, usually they have been appointed from among the staff of the *Service des Biens et Intérêts Privés,* in which case modest fees have been paid. The *rapporteurs* have not been required to have had legal training, although ordinarily this background has been considered desirable. As a matter of fact, most of them have had at least practical legal experience. Also, it has been unnecessary for them to be "fonctionnaires" in the French civil service system, although in fact they have often had this status because frequently they have been chosen from among the commission members. Interview with Dervieu, in Paris, June 21, 1969.

244 *Compare* note 255 *infra.*

245 Theoretically, expert witnesses have been restricted to presenting facts and not opinions, a distinction that doubtless has been difficult to maintain in practice at all times. At any rate, their testimony has had always to be in writing since at no time have they been allowed actually to participate in commission proceedings. When

has had to prepare a written "rapport," first, for annexation to the "dossier" (at least under the Cuban, Czech, Egyptian, and Hungarian commission Rules),[246] and second, for communication to the *commissaire du gouvernement*,[247] whose right it then has been to require the *rapporteur* to complete such information or obtain such additional expert testimony as the *commissaire* might deem appropriate. With this task done, the *commissaire* (who, it will be recalled, acts on behalf of all claimants) has had to prepare his "conclusions" (findings) and to transmit the "dossier" to the President of the commission.[248] Together, the "rapport" of the *rapporteur*

---

the commissions have been required to pay for their services, the cost has been charged against the lump sum fund. Otherwise, the claimant has borne the cost. Also, it may be noted that the commissions have usually avoided employing foreign expert witnesses because of diplomatic difficulties that sometimes have arisen when foreign experts request, as apparently they often do, to be paid in "Western" currencies. Interview with Dervieu, in Paris, June 21, 1969. On the use of experts by the British Foreign Compensation Commission and the United States Foreign Claims Settlement Commission, see G. WHITE, THE USE OF EXPERTS BY INTERNATIONAL TRIBUNALS 226–41 (1965).

[246] The "rapport" usually has been in written form even when the Commission Rules have not so required. Conversely, the "rapport" has been communicated orally sometimes even when the Commission Rules have required that it be in writing. Interview with Dervieu, in Paris, June 21, 1969.

[247] It has been an unwritten rule that the "rapport" is never to be communicated to the claimant. It is understood to be exclusively an "internal document." Interview with Dervieu, in Paris, June 21, 1969. *But cf. Consorts Eymond dits Griffon, infra* note 248.

[248] In *Sieur Lambert et autres,* [1963] Rec. Cons. d'Ét. 511, on appeal from the Romanian Commission, the *Conseil d'État* held that, to assure the adversarial character of commission proceedings, the written *conclusions* had to have been communicated to the claimant before the Commission rendered its decision. Failing such communication, the Commission's ruling was annulled. Five later cases decided by the *Conseil d'État,* all of them also on appeal from the Romanian Commission, had identical holdings. *See Société Fichet, Beau Huppert et Cie,* [1963] Cons. d'Ét., Section du Contentieux, No. 56,902 (unpublished mimeo.); *Compagnie de Saint-Gobain et Sieur Saporta,* [1963] Cons. d'Ét., Section du Contentieux, Nos. 55,415–55,416 (unpublished mimeo.); *Sieur Motte,* [1964] Cons. d'Ét., Section du Contentieux, No. 57,011 (unpublished mimeo.); *Société "Établissements Motte, Meillassoux et Caulliez,"* [1964] Cons. d'Ét., Section du Contentieux, No. 57,010 (unpublished mimeo.). *But cf., Société financière et industrielle des pétroles et commissaire du gouvernement près de la Commission de répartition de l'indemnité tchécoslovaque,* [1964] Rec. Cons. d'Ét., 233, wherein the *Conseil,* in a case on appeal from the Czech Commission, held, after conceding that the *conclusions* of the *commissaire du gouvernement* should ordinarily be communicated, that the non-communication of the *conclusions* in this instance "would not have had any influence" on the outcome of the case and that for this reason could not be said to have constituted "a vice of a kind to taint the regularity of [the Commission's] procedure."

In another case, related to the foregoing, the *Conseil d'État* held that a failure by the Romanian Commission to allow claimant examination of the "dossier" before

and the "conclusions" of the *commissaire du gouvernement* have served as the principal documents upon which the commissions have based their rulings.[249]

Final Examination (or Judgment) of the Claim[250]

At the outset, the President of each commission has had to fix the date for commission deliberation of the claim(s). To proceed, a quorum of at least three of the five commission members has been required; four out of seven in the case of the Egyptian Commission. None of the Rules states whether and at what point commissioners not initially sitting might join in the deliberations, or whether and at what point such commissioners might replace others who, for one reason or another, cannot attend.[251] Other organizational matters, however, are quite clearly detailed. Thus, commission sessions have been required to be closed to the public; the *commissaire du gouvernement*, the *secrétaire* of each commission (at least under the Bulgarian, Cuban, Egyptian, Hungarian, Romanian, and Yugoslav commission Rules), and the *rapporteur* (even when not a member of the commissions) have been the only persons *automatically* entitled to argue before or to assist the commissions. At their discretion, however, the commissions have been free to request the personal appearance of the claimant who, in turn, has been allowed to be accompanied or represented by any of a number of expressly

---

rendering its decision was sufficient to warrant annulment of the Commission's decision. *Consorts Eymond dits Griffon*, [1963] Cons. d'Ét., Section du Contentieux, Nos. 55,387–55,388 (unpublished mimeo.).

[249] Access to these documents by this writer has proven impossible. *See* Part I, note 15 and accompanying text.

[250] *See* Czech, Polish, and 1951 Yugoslav Commission Rules, *supra* note 233, arts. 15–32; 1950 Hungarian Commission Rules, *supra* note 233, arts. 14–27; 1963 Yugoslav Commission Rules, *supra* note 233, arts. 12–29; Bulgarian, Cuban, Egyptian, 1965 Hungarian, and Romanian Commission Rules, *supra* note 233, arts. 9–20.

[251] *Compare Société financière et industrielle des pétroles et commissaire du gouvernement près de la Commission de répartition de l'indemnité tchécoslovaque*, [1964] Rec. Cons. d'Ét. 233, wherein the *Conseil* held that the claimant *Société* was not justified in contending that the Commission was in error when, on ruling on the claim, it did not declare the names of the commissioners sitting at the date of the hearing. The *Société* alleged that the same commissioners did not sit in deliberation on the claim three months later. According to the *Conseil* "the commission sits validly if three of its members are present." *Contra, Sieur Revesz*, [1958] Rec. Cons. d'Ét. 43, wherein the *Conseil* annulled and returned a 1950 Hungarian Commission ruling on the grounds that the Commission's opinion failed to mention the names of the members who participated in the deliberation of the claim.

listed counselors: *avocats* at the *Conseil d'État* and the *Cour de Cassation; avocats* regularly enrolled in a French bar or, under the Bulgarian and Romanian commission Rules, in a bar of a member State of the European Community; *avoués* and *agrées* practicing in the *tribunaux de commerce;* law professors; the *Association Pour la Sauvegarde et l'Expansion des Biens et Intérêts Français a l'Étranger*;[252] the *Association Nationale des Sinistrés Français de Pologne* (under the Polish Commission Rules); the *Association Nationale des Porteurs de Valeurs Mobilières*[253] (under the Czech Commission Rules); and other generally interested and technically equipped individuals and groups authorized by the commissions.[254] Also, the commissions have been free, at their own initiative or at the request of the claimant, the *rapporteur,* or the *commissaire du gouvernement* (but at the expense of the claimant), to request oral and written testimony and to designate experts to inquire into, and report on, such technical problems as might be considered necessary.[255] Gaps, contradictions, and ambiguities in the Settlement Agreements—concerning which all the Rules have been silent—have had to be resolved by appropriate offices in the French Foreign Ministry.[256]

[252] *See* note 16 *supra.*

[253] *See* note 19 *supra.*

[254] A literal reading of the Commission Rules suggests that a claimant's personal appearance is a matter of privilege and not of right. Such at least was the thrust of the holding of the *Conseil d'État* in *Époux Cassel,* [1963] Cons. d'Ét., Section du Contentieux, No. 55–697 (unpublished mimeo.), an unsuccessful appeal from the Romanian Commission. Nevertheless, the commissions ordinarily have agreed to personal appearances whenever asked. The asking, however, has been infrequent. Interview with Branche, in Paris, July 10, 1969. *Accord,* Interview with Dervieu, in Paris, June 28, 1969.

[255] According to the *Conseil d'État,* in a case arising out of the 1951 Yugoslav Commission, it was unnecessary for the Commission—assuming no legislation to the contrary—to advise a claimant of diverse documents requested by it or voluntarily transmitted by the French Foreign Ministry. In the absence of a formal demand by the claimant, the Commission had complete discretion in this regard. *Sieur Campion,* [1960] Rec. Cons. d'Ét. 30.

[256] In three decisions, the *Conseil d'État* held that the Polish Commission could not itself determine, without exceeding its powers, whether non-French shareholders in a company under French control could share in the lump sum compensation of the 1948 Polish Accord, the provisions of the Accord not being clear on this point. *Sieur Pioton, ès-qualité de liquidateur de la Société anonyme polonaise des charbonnages, mines et usines de Sosnowice,* [1960] Rec. Cons. d'Ét. 632; *Sieur Pioton, ès-qualité de liquidateur de la Société des usines de fabrication de tubes et des forges de Sosnowice,* [1960] Rec. Con. d'Ét. 633; *Sieur Pioton, ès-qualité de liquidateur de la Société des mines et usines à zinc de Silesie,* [1960] Rec. Cons. d'Ét. 634. In an-

As for the deliberations and judgment proper, each has had to be restricted to the commission members alone,[257] although the *commissaire* and the *rapporteur* (when not a commission member) have had the right to serve in a consultative capacity at this juncture. Decisions have had to be by majority vote except when only three commissioners have deliberated, in which event a unanimous vote has been required. When the votes have divided equally, the President's vote has been decisive (under the Czech, Egyptian, 1950 Hungarian, Polish, and Yugoslav commission Rules). Alternatively, the "affaire" has been postponed to a later deliberative session (under the Bulgarian, Cuban, 1965 Hungarian, and Romanian commission Rules). Except in the case of the Egyptian Commission, when a required unanimous vote has failed the "affaire" has had to be postponed to a later deliberative session. Once made, the decisions have been required to be reasoned ("motivée"), signed by the President and "registered" along with the minutes ("procésverbal") of each session with the *secrétaire* who, in turn, has had to communicate the results of the commission's deliberations to the claimant and other concerned parties.[258] Thereafter, the commis-

---

other decision, the *Conseil* held that the Romanian Commission could not itself determine, without exceeding its powers, the effect of a Romanian currency devaluation upon the value of certain French debt claims entitled to benefit from the 1959 Romanian Accord, the provisions of the Accord not being clear on this point. *Sieur Pioton, ès-qualité de liquidateur de la Société industrielle des pétroles roumains,* [1962] Rec. Cons. d'Ét. 142. And in still another decision, the *Conseil* held that the 1963 Yugoslav Commission could not itself determine, without exceeding its powers, whether the date of nationalization of the claimant's property, for purposes of eligibility, should be the date of the nationalization authorization (antedating the 1951 Yugoslav Accord) or the date of actual loss (postdating the 1963 Yugoslav Accord), the 1963 Yugoslav Accord not being clear on this point. *Dame Kliks,* [1967] Cons. d'Ét., Section du Contentieux, No. 68,781 (unpublished mimeo.). In all of these decisions, the *Conseil d'État* designated the French Foreign Ministry as the appropriate interpreter.

[257] In two instances, the *Conseil d'État* has rejected appeals based on the argument that the *"secrétaire"* of the commission in question was not present at the time of the commissions' final deliberations. See *Société Anonyme Rhône-Poulenc,* [1963] Cons. d'Ét., Section du Contentieux, No. 57,024 (unpublished mimeo.), an appeal arising from the Czech Commission; *Sieur Steinberg,* [1963] Cons. d'Ét., Section du Contentieux, No. 59,621 (unpublished mimeo.), an appeal arising from the Romanian Commission.

[258] The opinions reflecting the commissions' decisions usually are prepared by the *rapporteurs* subject to correction by the commission members. Interview with Dervieu, in Paris, June 27, 1969. Failure to explain sufficiently the grounds for decision has resulted in "annulation" by the *Conseil d'État. See Dame Landau,* [1960] Rec. Cons. d'Ét. 199. Also, if not communicated to the claimant fast enough to allow the

sions have been free to order a provisional distribution to the successful claimant[259] who (at least under the Czech, 1950 Hungarian, Polish, and Yugoslav commission Rules) then has been free, in turn, to contest the provisional allocation as in the manner outlined above. After having ruled on all claims, including provisional allocation contests, the commissions have been required to draw up a definitive repartition statement for communication to the *Trésor* and for publication, with the *secrétaire* of each commission having to notify each of the claimants of the definitive statement as it concerns them.

Over-all, then, the French distributive (or decisional) context has been very much of a piece. Subject to the variations noted in connection with the Egyptian Commission, all the French commissions have borne great resemblance to each other—juridically, operationally, and structurally. *Juridically,* all have been both fish *and* fowl. Stemming neither from "l'ordre judicaire" nor from "la hiérarchie administrative,"[260] they were conceived as "organes administratifs juridictionnels, de caractère arbitral marqué."[261] It is because of this and because they were ordered to rule "souverainement" that they were called "Commissions Spéciales."[262] *Operationally,* as already suggested, all were inspired by "la notion d'arbitrage."[263] Individual claimants or their proper representatives have been able to present their demands directly to the commissions which, though without competence to rule on private law issues,[264]

---

claimant to make an appeal to the *Conseil d'État* within the time limits prescribed by law, the Government cannot then object to the appeal on the grounds of its being tardy. *See Sieur Block,* [1968] Cons. d'Ét., Section du Contentieux, No. 71,499 (unpublished mimeo.).

[259] In order to avoid overpayment, uniformly small percentages have been given out at a time. It is said that the reason for these provisional distributions has been the absence of interest payments. It also is reported that the procedure has created difficulties on occasion. "Claimants tend to believe that an amount paid once will be given again and again up to 100%, as if provisional distribution were a pension. When this is found not to be the case, sometimes claimants have written to their *députés.*" Interview with Dervieu, in Paris, June 28, 1969.

[260] VIENOT 231.

[261] Bindschedler, *supra* note 23 at 292. *Cf. Société "La Huta,"* [1961] Rec. Cons. d'Ét. 313, on appeal from the Polish Commission.

[262] *See* VIENOT 231.

[263] *Id.* 229.

[264] *Cf. Société des Laboratoires de Reuilly,* [1962] Rec. Cons. d'Ét. 629, wherein the *Conseil d'État* held that the Czech Commission was incompetent to pronounce upon the existence or validity of an agreement in private law for the purpose of

have been nonetheless free to render definitive rulings subject to review only by the *Conseil d'État*. Also, all have partaken of a mixed adversarial-inquisitorial process, with a *commissaire du gouvernement* designated by the Foreign Ministry assuming the role of advocate on behalf of all claimants, and the commissions themselves, at their own initiative, actively pursuing the discovery of relevant information. And *structurally*, as seen, the commissions have differed only in relatively minor degree. What decisions they have rendered, to what extent their decisions have also been of a parcel, and whether their decisions have been in keeping with both customary international practice and sound policy is the next and most important inquiry of this study.

---

choosing among competing claimants, and that such issues must be left to the civil courts. For discussion demonstrating a like approach in American practice, see LILLICH (U.S.) 58–62.

Part III

The Process of Claim

International law continues to be doubted not only because we yearn for centralized decision-making structures. Another, more subtle, reason is our general reluctance to rationalize satisfactorily the ambiguous, contradictory, and, above all, haphazard heap of horizontally produced communications which are, by and large, what we call international law. However much we may want to relate international law to the push and pull of the everyday world, rather helplessly we continue to talk in terms of the obfuscating classifications that are the traditional fare of the legal profession; we continue to talk as if law were not a function of social process.

In reporting the decisions of the French commissions, hopefully the pages following register sensitivity to, and escape from, this dilemma.[1] Drawing partly upon this writer's experience in trying to articulate a framework for analyzing how international law regulates the deprivation of foreign wealth worldwide,[2] they recommend an

---

[1] As will be seen, the efforts of this writer in this connection owe enormously to the contributions of professors Harold D. Lasswell and Myres S. McDougal of the Yale Law School, authors of what has recently been called, not altogether accurately, the "New Haven Approach" to law—*i.e.,* "configurative" and "policy-oriented" jurisprudence. *See* Falk, *On Treaty Interpretation and the New Haven Approach: Achievements and Prospects,* 8 VA. J. INT'L L. 323, 330 n.11 (1968). For the central initiatives of the "New Haven Approach," see M. McDOUGAL & ASSOCIATES, STUDIES IN WORLD PUBLIC ORDER (1960); M. McDOUGAL & W. BURKE, THE PUBLIC ORDER OF THE OCEANS: A CONTEMPORARY INTERNATIONAL LAW OF THE SEA (1962); M. McDOUGAL & F. FELICIANO, LAW AND MINIMUM WORLD PUBLIC ORDER: THE LEGAL REGULATION OF INTERNATIONAL COERCION (1961); M. McDOUGAL, H. LASSWELL, & J. MILLER, THE INTERPRETATION OF AGREEMENTS AND WORLD PUBLIC ORDER (1967); M. McDOUGAL, H. LASSWELL, & I. VLASIC, LAW AND PUBLIC ORDER IN SPACE (1963). *See also* the seminal study, H. LASSWELL & A. KAPLAN, POWER AND SOCIETY (1950).

[2] *See* Weston, *International Law and the Deprivation of Foreign Wealth: A Framework for Future Inquiry,* in 2 THE FUTURE OF THE INTERNATIONAL LEGAL ORDER 36 (R. Falk & C. Black eds. 1970) [hereinafter cited as "WESTON"]. For earlier efforts by this writer in this connection, see Weston, *Community Regulation of Foreign-Wealth Deprivations: A Tentative Framework for Inquiry,* in ESSAYS ON EXPROPRIATIONS 117 (R. Miller & R. Stanger eds. 1967).

approach to the study of the "Law of International Claims" (and "State Responsibility") which, by allowing descriptive rather than prescriptive organization of the French commission decisions, would seem better attuned to the needs of all who would affect and understand the interrelation of law and community process—of course, within the wealth deprivation setting to which the French commission decisions, with minor exception, have had to be confined.[3] Thus, against the tripartite backdrop just recounted, the ensuing discussion presumes a Process of Claim which, itself conducive to functional analysis, attempts simultaneously to isolate the claims brought to the French commissions and to relate these claims to the deprivative process out of which they arose (here using "claim" in the sense of demand rather than obligation). That is, the discussion presumes a sequence of interrelated events involving persons (Claimants) who, in quest of particular relief, assert varying demands (Objectives), within varying particularized contexts (Situations), with varying means (Base Values) and in varying ways (Strategies) that produce varying results (Outcomes). An abbreviated outline of this Process of Claim looks as follows:

> Claimants
> Claimant Objectives
>> Claims Relating to Deprivors
>> Claims Relating to Deprivor Objectives
>> Claims Relating to Situations Which Affect Deprivor Action
>> Claims Relating to Deprivor Base Values
>> Claims Relating to Deprivor Strategies
>> Claims Relating to Outcomes of Deprivation
> Situations Affecting Claimant Eligibility
> Claimant Base Values
> Claimant Strategies
> Outcomes of Claim

By framing our analysis along these lines, a framework that seeks both comprehensiveness and systematic specification of particular claims, hopefully we can begin to standardize our approach to the

---

[3] *See* text at Part II, notes 154–158.

"Law of International Claims" (and "State Responsibility") in a manner that other social scientists have long demonstrated is possible,[4] namely, through communication over time, across frontiers, and between institutions in functional and relatively norm-free language. The cumulative result, it is believed, would be an injection of commonsense clarity into a welter of technical confusion and, therefore, a heightened awareness about the horizontal possibilities for assuring and expanding world order.

Before turning to an examination of the French commission decisions, however, it is important to make three distinct but related comments concerning analytical perspective. Each is necessary for proper appreciation of the conclusions that are drawn hereinafter.

First, while naturally the discussion that follows accounts for the explicit decisions of the French commissions, it is not restricted to them. In order to present as comprehensive and realistic a portrayal as possible, it seeks also to extrapolate the implicit decisions of these commissions, even if such decisions have not been expressly required by the claimant petitions. In other words, notwithstanding that the manifest decisions of the French commissions have dealt with the specific application of particular norms, these applications themselves have been premised on a variety of public order assumptions which, although seldom the subject of commission speculation and usually to be inferred from prior diplomatic decision, may be said to constitute decisions in their own right and hence worthy, if not demanding, of attention. To uncover these assumptions, it has of course been necessary to look not simply to the commission opinions but, as well, to as many of the facts that have conditioned their writing as information and inference have allowed, including, obviously, the texts of the Settlement Agreements. The gain, it is believed, has been to facilitate a richer, albeit still modest, contribution to the "Law of International Claims" (and "State Responsibility") than would otherwise have been possible.

Second, the subsequent discussion is premised on the conviction that the French commission decisions, however much diplomatically or legislatively predetermined, have been international legal de-

---

[4] Lillich, it should be noted, already has made significant strides in this direction. *See, e.g.,* LILLICH (U.S.); LILLICH (G.B.); LILLICH & CHRISTENSON.

cisions, affected by, and in turn affecting, the law of international privilege and responsibility. To be sure, it would be wrong to overlook those disclaimers, whether capitalist, socialist, or Third World inspired, that insist that the "rules" proclaimed or inferred in lump sum settlement–national claims commission decisions, far from evincing international law, represent little more than voluntary concessions to socioeconomic and political expediency. Especially must we be cautious until after we have surveyed satisfactorily the wider practice of which they are a part.[5] Still, if we understand, as we should, that international law, like all law, is not simply a matter of rules from which parochial dissent can be had at will, but rather a special and oftentimes hazy mix of formal authority *and* effective control; and if we understand, further, that in our essentially horizontal world order, as on occasion in our domestic orders, the matter of control is often reduced to informal socioeconomic and political pressures ("sanctions") of one sort or another—then by and large the disclaimers must fail, especially if similar behavioral patterns can be discerned worldwide (although surely universality is not a *sine qua non* of "law"). This view, it should be added, is one which affects equally all sides of our ideologically cloven world. Were the French experience unique, which it is not,[6] then obviously conclusions other than those reached might have to be drawn—the emphasis being conditional and not absolute because, even then, the conditions of progress upon which major community-wide policies depend still must be clarified and taken into account.

Finally, the ensuing discussion proceeds on the assumption that the very real possibilities that horizontal decision-making can and does have for the enlightened development of the "Law of International Claims" (and "State Responsibility") can be advanced only slightly by merely reporting the decisions of national claims commissions. A primary requirement is a conscious commitment to, and a willingness to recommend, community policies that identify one more with the interests of the world community as a whole than with the interests of any particular group or groups—or, as Mc-

---

[5] A complete survey of this kind is, of course, beyond the scope of this volume. However, as much as possible, references will be made to what is said to be the international law in this area.

[6] *See, e.g.,* LILLICH (U.S.) and LILLICH (G.B.).

Dougal has put it, with "a world public order in which values are shaped and shared more by persuasion than by coercion, and which seeks to promote the greatest production and widest possible sharing, without discriminations irrelevant of merit, of all values among all human beings."[7] It is this writer's conviction that resolution of conflict in the context presented by postwar French international claims practice must favor, as in other contexts, the overriding goals of this "international law of human dignity," or in somewhat less abstract terms: minimizing the potential for resort to coercion in international economic interaction; promoting a viable international economy in which wealth, skills, enlightenment, and other important values can flow freely and abundantly across State lines; maintaining at least minimum public order within particular territorial communities; and securing optimum return from all domestic value processes. Of course, it is not enough to stop here. The essential next step—concededly no easy one—is to relate these broad preferences to the many concrete cases of explicit and implicit claim that can and do arise. It is, indeed, because this task is so difficult that its attempted performance hereinafter is undertaken in tentative rather than dogmatic spirit.

Now, bearing these perspectives in mind and following the outline set forth above, it is appropriate to consider the French commission decisions.[8]

[7] McDougal, *Perspectives for an International Law of Human Dignity*, in M. Mc-Dougal & Associates, *supra* note 1, at 987.

[8] As earlier mentioned, French officials have expressed great concern for claimant privacy. *See* text at Part I, notes 14–16. Deferring to this sentiment, except where claimant names have already been made public, the decisions of the French commissions are hereinafter referred to by number and year only. With prefixes designed to identify the particular French commissions, the decisions are hereinafter cited, for example, as follows:

Bulgarian Commission decisions	FB 1 (1960)
Cuban Commission decisions	FC 1 (1968)
Czech Commission decisions	FCz 1 (1952)
Egyptian Commission decisions	FE 1 (1969)
1950 Hungarian Commission decisions	FH 1 (1952)
1965 Hungarian Commission decisions	FH2d 1 (1967)
Polish Commission decisions	FP 1 (1952)
Romanian Commission decisions	FR 1 (1960)
1951 Yugoslav Commission decisions	FY 1 (1953)
1963 Yugoslav Commission decisions	FY2d 1 (1964)

Supplementing these citations will be references to 1950 Hungarian Commission decisions concerning claims based on bond and stock certificates ("titres et valeurs").

1. CLAIMANTS

The precise identification of persons who make claims to secure the prescription and application of relevant community policies, whether in original or substituted (*i.e.*, surrogate and successor) capacity, is a matter of no mere academic interest. Depending on the arena to which their claims are brought (*e.g.*, diplomatic or adjudicative, global or national, permanent or *ad hoc*), who claimants are can condition, *inter alia*, the character and intensity of their demands, the importance and wisdom—even the feasibility—of deciding for or against them, and of course the nature and degree of protection warranted, if any. At any rate, for the quasi-judicial and temporary French *commissions spéciales de répartition*, the job of claimant identification has been all-important. Simply put, the commissions have sought carefully to identify claimants in order to decide who, according to previously established tests, has had "personal standing" to benefit from the settlements that have been theirs to administer. They have not done so, however, in order to favor original over surrogate and successor claimants. Most of the Constitutive Laws have inferred and all the Commission Rules have expressly allowed that original claimants could be represented by their legal proxies[9] (naturally on the assumption that these persons—*i.e.*, administrators, guardians, trustees, and other legal representatives—would succeed or fail to the same extent as their principals). And while only the 1950 Czech Accord explicitly authorized lump sum distributions to some successor interests (by way

Unlike the other French commissions, the 1950 Hungarian Commission chose to number and file these decisions separately from the others it rendered. Accordingly, these decisions are hereinafter separately cited, for example, as "FH TV1 (1955)."

The decisions of the French commissions are available for inspection, upon permission, in the commissions' separate *Extraits du Registre des Décisions Juridictionelles* housed at the commissions' secretariats, most of whose addresses have already been noted. *See* Part II, note 233. The secretariats of the Bulgarian, Czech, and Romanian commissions, whose addresses are not set forth above, are all located at 80, Rue de Lille, Paris VII.

Decisions of the *Conseil d'État*, where published, are cited to the *Recueil des Décisions du Conseil d'État*, the annual series in which some of the decisions of the *Conseil* are published in chronological order. Most of these published decisions also can be found in the Sirey and Dalloz collections. Unpublished decisions of the *Conseil d'État* are hereinafter so identified and can be obtained free of charge from the *Centre de Coordination et de Documentation* of the *Conseil d'État* (Paris I).

[9] *See* text at Part II, note 167 and notes 251-254.

of limitation),[10] nevertheless all the commissions have recognized the standing of heirs, successor companies, assignees, subrogees, and other successor claimants to establish their claims.[11] In sum, although personal eligibility may be restricted to original claimants within some legal regimes (for example, when non-assignable causes-of-action prevail), at no time have surrogate or successor claimants been denied access to the French commissions by reason of their substituted status *per se*.[12] However numerous the tests of personal eligibility could have been, in fact they have been limited exclusively, and without regard to the substance of the claims involved, to proof of claimant ownership or representative authority, nationality, and, to lesser extent, residence and legal personality.

Ownership–Authority

As indicated, both original and substituted claimants have had standing to benefit from France's lump sum settlements in principle. More or less explicit in all the Settlement Agreements, however, as well as in most of the other Controlling Texts, has been the patently rudimentary requirement that no claimant should have the right to share in the lump sum distributions without ownership of the claim in question or without delegated authority to petition on the owner's behalf.[13] Consistent therewith, the commissions have declined to

10 *See* 1950 Czech Accord, Additional Protocol No. I, para. 1(a). In no known case was this provision, limiting eligibility to those successors whose "right of succession has come into being before the occurrence of the [deprivative] measures mentioned in [Article 1 of the 1950 Accord]," ever the subject of discussion by the Czech Commission. In any event, it does not appear to have foreclosed recovery at any time. Accordingly, its importance is open to question.

11 For indication of this recognition, see text at notes 46–51 *infra*.

12 In the case of surrogate claimants, this freedom of access assumes of course that their principals have not themselves already secured a commission ruling in their own behalf, in which event, obviously, the surrogate claimants have had no standing. *See* FB 10 (1961); FR 5870 (1965), 6430 (1966). Likewise, when surrogate claimants already have secured a commission ruling on behalf of their principals, the latter have not had standing. *See* FR 5384 (1965). Unclear is whether a principal has been entitled to replace his surrogate or a surrogate has been entitled to replace his principal *before* a decision has been rendered, the commissions apparently never having addressed themselves to this circumstance. According to one informed source, however, this would present no problem. Interview with Dervieu, in Paris, June 23, 1969.

13 *See* 1955 Bulgarian Accord, preamble and arts. 1–5; 1967 Cuban Accord, preamble and art. 1; 1950 Czech Accord, preamble and arts. 1–2; 1966 Egyptian Accord, arts. 1–3; 1950 Hungarian Accord, preamble and art. 3; 1965 Hungarian Accord,

indemnify not only when title or delegated authority has been absent in fact,[14] but also, demonstrating the degree of their commitment to this proposition, when title or delegated authority has been unproved.[15] Illustrative are cases in which the commissions have denied

preamble and art. 1; 1948 Polish Accord, preamble and arts. 2–4; 1959 Romanian Accord, arts. 1–3; 1951 Yugoslav Accord, preamble and arts. 2 and 5; 1963 Yugoslav Accord, preamble and art. 2. *See also* text at Part II, notes 167 & 235.

[14] FB 5 (1961); 61, 70, 75 (1962); 116, 134 (1963); 144, 160, 162 (1964)/FC 1 (1968)/FCz 13 (1953); 34 (1954); 177, 179, 206 (1957); 319, 420, 654 (1958); 726, 772, 789–90, 799, 832, 906 (1959); 1013–14 (1960)/FE 4, 8, 78 (1969)/FH 328 (1955); 346 (1957); TV128–282, TV384–438 (1955); TV384, TV507, TV735–36 (1956)/FH2d 18, 20, 25, 29 (1967); 68 (1968)/FP 55, 57, 60, 99 (1953); 114 (1954); 190, 192 (1955)/FR 3, 21, 83 (1960); 893, 1236, 1892 (1962); 2441, 2848, 2850, 2924 (1963); 3477, 3598, 3720, 4009, 4135 (1964); 7013 (1966)/FY 85 (1953); 100, 117 (1954); 175 (1955); 335 (1956); 415 (1957). Three of the Romanian Commission decisions cited (FR 3477, 3598, and 3720), each demonstrating the nature of some of the problems involved, were appealed to the *Conseil d'État*. In the first, the *Conseil* affirmed that a unilateral cancellation of a stock transfer agreement, allegedly pursuant to the agreement but 21 years after its making (*i.e.*, after the nationalization of the stock company and after the entry into force of the 1959 Romanian Accord), did not reinstate ownership status for the purpose of establishing compensatory eligibility. *Compagnie internationale des ciments (INTERCIME)*, [1966] Cons. d'Ét., Section du Contentieux, No. 63,585 (unpublished mimeo.). In the second, the *Conseil* affirmed that ownership based on a "reciprocal contract" (*acte synallagmatique*) could not be maintained for distributive purposes because the titular contract had not been registered as required by the French *Code Civil*. *Dame Bouchet*, [1966] Rec. Cons. d'Ét. 116. In the third case, similar to the second, the *Conseil* affirmed that ownership based on an *inter vivos* "gift deed" could not be maintained for distributive purposes because the deed in question had not been executed according to the formalities required by French law. *Sieur Sclia-Balaceano*, [1966] Cons. d'Ét., Section du Contentieux, No. 64,570 (unpublished mimeo.). Bulgarian Commission decision FB 144, *supra*, was affirmed by the *Conseil d'État* without supplementary discussion. *See Dame Arié*, [1965] Cons. d'Ét., Section du Contentieux, No. 64,555 (unpublished mimeo.). For related discussion, see text at note 270 *infra*.

[15] FB 25, 29, 33, 37, 38 (1961); 62, 80, 87 (1962); 97, 98, 112–13, 115, 119, 126 (1963); 139, 145, 147 151, 172 (1964); 201 (1966)/FCz 8, 11, 12 (1953); 50, 63 (1955); 85, 125, 136, 141 (1956); 185, 208, 221 (1957); 264, 319, 322, 326, 347, 395, 404, 415, 417, 422, 647–49 (1958); 684–85, 718–21, 729, 738–65, 773, 792, 807–11, 831, 887–88, 906, 954, 963, 975, 977–80, 982 (1959); 1102, 1168–73, 1191, 1193–96 (1960); 1284–88, 1300, 1314 (1961); 1328 (1962); 1348 (1963); 1357 (1964)/FH 53, 74, 80, 150–52 (1953); 173, 257–58 (1954); 279, 286 (1955); 348–49, 351 (1957); TV439–86, TV710, TV714, TV730–31, TV734, TV736 (1956)/FH2d 24, 27, 39, 44, 50 (1967)/FP 63, 97 (1953); 117–18, 120–21, 125, 156–58 (1954); 190, 192, 203, 211 (1955); 297 (1957); 354, 367, 386, 389, 400, 403 (1958); 409–10 (1959); 474, 482, 483 (1960); 499 (1961); 521, 532–35, 538 (1962); 545 (1963)/FR 7 (1960); 305, 361, 368, 401, 467, 544, 577, 580, 639, 694, 759, 673 (1961); 970, 973, 1030, 1360, 1713, 1851, 1919, 1983 (1962); 2110, 2179, 2376, 2558, 2560–61, 2847, 2923, 2986–87, 3094–96 (1963); 3345, 3374, 3638, 3744, 4133, 4153, 4253, 4258 (1964); 4510–11, 4515, 4639, 4642, 4645, 4770–71, 4774, 4777–78, 4812, 4900–902, 5063, 5065, 5069, 5248, 5289, 5501, 5545–46, 5589, 5716, 6023–24 (1965); 6168–71, 6304, 6307, 6560, 6678–79, 6786, 6805, 6914, 7051 (1966); 7125, 7136, 7212, 7297–98, 7385 (1967)/ **FY** 85, 86 (1953); 171 (1954); 204–11 (1955); 240, 243, 247, 256, 316, 328–29,

relief to claimants whose "dossiers," because of neglect to reassert "rights" previously abandoned or taken, revealed constructive waivers of proprietary interest.[16] Save mentioning that to establish title or authority the commissions have had to investigate French and other municipal laws, to refer apparent disputes to French civil court adjudication (the commissions themselves being theoretically without competence to rule on "private law" issues[17]), and, on final analysis, to adopt a flexible rather than a rigid approach to problems of proof,[18] the point is too elementary to require further elaboration.

Nationality

Except in two situations, only persons having French nationality have had standing to share directly in the lump sum distributions

331 (1956) ; 342, 396, 427, 441 (1957)/FY2d 21, 32, 33 (1965) ; 35, 36, 38, 40, 41, 45, 57, 59 (1966).

[16] FB 65, 91 (1962) ; 117–18, 124, 131 (1963) ; 170 (1964) ; 178 (1965)/FCz 6 (1953) ; 222 (1957) ; 224 (1958)/FH 40, 64, 150–52 (1953) ; 273–74, 334–36 (1956)/ FP 44, 56, 63, 71, 89 (1953) ; 103 (1954) ; 532 (1962)/FR 2985 (1963). In a number of these cases, the commissions were asked, for the purpose of establishing title, to ignore that the claimants' predecessors-in-interest had failed to reassert "rights" at first seized by the German occupation forces and later, after World War II, "sequestered" or placed under "temporary management" by the payor governments. Of course, express waivers of proprietory interest have likewise been deemed to preclude a claim to ownership. See FH 289 (1955)/FP 288 (1957) ; 481 (1960).

[17] See Part II, note 264 and accompanying text. Thus, in the only known decisions of the Conseil d'État concerning specifically the validity or scope of surrogate authority, the Conseil held that the Polish Commission had "exceeded its competence" in interpreting certain ambiguous provisions of a judgment of the Tribunal de Commerce de la Seine which purported to limit the mandate of the surrogate in question. The commission, the Conseil observed, should have suspended judgment until after the civil court had clarified the matter. Sieur Pioton, ès-qualité de liquidateur de la Société anonyme polonaise des charbonnages, mines et usines de Sosnowice, [1960] Rec. Cons. d'Ét. 632 ; Sieur Pioton, ès-qualité de liquidateur de la Société des usines de fabrication de tubes et forges de Sosnowice, [1960] Rec. Cons. d'Ét. 633 ; Sieur Pioton, ès-qualité de liquidateur de la Société des mines et usines à zinc de Silesie, [1960] Rec. Cons. d'Ét. 634. But cf. the decisions of the Conseil d'État cited at note 14 supra.

[18] See, e.g., FB 172 (1964) wherein the Bulgarian Commission accepted as proof of title to 50 shares in the nationalized Bank of Bulgaria the fact that the claimant stockholder was also "administrator" of the Bank; FP 137 (1954) wherein the Polish Commission observed that "despite the lack of authentic documents proving her position as proprietor, the claimant presents sufficient evidence to establish her good faith." That the French commissions uniformly have taken into account the intention and situation of the claimant in matters of proof has been confirmed by interviews had with French officials, public and private—in particular: Interview with Dervieu, in Paris, June 23, 1969; Interview with Henri Glaser, "Secrétaire General"

of the *commissions spéciales*.[19] Whether they have appeared in original or substituted capacity and whether their claims were born of "wartime" or "peacetime" deprivation has been immaterial. The reason is clear. Generally speaking, consistent with the proposition that only French nationals should be entitled to benefit from French diplomatic protection, all the Settlement Agreements (as well as the ensuing Statutory Instruments and Commission Rules) have expressly required possession of French nationality as a condition precedent—arguably *the* condition precedent—to compensatory eligibility.[20] The French commissions, obliged to "execute" these accords, have complied meticulously, refusing eligibility not only to foreign nationals[21] and stateless persons (*apatrides*)[22] but, as well, to claimants who have been unable to prove or who have failed to prove the French nationality they alleged.[23] Even Moroccan nation-

---

of the *Association Pour la Sauvegarde et l'Expansion des Biens et Intérêts Privés Français à l'Étranger,* in Paris, July 8, 1969.

[19] Of course, foreign companies have benefited indirectly to the extent that their French shareholders have been able to share in the lump sum distributions. For discussion concerning shareholder eligibility, see text at notes 394–414 *infra.*

[20] *See* 1955 Bulgarian Accord, preamble and art. 1(a); 1967 Cuban Accord, preamble and art. 1; 1950 Czech Accord, preamble and arts. 1–2; 1966 Egyptian Accord, preamble and arts. 1–2, 4; 1950 Hungarian Accord, preamble and art. 3; 1965 Hungarian Accord, preamble and art. 1; 1948 Polish Accord, preamble and arts. 1 and 4; 1959 Romanian Accord, arts. 1, 3, and Exchange of Letters No. 1; 1951 Yugoslav Accord, preamble and art. 2; 1963 Yugoslav Accord, preamble and art. 2. A like stipulation is to be found in the 1961 German Accord, *supra* Part I, note 10. For indication that this requirement has been reiterated, implicitly if not always explicitly, in the Statutory Instruments and Commission Rules, see text at Part II, notes 167 & 238.

[21] FB 6 (1960); 11 (1961); 157 (1964)/FCz 176–77 (1957); 260, 423, 623 (1958); 868–69 (1959)/FE 52, 59 (1969)/FH 284 (1955); TV740, TV745, TV751, TV756 (1956)/FH2d 4 (1967)/FP 111 (1954); 170–72, 205 (1955); 221, 229, 255, 258 (1956); 271 (1957); 339, 371 (1958)/FR 233, 356, 544, 597 (1961); 920, 1125, 1745 (1962); 2873, 3180 (1963); 5720, 5905 (1965); 6563, 6918, 7029 (1966); 7316, 7389 (1967)/FY 49–52 (1953); 202 (1955); 234, 321 (1956); 392, 405, 416–17, 423 (1957); 521 (1958).

[22] FE 50 (1969)/FP 345 (1958)/FY 247 (1956). *See also* FCz 206 (1957) wherein a grantee was denied compensation for deprivations sustained by the grantor because the grantor was a "stateless person" at the time of loss. For additional decisions concerning the nationality-eligibility of successor claimants, see notes 46–51 and accompanying text *infra.* Also, it merits notice that "stateless persons" residing in French territory as of March 20, 1958 (a functional equivalent to a claim accrual date) have been authorized to share in the lump sum transferred under the 1961 German Accord (as to which, see Part I, note 10).

[23] FB 29, 37, 38 (1961); 62, 69, 84 (1962); 113–15 (1963); 161–62, 168 (1964) 201 (1966)/FCz 162, 168 (1957); 322, 326, 347, 408, 422, 647 (1958); 685, 718–21,

als, "protected" by the French until 1956, and Monegasques, over whom France long has exercised certain "sovereign" powers (including the power to tax), have not been deemed "French" for purposes of lump sum distribution.[24] In short, in respect of only two special groups of claimants—"[foreign] companies under French control" (eligible in principle under the 1948 Polish Accord)[25] and

---

738–43, 792, 808–11, 975, 977–80, 982, 992 (1959); 1169–73, 1193–96 (1960); 1287, 1300 (1961); 1348 (1963)/FH 264 (1955); TV741, TV747, TV754 (1956)/FP 67 (1953); 102–104, 118, 120–21 (1954); 361 (1958); 409 (1959)/FR 2847 (1963); 3345 (1964); 4639, 4642, 4900, 5377, 5545–46, 5559, 5716, 6023–24, 6168–71 (1965); 6434, 6678–79, 6786, 6914 (1966); 7125, 7212, 7297–98 (1967)/FY 100 (1954); 201, 204–205 (1955); 316, 331–32 (1956); 342, 392, 423 (1957); 521 (1958)/FY2d 11 (1965). As with other matters of proof, rather than rely solely on the documentation furnished by the claimants the French commissions themselves have made inquiries to research the presence or absence of French nationality. *See, e.g.,* FH 34 (1953) wherein the 1950 Hungarian Commission, faced with insufficient evidence, deferred a final decision until after a "complementary investigation" could be made. Again, too, they have demonstrated sensitivity to claimant intention and circumstance. *See, e.g.,* FY 321 (1956) wherein the 1951 Yugoslav Commission, in recognizing the eligibility of the French Red Cross in respect of a shareholder claim acquired through an anonymous gift, observed that "in all probability, these shares belonged to a French national who did not want to reveal his irregular situation regarding assets held in a foreign country." However, when claimant nationality has been contested, the commissions, being more of the "ordre administrative" than of the "ordre judiciare," have not been free to resolve the issue. This task has belonged to the ordinary civil tribunals. *See Dame veuve Deltel*, [1957] Rec. Cons. d'Ét. 512; *Dame veuve Rubel*, [1958] Rec. Cons. d'Ét. 33. *See also* C. civ. art. 125 (67e. ed. Petits Codes Dalloz 1967–68). For related remarks, see note 62 and accompanying text *infra*.

24 FP 111 (1954); 170–72 (1955); 255, 258 (1956); 271 (1957)/FR 1745 (1962)/ FY 405 (1957). By way of some contrast, the British Foreign Compensation Commission, in accordance with the British Nationality Act, has accepted as within the term "British national" all " 'persons in those self-governing Dominions which were in existence at the date of the [lump sum] Agreement,' as well as citizens of the United Kingdom and British protected persons." LILLICH (G.B.) 33. For related comment, see note 62 *infra*.

25 1948 Polish Accord, art. 4(c). To these claimants must be added four apparently French-controlled Polish companies actually named in the agreement: "the *Compagnie franco-polonaise des chemins de fer* for the withdrawal of its concession as well as for the nationalized assets," "the *International Ship-Building Company de Gdansk* for the French share in this company and concession," "the *Société Skarboferm* for the final termination of its concession," and "the *Société Hohenlohe* . . . for the French share in this company and all other rights." *Id.* art. 4, subparas. 1–4. (Emphasis added.) Only the first of these companies actually petitioned the Polish Commission in its own name. *See* FP 294 (1957). The French interests in the three other companies were defended by surrogates acting on behalf of the French stockholders. *See* FP 261 (1956); 323 (1957).

It merits notice that, notwithstanding the quoted language of Article 4(c) of the 1948 Polish Accord, Polish companies under French control have not been eligible to petition on behalf of their French stockholders in their capacity as stockholder of another company. *See, e.g., Sieur Pioton, ès-qualité de liquidateur de la Société*

several French-controlled foreign companies eligible for relief under the 1950 Czech Accord[26]—have different results been authorized, and then only to the extent of the aliquot share of the French interests participating.[27]

---

des mines et usines à zinc de Silesie, [1964] Cons. d'Ét., Section du Contentieux, No. 55,619 (unpublished mimeo.) ; *Sieur Pioton, ès-qualité de liquidateur de la Société des charbonnages, mines et usines de Sosnowice et de représentant de ses actionnaires ou de ses créanciers,* [1964] Rec. Cons. d'Ét. 458.

[26] *See* 1950 Czech Accord, "Lettre-Annexe No. 2," para. 3 which, reflecting a French-Czech willingness to "pierce the corporate veil" in order to protect an important bloc of French stockholders, provided "that the provisions of the Agreement apply to certain participations in Czechoslovak enterprises held indirectly by French parties, which are: participations in the enterprise *Tiberghien-Synovia,* all considered as French, participations in the *première fabrique tchéque de soie artificielle* held by the *Société Viscose Suisse S.A.,* the *Société privée de gestion S.A.,* the *Société Holva S.A.,* equally considered as French." (Emphasis added.) Although a literal reading of this language suggests that only the shareholder interests in these companies were to have standing to petition the Czech Commission, in fact the three named Swiss companies did so on their own behalf. In so doing, however, they were thoroughly exposed to the systemic framework of the Czech claims program. Initially granted compensation by the Czech Commission pursuant to the "Lettre-Annexe" [*see* FCz 146–48 (1956)], they were later denied relief [*see* FCz 1316–18 (1961)] by virtue of a decision rendered by the *Conseil d'État.* Decisions FCz 146–48 simultaneously were appealed to and "annulled" by the *Conseil* on the grounds that the "Lettre-Annexe" never had been officially published in the French *Journal Officiel.* According to the *Conseil,* this non-publication meant that the "Lettre-Annexe" had no "legal effect" within France and that the claimant Swiss companies therefore could not be "equally considered as French." *Commissaire du gouvernement près de la Commission de répartition de l'indemnité des nationalisations tchécoslovaques,* [1959] Rec. Cons. d'Ét. 674.

Subsequently, in 1963, the "Lettre-Annexe" was published officially in the French *Journal Officiel,* and the claimants thereafter recovered the indemnity originally awarded. FCz 1358–60 (1964). It should be noted, however, that the *Conseil d'État* decisions foreclosing relief to the claimant Swiss companies prior to the official publication of the "Lettre-Annexe" did not make the benefits of the 1950 settlement available to the companies' controlling French stockholders. In rejecting an appeal arising out of FCz 1325 (1961), the *Conseil* upheld the Commission's ruling that Article 3(b) of the Czech Commission Constitutive Law (see text at Part II, note 167) was designed only to facilitate representation of French or French-controlled companies and that it did not give to the claimant stockholder a personal right to relief under the 1950 Accord which, if granted, would make impossible the Swiss companies ever invoking their primary rights under the "Lettre-Annexe" once the "Lettre-Annexe" was officially published. *S. A. Rhône-Poulenc,* [1963] Cons. d'Ét., Section du Contentieux, No. 57,024 (unpublished mimeo.). For related discussion, see text at notes 394–414 *infra.*

[27] *See, e.g., Sieur Pioton ès-qualité de liquidateur de la Société des mines et usines à zinc de Silesie,* [1964] Cons. d'Ét., Section du Contentieux, No. 55,619 (unpublished mimeo.) ; *Sieur Pioton ès-qualité de liquidateur de la Société des usines de fabrication de tubes et forges de Sosnowice,* [1964] Cons. d'Ét., Section du Contentieux, No. 55,620 (unpublished mimeo.) ; *Sieur Pioton ès-qualité de liquidateur de la Société des charbonnages, mines et usines de Sosnowice et de représentant de ses*

In other words, with minor *formal* exception, France has followed what is said to be the traditional international law rule that States shall espouse only the claims of their nationals,[28] which in postwar French practice has meant that only French nationals have been entitled to lump sum protection. The "rule," of course, consistent with American and British practice[29] but increasingly open to question in light of the *Nottebohm* and *Reparations* cases,[30] is less an expression of principle than it is a recognition of the demands of practicality and the limitations of power. Still, it has to be pointed out that France has not adhered completely to the tradition—notably in her Egyptian and German claims programs[31]—and that this departure suggests a developing sensitivity to the needs of many persons who in this century have been the objects of forced change in nationality and other aspects of the human condition, a sensitivity that obviously will not be free to flourish until after more effective cooperation is achieved among claimant States.

Of course, to have conditioned eligibility upon proof of French nationality presumes that claimants must have been French at some time. Nationality does not exist *in vacuo*. Accordingly, bearing in mind that eligibility appears never to have depended on the presence of French nationality at any time following the date of lump sum

---

actionnaires ou de ses créanciers, [1964] Rec. Cons. d'Ét. 458. Each of these cases was appealed from the Polish Commission.

It should also be noted that, although undisposed to detail the criteria by which they have determined the existence of "French control," it appears that the Polish and other commissions for whom this issue has for one reason or another been relevant have based their decisions mainly on the presence or absence of a simple French shareholding majority. Interview with Dervieu, in Paris, June 25, 1969.

28 *See* 1 M. SIBERT, TRAITÉ DE DROIT INTERNATIONAL PUBLIC 560-72 (1951) [hereinafter cited as "1 SIBERT"]; 2 D. O'CONNELL, INTERNATIONAL LAW 1116-17 (1965) [hereinafter cited as "2 O'CONNELL"]. Traceable to Vattel, the doctrine was once famously justified by Umpire Parker of the United States–German Mixed Claims Commission on the grounds that "[a]ny other rule would open wide the door for abuses and might result in converting a strong nation into a claim agency in behalf of those who after suffering injuries should assign their claims to the nationals or avail themselves of its naturalization laws for the purpose of procuring its espousal of their claims." Administrative Decision No. V, 7 U.N.R.I.A.A. 119, 141 (1924). *See also* Panevezys-Saldutiskis Railway Case, [1939] P.C.I.J., ser. A/B, No. 76, at 16.

29 *See* LILLICH (U.S.) 76–101; LILLICH (G.B.) 24–59; LILLICH & CHRISTENSON 7–39.

30 *See* Nottebohm Case (Preliminary Objection), [1953] I.C.J. 111; Reparations for Injuries Suffered in the Service of the United Nations Case, [1949] I.C.J. 174.

31 For an inroad made under the Egyptian claims program, see text at note 33 *infra.* For an inroad made under the German claims program, see note 22 *supra.*

settlement,[32] what specific point or points in time have in fact proved decisive for recovery?

For the vast majority of claimants, happily the answer to this question has never been much in doubt. Excepting individuals who, under the continuing Egyptian claims program, may have acquired French nationality after August 22, 1958 (the signature date of the 1958 Zurich Accord)—these persons being eligible for relief under the 1966 Egyptian Accord provided proof of French nationality and permanent French residence can be shown to have existed prior to the entry into force of the 1966 Accord[33]—all claimants who have petitioned not only the Egyptian Commission but also the Bulgarian, Cuban, Czech, 1965 Hungarian, Romanian, and two Yugoslav commissions have had to demonstrate French nationality, at risk of forfeiture, both at the date of claim accrual (or a functional equivalent thereof)[34] and at the date of agreement signature or entry into force.[35] Why? Because, in the case of the Eastern European claims programs, the Settlement Agreements expressly so

[32] See, e.g., FCz 63 (1955)/FP 203 (1955); 221 (1956); 367 (1958) wherein the Czech and Polish commissions granted compensation notwithstanding that the claimants were not French nationals after the signature or entry into force of the relevant Settlement Agreements. While no other such decisions have been found, it is said that like results probably would obtain among the other commissions. Interview with Branche, in Paris, July 11, 1968.

[33] See 1966 Egyptian Accord, Protocol Annex, art. 11; Decree No. 68–103 of January 30, 1968, art. 5, [1968] J.O. 1228 (the Egyptian Commission Constitutive Law). See also FE 4 (1969), as of this writing the only case wherein compensation has been extended under these circumstances.

[34] Certain persons holding "ordinary" (i.e., non-deprivative) debt claims against the Yugoslav Government have been entitled to benefit from the 1963 Yugoslav settlement subject to proof of French nationality as of May 15, 1945, a functional equivalent to a claim accrual date. See 1963 Yugoslav Accord, art. 2.

[35] The cases in which the dual time requirements have been met are far too many to enumerate. Cases wherein one or both of the time requirements have not been met, however, are as follows: FB 2 (1960); 107, 125 (1963)/FCz 6, 7 (1953); 18, 28 (1954); 95, 115, 130, 136–37 (1956); 176–77, 183, 207, 215–17, 220 (1957); 260, 319–20, 348, 366–69, 395, 423, 611–12, 616, 623, 650 (1958); 680, 684, 730, 766–69, 868–70, 954, 956, 964 (1959); 1011, 1125, 1177 (1960); 1325 (1961); 1327 (1962)/ FH 54, 58, 59, 67, 74, 83, 106, 128, 132–33 (1953); 163, 193, 197, 237 (1954); 264, 297 (1955)/FH2d 3, 5, 7, 10, 11, 19 (1967)/FP 6, 15, 40 (1952); 59, 74 (1953); 115, 125 (1954); 191, 245 (1955); 289 (1957); 374, 388 (1958)/FR 6, 21, 34, 35, 74, 75, 85–87 (1960); 118, 120, 148–52, 232, 239, 257–58, 302, 354, 471, 582–83, 636–38 (1961); 893, 1236, 1354, 1576, 1789, 1915, 1982 (1962); 2109, 2176–77, 2242, 2244, 2923, 2949 (1963); 3388, 3511, 3720, 4383 (1964); 4510, 5063, 5715 (1965); 6303, 6467 (1966)/FY 54, 57, 62 (1953); 93 (1954); 188 (1955); 233, 244, 311, 321 (1956); 392 (1957); 516 (1958); 855 (1961)/FY2d 2, 8, 9, 16 (1965); 63 (1967).

required;[36] in the case of the Cuban and Egyptian claims programs, because the Cuban Commission Rules and the Egyptian Commission Constitutive Law unequivocally substituted a two-pronged time requirement for what appears to have been no more than a single time requirement in the Cuban and Egyptian accords[37]—thereby demonstrating, incidentally, the prerogative role left to France in fixing eligibility terms no less stringent than those called for in her international agreements.[38]

Regrettably less clear, however, are the nationality time requirements that have regulated the remaining 1950 Hungarian and Polish claims programs. Looking, as above, to all their Controlling Texts, one finds but one date upon which claimants must have been French in order to share in the lump sums: the date of claim accrual, explicitly in the case of the 1950 Hungarian claims program and implicitly in the case of the Polish claims program.[39] Nowhere in these texts is it stated or even implied that still another date might be dispositive. Yet in every instance in which claimants have been deemed eligible, they appear to have been French both at the initial date prescribed and at the date of the signature or entry into force of the relevant agreement. Perhaps this fact is mere coincidence. Except in one case in which the 1950 Hungarian Commission denied relief because French nationality, present "at the moment . . . rights to indemnification arose," had not been established at the date upon which "[the 1950 Accord] was concluded,"[40] eligibility has always

36 *See* 1955 Bulgarian Accord, art. 1(a); 1950 Czech Accord, art. 2; 1965 Hungarian Accord, art. 1; 1959 Romanian Accord, Exchange of Letters No. 1; 1951 Yugoslav Accord, art. 2; 1963 Yugoslav Accord, art. 2.

37 *See* Cuban Commission Rules, art. 4(1), Part II, note 233; Decree No. 68–103 of January 30, 1968, art. 5, [1968] J.O. 1228 (the Egyptian Commission Constitutive Law).

38 It will be recalled that the French commissions have themselves been obliged to draw up their Rules of Procedure. Accordingly, the two-pronged time requirement stipulated in the Cuban Commission Rules is evidence that this prerogative role extended all the way down to the commissions.

39 *See* 1950 Hungarian Accord, art. 3; 1948 Polish Accord, preamble and arts. 2–3. The 1950 Hungarian Accord provision requiring French nationality "at the moment their rights to indemnification arose" of course left wholly unclear whether this was intended to mean the date of loss, the date of claim, the date of decision or any other of a number of possible times. *But cf.* note 45 *infra*.

40 FH 264 (1955). This case was appealed to the *Conseil d'État*, on unrelated grounds. *See Dame veuve Rubel, supra* note 23.

been disallowed because the claimants have been unable to demonstrate French nationality at the prescribed initial date.[41] The exception, however, may prove the rule. Wholly without textual constraint, albeit as *dictum*, the 1950 Hungarian and Polish commissions have repeatedly invoked the norm, prevailing among the majority claims programs, that French nationality must be shown both at the date of claim accrual and at the date of treaty signature or entry into force.[42]

Strict constructionists doubtless would insist that nothing can be drawn from these repeated invocations. On the other hand, considering (1) that all the other claims programs (including, significantly, the 1965 Hungarian) have conditioned eligibility on proof of French nationality at a minimum of two dates, (2) that among them the Cuban and Egyptian (like the 1950 Hungarian and Polish) spoke initially in terms of one date only,[43] and (3) that the "exceptional" Hungarian decision noted must otherwise remain a curious anomaly—considering, that is, the total context within which nationality-eligibility has been treated, then it is not unreasonable to look upon the 1950 Hungarian and Polish commission *dicta* as expressions of more than a prevailing rule of postwar French practice. In short, special treaty reservations excepted (*e.g.*, Article 11 of the Protocol Annex to the 1966 Egyptian Accord), French nationality both at the date of claim accrual and at the time of agreement signature or entry into force appears to have been in deed, if not always in word, the exclusive rule of post-war French practice, similar if not wholly identical to that found in American and British practice.[44] Lacking explicit confirmation, of course, this judgment is not wholly conclusive. If accurate, however, it necessarily implies that costly and time-wasting energies have been expended by many of the claimants who have petitioned the 1950 Hungarian and Polish commissions. Since the opinions of these commissions never have been published, few if any of the claimants could have known in advance the precise conditions that they have been required to fullfill in fact.

[41] See the 1950 Hungarian and Polish commission decisions cited in note 35 *supra*.
[42] *Id.*
[43] *Compare* 1967 Cuban Accord, art. 1 and 1966 Egyptian Accord, Protocol Annex, art. 11, *with* the references cited in note 37 *supra*.
[44] *See* note 29 *supra*.

For most if not all claimants, then, proof of French ownership at both the accrual and settlement dates has been an indispensable first step toward establishing a successful claim.[45] But has this two-pronged time requirement necessitated French nationality continuously from the time of claim accrual to the time of settlement? Surprisingly, considering the large number of cases that they have been called upon to decide, the French commissions appear never to have been obliged to rule upon this issue. In each instance where the claim has been owned only by one person, as in most of the cases decided as of this writing, either the claimant has failed to prove French nationality at one or both of the key dates or he has been French, as a matter of fact, throughout the relevant period. And in all the remaining cases, where two persons have figured in the chain of title, the decisions have turned exclusively on the nationality of the original owner at the time of claim accrual or the nationality of the successor owner at the time of settlement, a fact which the following table concerning the nationality-eligibility of heirs and other successor claimants (successor companies, surviving partners, assignees, and subrogees) makes clear:[46]

[45] Conceding that the date of treaty signature or entry into force has presented no interpretative difficulty, it still merits asking what operational meaning has been given to the date of claim accrual, variously referred to in the Settlement Agreements and other Controlling Texts as "the date the measures were taken" or "the date the rights to indemnification arose." Regrettably, the commissions have not been very lucid by way of answer. With compounding ambiguity, repeatedly they have spoken of "the date of nationalization," "the date of expropriation," "the date of confiscation," and the like. However, two decisions of the Czech Commission infer what probably has been the preference throughout, *i.e.,* the date of effective deprivation. Thus, in FCz 50 (1955) the Czech Commission referred to the date when the claimant's wealth was "put under Czechoslovak sequestration pursuant to a decree of the Ministère de la Prévoyance Nationale." Similarly, in FCz 52 (1955) the Czech Commission referred to the date when "in accordance with Law No. 115 of 28 April 1948, the nationalization [of the claimant's wealth] was officially called for by decree No. 1232 . . . published in the Czechoslovak Official Journal." For other decisions that appear to support this conclusion, see FB 125 (1963); 157 (1964)/ FC 3 (1968); 5 (1969)/FCz 24 (1954); 53 (1955); 149 (1956); 160 (1957)/ FE 1, 4, 8 (1969)/FH 54, 58, 59, 83, 106 (1953); 197 (1954); 297 (1955)/FH2d 3, 4, 7 (1967); 68 (1968)/FP 6, 15 (1952)/FR 21 (1960); 471, 582, 636–37 (1961); 2949 (1963)/FY 233, 244, 321 (1956); 516 (1958)/FY2d 2, 9 (1965); 74 (1968).

[46] As may be deduced from the citations following, no known decision involving successor claimants has been rendered as of this writing by the Cuban and Egyptian commissions. However, there is nothing to suggest that these commissions would decide any differently than the other commissions. It may be noted that the same pattern has obtained in American and British practice. *See* note 29 *supra.*

Original Owner at Time of Claim Accrual	Successor		Decision
	At Time of Succession	At Time of Settlement	
Non-French	Non-French	Non-French	Ineligible[47]
	Non-French	French	Ineligible[48]
	French	French	Ineligible[49]
French	Non-French	Non-French	Ineligible[50]
	French	French	Eligible[51]

Suppose, however, that a French national owning property in Czechoslovakia, nationalized in 1945, were to have lost French nationality through marriage in 1949, but to have regained such status before October 19, 1951 (the date of the entry into force of the 1950 Czech Accord)? Or suppose that a French national owning property in Czechoslovakia, nationalized in 1945, were in 1949 to have assigned such rights as he may then have had in the property to a Swiss national who thereafter, but before October 19, 1951,

[47] *Heirs:* FB 6 (1961).

[48] *Heirs:* FR 1982 (1962)/FY2d 63 (1967).

[49] *Heirs:* FB 1 (1960); 55 (1962); 99, 127 (1963); 162 (1964)/FCz 208 (1957); 625 (1958); 690 (1959); 1177 (1960)/FH2d 20 (1967)/FP 105 (1954); 203 (1955); 479 (1960)/FR 84 (1960); 119, 299, 308–309, 502, 579, 791 (1961); 1787 (1962); 4812, 5248 (1965)/FY 54 (1953); 245, 321 (1956). *Assignees:* FCz 206 (1957)/FH TV740 (1956)/FR 920 (1962); 3598 (1964); 6427 (1966)/FY 392 (1957). *Subrogees:* FCz 85 (1956). Polish Commission decision FP 479 (1960), cited above, was affirmed on appeal by the *Conseil d'État. Sieurs Bernard et Georges Wilner,* [1963] Cons. d'Ét., Section du Contentieux, No. 54,761 (unpublished mimeo.). Romanian Commission decision FR 1714 (1962), not cited above, appears to be the only French commission decision to have reached results inconsistent with the foregoing decisions. The Commission granted compensation to two French heirs notwithstanding that their Romanian ancestor was alive and the sole owner of the property in question at the time of nationalization. While the Commission stressed that the heirs themselves were French at the time of nationalization, this fact does not appear to distinguish this decision from the others herein cited. Accordingly, for lack of further details, the decision remains a curious anomaly.

[50] *Heirs:* FCz 157 (1957).

[51] *Heirs:* FB 34 (1961); 48 (1962); 92, 94, 108, 125–26 (1963); 142, 148–51, 154, 160 (1964)/FCz 84 (1956); 218 (1957); 258 (1958); 805–806, 880, 969, 971 (1959); 1355 (1964)/FR 13, 66, 69 (1960); 255, 363, 464, 504, 635 (1961); 1441, 1603, 2049 (1962); 2490–91, 2590, 3222 (1963); 3510 (1964)/FY 252 (1956); 426 (1957). *Successor companies:* FB 47 (1961)/FCz 778 (1959)/FR 1579 (1962). *Surviving partners:* FCz 125 (1956). *Assignees:* FR 7387 (1967). *Subrogees:* FP 264–65 (1956)/ FR 7387 (1967). It is necessary to point out that for lack of eligibility in other respects not all of these decisions resulted in actual awards. Also, consider the above-cited Czech Commission decisions in light of note 10 and accompanying text *supra.*

were to have (a) acquired French nationality by naturalization or other means or (b) reassigned his newly acquired rights (i) back to the original French owner or (ii) to another French national. What decisions? Assuming otherwise eligible claims, arguably a "plain and natural" reading of Article 2 of the 1950 Czech Accord[52] would authorize an award in all these cases. For that matter, subject to obvious necessary differences, so would a literal reading of all the Controlling Texts and commission rulings that have conditioned eligibility on proof of French nationality at the claim accrual and settlement dates.[53] A continuous nationality interpretation of these provisions, however, would not. Continuity of French nationality from time of claim accrual right down to time of settlement clearly having been interrupted, none of these cases would succeed. As indicated, however, the French commissions have not been called upon to decide this issue. At most—understandably given the cases they have had to decide—they have but reiterated *verbatim* the two-pronged time requirement language that has been set forth in their Controlling Texts. Accordingly, whether a thoroughgoing continuous nationality rule has prevailed in theory must be left an open question.[54] If so, and there is some reason to believe as much,[55] it will have placed postwar French practice in a position consistent with present American and past British practice,[56] as well as with customary practice generally.[57] Nonetheless, as Lillich's critique of equivalent British practice (suitably amended) makes abundantly

[52] The provision reads: "Considered as French interests for the purposes of the present Agreement are interests belonging to natural or juridical persons of French nationality on the date of the Czechoslovak measures mentioned [in Article 1] and on the date the present Agreement enters into force."

[53] See the provisions cited in notes 36, 37, & 39 *supra*.

[54] Perhaps indicative of French perspectives in this respect is Article 8 of the 1966 Egyptian Accord, applicable to post-1958 wealth-deprivation claims (not within the distributive competence of the Egyptian Commission), which provides that "[t]he conditions of nationality required of natural persons and the conditions of *siège et de majorité* required of juridical persons according to the terms of the preceding paragraph [concerning French property, rights, and interests affected by measures after August 22, 1958] must have been met from the date of the measure affecting their property, rights, and interests until the day of the entry into force of the present Agreement."

[55] *See* FR 4775 (1965) wherein the Romanian Commission assumed the dual time requirement language to mean "having had and still enjoying" French nationality between the two key dates.

[56] *See* note 29 *supra*.

[57] *See* 2 O'CONNELL 1117–24.

clear, it would be open to serious and valid criticism as a matter
of sound policy:

> Assuming that the original claimant was British [or French] at
> the time of loss, there seems little reason why the eventual allowance
> or denial of the claim should turn on the fortuitous factor of his lon-
> gevity. Indeed, rendering an award to a nonnational who succeeded
> to the claim of a British [or French] national after the settlement
> agreement can hardly be squared with the standard rationale of the
> traditional rule, i.e., "that, in the end result, the slice of the cake
> should pass to British [or French] nationals." Only by requiring . . .
> what traditional international law and the agreements clearly do not,
> namely, continuous British [or French] ownership of the claim from
> the time of loss right down to the payment of the final installment
> on the adjudicated award, could this objective be met.[58]

And to this Lillich adds:

> Furthermore, the . . . long delay before claims are settled, coupled
> with the increased movement of people across national lines, both of
> which serve to bring nonnationals into the claims picture, renders
> the desirability of the objective questionable. Requiring nationality
> only at the time of loss seems a preferable approach in that it retains
> the essence of the nationality requirement while eliminating a second,
> arbitrary cut-off date, thus precluding fortunate claimants against a
> limited lump sum from receiving increased dividends on their awards
> following the untimely deaths of their fellow claimants. If lump sum
> settlements cannot be negotiated along such lines, however, an equi-
> table application of the . . . two-pronged [noncontinuity] test at
> least may mitigate the harshness of the strict continuity of national-
> ity rule in an appropriate situation.[59]

It remains finally to consider what content the French commissions have given to the term "French national." Obviously, to satisfy the nationality prerequisite, however applied, a definition of
"French national"—or, more precisely, "French natural and juridical persons"—has been needed. Contrary to what might be supposed, however, neither the Settlement Agreements nor any of the

---

[58] LILLICH (G.B.) 28. As to the relevance of this observation in the context of
postwar French international claims practice, consider note 32 and accompanying
text *supra*.

[59] LILLICH (G.B.) 28–29.

other Controlling Texts have been of any help in this regard. Indeed, nowhere among them is there even a hint as to where a definitional search might begin.[60] In other words, the commissions have been free—perforce obliged—to determine the conditions of French nationality for themselves. Undisposed in the vast majority of cases to detail the bases of their findings, however, perhaps to save time they appear to have been content simply to accept *prima facie* evidence of nationality.[61] Still, assuming that we can generalize from expressed particulars, it is clear that the commissions have uniformly looked to French law, including French "private international law." The French law of nationality being beyond the scope of this study, however, suffice it to say that the commissions have readily recognized French nationality, in the case of natural persons, whenever the *Code de Nationalité* has so required,[62] and, in the case of juridical persons, usually when the *société* or *association* has maintained a French *siège social* and occasionally when French management and control have been additionally substantiated.[63] Conversely, they have been quick to refuse such recogni-

60 It may be noted that the treaty provisions leaving lump sum distribution within the sole competence of the French Government have been altogether silent in this connection. See the provisions cited in Part II, note 136.

61 A possible explanation for this *prima facie* acceptance seems to lie in the fact that contests over nationality have been required under French law to be adjudicated in the ordinary civil tribunals, a process that obviously necessitates delay and inconvenience. For related remarks, see note 23 and accompanying text *supra*.

62 Thus, French nationality has been recognized whenever the Code's conditions of "birth," "filiation," "marriage," "naturalization," "reintegration," "territorial annexation," and other such contingencies have been fulfilled. The present Code of Nationality was brought into force by an *ordonnance* of October 19, 1945. It is most easily referred to, with its subsequent modifications, in Code Civil (67e ed. Petits Codes Dalloz 1967–68), at 16–46. The *ordonnance* is found at *id.* 13–16. Ordonnance No. 62–825 of July 21, 1962 [*id.* at 44], it may be noted, allows French residents in Algeria to retain citizenship in certain cases, even if they become Algerian citizens. For related remarks, see note 24 and accompanying text *supra*.

63 This view is consistent with both French law and "private international law" generally. See H. Batiffol, Droit International Privé 223–34 (4th ed. 1967); Loussouarn, *Nationalité des Sociétés*, 6 Juris-Classeur de Droit Int'l, Fasc. 564–A. Generally, of course, there exist a number of criteria according to which the nationality of a juridical person has been determined. Different legal systems have different approaches to the problem. It is fair to say, however, that the nationality of juridical persons usually has been determined either by reference to the State under whose law the entity has been constituted or by reference to the State where the entity maintains its headquarters (or *siège social*). Ordinarily these criteria point to the same State. However, because this focus is not always to be found, with the result that complex choice-of-law problems have arisen, recently efforts have been bent toward

tion whenever, according to French law, the necessary attributes have been lacking. In short, despite the absence of explicit directives in the Settlement Agreements and other Controlling Texts, the task of nationality identification has presented few problems. Only when a possibility of dual nationality has arisen, which as of this writing has yet to be the subject of any explicit discussion or known decision, has more than routine inquiry been required.[64]

Residence

Except for the 1966 Egyptian Accord, neither the Settlement Agreements nor any of their complementary Controlling Texts have made French residence a prerequisite to compensatory eligibility (unless of course one is to equate *siège social* with corporate res-

---

reconciling these criteria. Thus, Article 1 of the 1956 Convention on Recognition of the Legal Personality of Foreign Companies (Sociétés), Associations and Foundations combines the two criteria. Official French text in CONFERENCE DE LA HAYE DE DROIT INTERNATIONAL PRIVÉ, RECEUIL DES CONVENTIONS DE LA HAYE 28 (1961); unofficial English text in draft, but identical, form in 1 AM. J. COMP. L. 277 (1952). Article 2 of the 1960 International Law Association's Draft Convention on Conflicts of Law relating to companies gives a preference to the "law of incorporation." I.L.A., REPORT OF THE FORTY-NINTH CONFERENCE ix (Hamburg 1960). So also does the 1965 Resolution of the Institut de Droit International on Companies in Private International Law, 51 ANNUAIRE DE L'INSTITUT 272 (II–1965). Common to all three efforts, however, has been a willingness to make adjustments for companies whose central administrations are not located within the "incorporating State," a willingness that is expressed also by the International Court of Justice, albeit within carefully defined limits, in the recent second phase of the Barcelona Traction Case, reported in [1970] I.C.J. 3. The French commission decisions thus appear by and large within the framework of current international patterns and trends. For decisions utilizing more than *siège social* as the basis for establishing corporate nationality, see FB 28, 34, 46 (1961); 155, 157, 159 (1964)/FH 78 (1953)/FP 100 (1953); 205 (1955)/FY 49, 51, 52 (1953); 202 (1955).

[64] The failure of the French commissions to elaborate on the dual nationality problem probably is due, it seems, to their not yet having been confronted with a proven case of dual nationality. At any rate, their Controlling Texts having laid down no rules in this connection, one is virtually at a loss to know whether the commissions, given claimants possessed simultaneously of French and payor State or other State nationality, would opt in favor of the dual national for distribution purposes. On the other hand, recalling that the Settlement Agreements have authorized compensation to "French nationals" and that the commissions have tended to accept *prima facie* evidence of French nationality, it is not unreasonable to assume that the French commissions, like their American and British counterparts, would not consider dual nationality a bar to eligibility as a general rule, or at least not when the claimant's dominant nationality is French. For details concerning American and British commission practice in respect of dual nationals, see LILLICH (U.S.) 83–84 and LILLICH (G.B.) 31–33.

idence).[65] In literally dozens of cases, apparently without regard to whether foreign residence has obtained at the time of post-settlement claim presentation, adjudication or any other time, the Eastern European and Cuban commissions have acknowledged the eligibility of claimants who have lived or have been living abroad,[66] a sensible and desirable pattern that appears to have prevailed in counterpart American and British practice as well.[67]

The French residence requirement of the Egyptian claims program has had as its source a provision of Article 4 of the 1966 Egyptian Accord: "The [lump sum] . . . will be paid . . . to an account opened in the name of the Government of the French Republic, which will proceed by its own authority to the distribution of this amount among the claimants *residing in France* whom it will designate."[68] The language, reflecting Egyptian reluctance or unwillingness to indemnify French Jews who had not fully departed from Egypt or the other Arab countries, appears firm enough at first glance. However, concerned to prevent gross discrimination while at the same time adhering to French treaty obligations, the Egyptian Commission has narrowly (*i.e.*, humanely) construed these words to refer to French claimants having *permanent legal residence* in France apparently *as of the entry into force of the 1966 Accord*[69]—an interpretation which, it seems, can fairly be read to have

---

[65] *But cf.* the 1961 German Accord (Part I, note 10) which requires that stateless persons seeking to benefit from the settlement also must have been French residents as of March 20, 1958 (a functional equivalent to a claim accrual date).

[66] FB 101 (1963); 143, 146, 154, 159, 162, 173–76 (1964)/FC 3 (1968)/FCz 59 (1955); 82 (1956); 201 (1957); 869 (1959)/FE 2, 3, 33 (1969)/FH 1–17 (1952); 19–22, 35, 37, 42, 48, 52, 61–63, 80, 82, 89, 90, 102, 113, 115–16, 121, 127, 134–35, 137, 139, 140–41, 144, 146 (1953); 174, 198, 241 (1954); 281, 283, 293, 332 (1956); 358 (1957)/FH2d 32, 33, 52, 55 (1967); 72 (1968)/FP 124, 133, 137 (1954); 203 (1955); 400 (1958); 521 (1962)/FR 1240, 1359–60, 1649 (1962); 2924 (1963); 5719 (1965); 6306 (1966)/FY 136, 169 (1954); 172 (1955); 232, 243, 311 (1956); 418, 426 (1957)/FY2d 16 (1965); 47, 57 (1966).

[67] None of the companion studies concerning equivalent American and British practice make any mention of this issue, leading one to conclude that residence has never been a test of eligibility before the United States Foreign Claims Settlement Commission or the British Foreign Compensation Commission.

[68] Emphasis added.

[69] *See* FE 2, 3, 10, 33, 46 (1969). A more recent decision, FE 57 (1969), casts doubt on the conclusion that French residence has had to be established as of the entry into force of the 1966 Accord. In this decision, the Commission made a point of asking for a Quai d'Orsay interpretative opinion on precisely this question. Unfortunately, the opinion is unavailable as of this writing.

equated legal residence with legal domicile[70] and thereby to have liberalized the opportunity to share in the Commission's lump sum distributions. Silent on its source for defining "French resident," presumably, as with "French national," the Commission has looked to French law to give it content.

Legal Personality

Again excepting the 1966 Egyptian Accord, all the Settlement Agreements have authorized compensation in principle to both natural and juridical persons ("personnes physiques" and "personnes morales").[71] Accordingly, save under the Egyptian claims program, no claimant—individual or group—has by reason of legal personality alone been declared ineligible to share in the commission distributions.[72]

The 1966 Egyptian Accord made exception to this pattern by way of implication. Without actually stating that only individuals might benefit from its provisions, by stipulating that "indemnities due" to deprived "companies" would be "settled in accordance with the terms of the Zurich agreements and the special agreements which have been concluded with the interested parties"[73] (e.g., the 1964 Egyptian Accord),[74] it left little doubt that this restriction was to be the rule. At any rate, such was the interpretation given by French ministerial decree. Expressly restricting indemnification

[70] See, e.g., FE 33 (1969) wherein the Egyptian Commission, in extending relief, remarked that the claimant "is only in Italy for his profession and has not lost his French residence where he keeps his principal establishment." Doubtless the same humanitarian concern that impelled this solicitous interpretation also explains a complementary need for statutory flexibility and therefore the absence of the French residence requirement in the Egyptian Commission Constitutive Law where, in light of earlier discussion (see text at Part II, notes 213–232), logically it should have appeared.

[71] See 1955 Bulgarian Accord, preamble and art. 1(a); 1967 Cuban Accord, art. 1; 1950 Czech Accord, art. 2; 1950 Hungarian Accord, art. 3; 1965 Hungarian Accord, art. 1 and Exchange of Letters No. 1; 1951 Yugoslav Accord, art. 2; 1963 Yugoslav Accord, art. 2.

[72] For a preliminary indication of the variety of juridical persons recognized by French law (and therefore authorized to share in the lump sum distributions), i.e., sociétés, associations, and fondations, see F. LAWSON, A. ANTON, & L. BROWN, AMOS AND WALTON'S INTRODUCTION TO FRENCH LAW 47–57, 345–55 (3d ed. 1967). See also G. RIPERT, TRAITÉ ÉLEMENTAIRE DE DROIT COMMERCIAL 289–717 (1959).

[73] 1966 Egyptian Accord, art. 5.

[74] See Part II, note 56.

to "personnes physiques," the Egyptian Commission Constitutive Law put all doubts to rest.[75] Consistent therewith, to date in two cases, the Egyptian Commission has declared "irrecevable" the claims of two French "sociétés" for property "liquidated" by the Egyptian Government.[76]

2. CLAIMANT OBJECTIVES

The principal objective of French commission claimants has been, obviously, to secure compensation for deprivations sustained.[77] Of course, given the decisions reached earlier at the diplomatic level, the claimants have had no cause to expect "full" compensation, a circumstance which doubtless has left many dissatisfied. Still, if they were to partake of even the limited amounts that have been available for distribution, they have had to convince the commissions that the "rules of State Responsibility" (and the privileges of diplomatic protection) have been on their side. Accordingly, their ultimate goal—indemnification—may be seen to have hinged upon winning acceptance of a number of arguments and assumptions which, sometimes articulated, sometimes not, have been at the heart of their claims for compensation, even if not always fully recognized by the claimants themselves. In keeping with the goal of this study of relating law to social process in a manner that encourages comparative analysis, it is helpful to reduce these arguments and assumptions to a series of subsidiary claims (or demands) that are organized around the key phases of the deprivative process out of which most of the claimant grievances have arisen.

A. Claims Relating to Deprivors

Throughout history, all categories of persons who have engaged in transnational economic activity also have undertaken foreign-wealth deprivations—nation-states, subnational entities, mixed governmental–non-governmental agencies, private associations, in-

---

[75] See Decree No. 68–103 of January 30, 1968, art. 5(a), [1968] J.O. 1228. See also text at Part II, notes 227–228.

[76] FE 5, 44 (1969).

[77] This statement does not apply, of course, to claimants who have sought compensation for "ordinary" debt claims under the 1963 Yugoslav Accord.

dividual human beings, and even international governmental institutions.[78] Accordingly, claims commonly have arisen concerning the
identification of parties legally competent to deprive and legally
responsible for the infliction of foreign-wealth losses. However, because the French appear never to have challenged seriously the legal
capacity of Eastern Europe, Egypt, or Cuba to appropriate the
property, rights, and interests covered by the Settlement Agreements (except, of course, in the case of "wartime" deprivations),
and because the Settlement Agreements themselves have demonstrated payor government willingness to account for deprivations
imposed *by them*, the decisions of the French commissions have
borne exclusively on the finding and placement of responsibility
where deprivative liability has been ostensibly in doubt.

*Claim That Changes in a "State's" Constitutive Attributes do Not
Release the "State" from Legal Responsibility for Deprivations
Imposed Before Such Change*

Doctrinal strictures about "State continuity" and "corporate personality" aside, the founding of the postwar Eastern European
Peoples' Republics, Nasser's Egypt, and Castro's Cuba heralded
new social orders. Each of these "successions" represented fundamental constitutive departures for the nations involved. Only in
Eastern Europe, however, were French property interests subjected
to deprivation before these basic changes took place—in the case
of Czechoslovakia, Poland, and Yugoslavia because of wartime German occupation policies, additionally in the case of Czechoslovakia
because of pre-Communist (Beneš) economic reforms and, finally,
in the case of Bulgaria, Hungary, and Romania because of wartime
Axis policies. It therefore has been only for the Eastern European
commissions to be concerned with the claim here posed. As inferred,
it has been implicated in three ways.

First, although never so precisely put, the claim has been hinted
at in a number of the decisions of the Czech, Polish, and two Yugoslav commissions involving wealth losses that arose not from Czech,
Polish, or Yugoslav governmental policies but from measures taken
by wartime German occupation authorities,[79] the controlling elites

---

[78] For details, see WESTON 42–52.
[79] *See* FCz 39 (1954); 78, 79, 136 (1956); 160, 179, 190, 215–17 (1957); 320, 322,

in "Czechoslovakia," "Poland," and "Yugoslavia" between, roughly, 1938 and 1945. In almost all cases the losses have been held ineligible for compensation, the three commissions likening them to "war damages" over which the Czechs, Poles, and Yugoslavs had had little or no control and whose reparation had to be secured through other channels.[80] The sole exceptions, if in fact they can be called such, are cases that were decided by the Czech Commission, consistent with Article 1(c) of the 1950 Czech Accord, in which the properties in question had been subsequently "sequestered" or otherwise appropriated by the Czech authorities and concerning which the claimants had already instituted restitution proceedings in Czechoslovakia.[81] As for the principal holdings, they too were compelled by treaty stipulations agreed to earlier. The 1950 Czech Accord, the 1948 Polish Accord, and the two Yugoslav accords—each have limited recovery to losses caused only by Czech, Polish, and Yugoslav deprivative measures.[82] Also, because the three countries never had joined the Axis alliance, these agreements made no provision for "war damage" compensation. The conclusion is clear: Communist Czechoslovakia, Communist Poland, and Communist Yugoslavia were not to be held responsible for deprivations imposed by predecessor governing authorities whose exclusive or near-exclusive control over population and territory had been won through international military coercion or conquest.

In marked contrast, second, was the uniformly affirmative reply of the Czech Commission to the literally hundreds of claims that were generated by the October 1945 and other deprivative measures of the pre-Communist Beneš regime of 1945–48, far too many to cite here. Again the 1950 Czech Accord controlled.[83] However much it represented a constitutive departure from the past, still, Communist Czechoslovakia was willing, if not legally required, to answer for the acts of the predecessor Beneš regime.[84]

349, 403, 416–17, 421 (1958); 729, 778, 883 (1959)/FP 71, 77, 97 (1953); 101, 102, 108 (1954); 355 (1958)/FY 269 (1956); 436 (1957); 660 (1959); 749 (1960); 853, 863 (1961)/FY2d 8 (1965); 54 (1966).

[80] See text at notes 152–158 infra.

[81] FCz 50 (1955); 322, 403, 417 (1958).

[82] See 1950 Czech Accord, preamble and art. 1; 1948 Polish Accord, preamble and arts. 2–3; 1951 Yugoslav Accord, preamble and art. 2; 1963 Yugoslav Accord, art. 2.

[83] See 1950 Czech Accord, art. 1(a) and (c).

[84] That these holdings may not have been required as a matter of customary inter-

Likewise contrasting sharply with the first group of cases mentioned (although for precisely opposite reasons) have been, finally, the scores of cases in which the Bulgarian, 1950 Hungarian, and Romanian commissions have granted compensation for deprivations sustained in formerly Axis Bulgaria, Hungary, and Romania during World War II.[85] These results have been prompted, of course, by the 1947 Peace Treaty commitments that were assumed by, or imposed upon, these countries and incorporated by reference into their respective Settlement Agreements.[86]

The implications that each of these groups of decisions bear for the "Law of State Succession" and the "doctrine of acquired rights" should be apparent. Of course, just how far they extend necessarily depends upon a detailed investigation of past practice in like situations, beyond the scope of this study. As D. P. O'Connell has correctly observed, "[t]he attempt to decide whether one particular treaty [or decision] substantiates a principle [of State succession] or creates an exception to another principle [of State succession] leads only to a vicious circle."[87] On the other hand, it is necessary to acknowledge that postwar French practice has not been alone in resolving these matters in these ways, especially as concerns "war damage" claims.[88] From the standpoint of sound policy, the important question is the extent to which decisions facilitate the attribution of liability in order to minimize loss without redress while at the same time assuring freedom for change among societies where change is necessary to achieve a wider shaping and sharing of values.

---

national law is given oblique support by a Bulgarian Commission decision wherein the Commission, in refusing to extend relief to a creditor claimant deprived by virtue of the "liquidation" of a debtor firm and a subsequent "blocking" of transfers outside Bulgaria, stated that "the liquidation . . . took place prior to the socialist reorganisation measures of the Peoples' Republic of Bulgaria," thus placing the claim outside the terms of the 1955 Bulgarian Accord. FB 79 (1962). *See* 1955 Bulgarian Accord, preamble.

[85] *See* note 153 *infra*.

[86] *See* 1955 Bulgarian Accord, preamble and art. 1(b); 1950 Hungarian Accord, preamble; 1959 Romanian Accord, art. 1(b). It may be noted that "war damage" claims brought before the 1965 Hungarian Commission have been treated either as tardy claims or as claims over which the Commission has had no jurisdiction because they were scheduled for compensation only under the 1950 Hungarian Accord. *See* text at note 338 *infra*.

[87] 1 D. O'CONNELL, STATE SUCCESSION IN MUNICIPAL LAW AND INTERNATIONAL LAW 28 (1967).

[88] *See, e.g.,* LILLICH (G.B.) 105–11; LILLICH & CHRISTENSON 66–67.

Claim That Legal Responsibility for Deprivations Imposed by One Party is Attributable to Another

Due mainly to wartime and postwar cessions, annexations, and other such measures, only the Eastern European commissions appear to have been called upon thus far, albeit again inferentially, to consider this claim. They have done so, cumulatively and in varying degree, in three distinct contexts.

First and most conspicuous, each of the Eastern European commissions has been asked to grant compensation for deprivations ostensibly initiated by other than Bulgarian, Czech, Hungarian, Polish, Romanian, and Yugoslav officials; that is, for claimed losses sustained presumably at the hands of third countries, often the Soviet Union which acquired portions of the territory of some of these Eastern European countries at the close of World War II.[89] Their responses have been uniform and unequivocal. Correctly observing, in cases of "peacetime" deprivation, that the respective Settlement Agreements authorized indemnification only if these measures were imposed by the payor countries,[90] they have declared the petitions "irrecevable,"[91] even when the concerned third countries had themselves negotiated lump sum settlements with France.[92] In the case of "wartime" deprivations, they have held the claims eligible for relief irrespective of who actually imposed the losses sustained— assuming, of course, that they were sustained in Axis Bulgaria, Hun-

[89] For example, in 1939, shortly after Munich and the cession of the Sudetenland, Hitler and Mussolini conveyed some 4,000 square miles of Czechoslovakia—Ruthenia (also known as the Carpathian Ukraine and Sub-Carpathian Russia)—to their Hungarian ally. In 1945, after the Hungarian surrender, the region was absorbed into the Soviet Union which, wanting to consolidate its control, thereafter undertook economic reforms in its newly acquired territory. Thus, since Ruthenia had not been a part of Czechoslovakia since 1939, the Czech Commission quite logically concluded that the injuries complained of had been sustained, if at all, at the hands of Soviet rather than Czech officials.

[90] *See* 1950 Czech Accord, preamble and art. 1; 1950 Hungarian Accord, preamble; 1948 Polish Accord, preamble; 1959 Romanian Accord, art. 1.

[91] FCz 7 (1953); 86 (1956); 399, 652 (1958)/FH 74 (1953); 278, 284, 288, 300 (1955); TV652 (1956)/FP 22 (1952); 38, 43, 53, 92, 94 (1953); 101 (1954); 177 (1955); 259 (1956); 354, 369, 373 (1958); 499 (1961)/FR 2, 5, 32, 33, 36, 71–73, 77 (1960); 303, 545 (1961); 1982 (1962); 2506 (1963); 6025 (1965); 6916 (1966); 7129, 7136 (1967). Similar logic has worked to reject claims based on non-deprivative, "ordinary" debts owed by third countries or their nationals. *See* FH TV597–600, TV701, TV715, TV727 (1956)/FP 499 (1961)/FR 545 (1961); 2506 (1963); 7129 (1967).

[92] *See* FR 545 (1961), involving a debt claim against Bulgaria; FR 7129 (1967), involving a stockholder claim against Poland.

gary, and Romania.[93] Provided that the losses inflicted in these three countries had been caused by World War II or by measures directed toward property during the war, thus bringing the claims under the protection of the incorporated 1947 Peace Treaty provisions,[94] it has mattered not at all whether the damages were imposed by these former Axis Powers themselves or by their World War II allies or enemies.[95] Only if at the time of loss these countries had quit the Axis alliance and joined the Allies, as did both Bulgaria and Romania in 1944, have different (but not inconsistent) results been reached.[96]

Second, the Czech and Romanian commissions have had to consider, each on one known occasion, whether the French Government had intended to hold Prague and Bucharest responsible, respectively, for wealth losses perpetrated by relatively minor Czech and Romanian officials. Their decisions differed. By way of *dictum*, the Czech Commission observed that a claim for personal possessions "taken away 'in the spring of 1945' by a Czechoslovak police chief" was not of a kind for which compensation was authorized under the 1950 Czech Accord.[97] In contrast, the Romanian Commission allowed recovery for peacetime "looting carried out by national guards."[98] However, the contradiction seems explained by the fact that the 1950 Czech Accord authorized indemnification for, *inter alia*, deprivative measures "bearing [only] upon reforms directed

[93] For by now obvious reasons, the Czech, Polish, and two Yugoslav commissions have always refused to extend relief for "war damages" sustained within Czechoslovakia, Poland, and Yugoslavia, respectively. *See* text at notes 154 & 338 *infra*.

[94] *See* note 86 *supra*.

[95] *See* the cases cited at note 153 *infra*, many of them involving third-State elements either because of general bombardments or nationally identifiable "requisitions."

[96] *See* FR 30 (1960) wherein the Romanian Commission denied relief for "war damage" sustained in but not at the hands of Romania, because "the claim cannot concern Romanian authorities who did not take repossession of the city of Cluj until the following October 10 [1944]." *See also* FR 18 (1960), wherein the Romanian Commission withheld an award because the measures complained of were taken by Hungarian "occupation authorities." The claimants' losses in these cases were sustained after the time when then King Michael, with Soviet help, overthrew the fascist Antonescu government. Given Romania's change of status, the decision is of course to be assimilated with the unsuccessful "war damage" claims registered with the Czech, Polish, and Yugoslav commissions. For related discussion, see text at notes 153 & 338 *infra*.

[97] FCz 350 (1958).

[98] FR 10 (1960).

at the Czech economic structure,"[99] whereas the 1959 Romanian Accord contained no such limitation. That is, the decisions were diplomatically predetermined. Hence, assuming agreement—even tacit agreement—at the diplomatic level, responsibility for the deprivative acts of minor officials appears to have been attributed to the national government, even when, as seems to have been true in the Romanian case, the officials acted in unofficial capacity. Especially noteworthy, however, is that the Romanian Commission, without benefit of explicit diplomatic directive, chose to exercise its interpretative option the way it did; it could reasonably have held the looting claim beyond the purpose and purview of the 1959 Romanian Accord.[100]

Contrary reasoning appears to have been at work in the remaining group of decisions alluded to (five by the Czech Commission and one each by the Polish, Romanian, and 1963 Yugoslav commissions), all of them involving acts of "looting," "theft," or other "taking" at the hands of presumably private persons locally situated. As in the preceding cases, the Czech Commission refused to impute liability to Prague, contending that these losses fell outside the 1950 Czech Accord, *i.e.*, that they were not due to "reforms directed at the Czech economic structure."[101] Similarly, the Polish Commission denied compensation because the losses did not arise from the Polish nationalization law of January 3, 1946, as required by the 1948 Polish Accord.[102] Finally, although unencumbered by such explicit treaty restrictions, the Romanian and 1963 Yugoslav commissions withheld protection apparently because the losses were not the result of governmental conduct,[103] an implicit condition of the 1959 Romanian and 1963 Yugoslav accords.[104] In short, because

[99] 1950 Czech Accord, art. 1(b).

[100] The argument might be made, for example, that the 1959 Romanian Accord, authorizing compensation per Article 1 for losses resulting from "Romanian measures of nationalization, expropriation, requisition, and other similarly restrictive measures," was intended to cover only official governmental undertakings.

[101] FCz 39 (1954); 59, 61 (1955); 219 (1957); 320 (1958).

[102] FP 222 (1956). *See* 1948 Polish Accord, preamble and arts. 2–3. The 1951 Polish Protocol, it will be recalled, was not effective until 1957. *See* Part II, note 61. Possibly this ruling would have been reversed on a post-1957 rehearing, but there is no evidence that a rehearing was ever requested.

[103] FR 307 (1961)/FY2d 42 (1966).

[104] *But see* FR 1788 (1962) wherein compensation again was granted for "looting,"

of diplomatic decisions reached earlier, responsibility for private spoliations was not to be attributed to the payor governments.

Summarizing, can it be said that postwar French practice has conformed to what are said to be contemporary international law rules concerning the attribution of State Responsibility? At the interpretative arbitral level, albeit on the basis of slim evidence, the answer must be in the affirmative, the tendency thus far having been to impute governmental liability for "public" deprivative acts, however "unofficial," and to withhold such imputation in the case of private spoliations[105]—a desirable trend, at least in the first instance, in an era in which even the most influential stagger at the complexity of holding government accountable and when demands for the official protection of basic human values each day join a rising chorus. At the prescriptive diplomatic level, however, the answer—to the extent that an answer is even possible—must be mixed. Insofar as they have allowed the French commissions to facilitate accountability, manifestly the Settlement Agreements have made a positive contribution. Where they have not—for example, by the 1950 Czech Accord limitation concerning measures "bearing upon reforms directed at the Czech economic structure"—arguably they have fallen short of the supposed norms. In making this judgment, however, the difficulties in reaching settlement have to be recalled and like efforts elsewhere taken into account.

B. Claims Relating to Deprivor Objectives

The immediate objective of any deprivor, nation-state or otherwise, is, obviously, to deprive. But further reflection points up that a great deal more is involved. Generally, recognizing that wide variations can and do exist from case to case, deprivor goals embrace all the demands that commonly are projected throughout the world for the protection and enhancement of wealth, power,

---

this time at the hands of private parties. Reading between the lines, however, it is likely that this award was based on the "war damage" provisions of the 1959 Romanian Accord.

[105] For relatively recent discussion of these "rules," see generally 2 O'CONNELL 1019–56; 1 SIBERT 309–40.

respect, and other values.[106] Of course, international law has long been concerned with the propriety of these demands; hence the multi-claim encompassing—but therefore analytically sterile—"public purpose" doctrine. What or why something is wanted, in both absolute and relative terms, is a question that is basic to all legal systems. As potential challenges to authority about what values may be lawfully reserved—exclusively or inclusively and in relation to the expansion, conservation, or destruction of other values—particular objectives condition not only our perspectives about the permissibility of given initiatives but also the correctness of individual and group reactions to them.

Significantly, among the diverse values that stirred Eastern Europe, Egypt, and Cuba to action against French property, rights, and interests—e.g., economic and political security or survival (well-being), global prestige (respect), ideological fidelity (rectitude), unity of nationhood (affection/solidarity), and others too commonly disregarded under the "public purpose" doctrine—none appear to have been regarded by France as illegitimate per se, however much exclusively or inclusively demanded and however much involving the expansion, conservation, or destruction of other values (excepting, of course, the goals of military conquest during World War II and to some extent the aims of Nasser's Egypt in 1956). On the other hand, as the Settlement Agreements themselves bear witness, neither have they offered escape from French expectations of payment—or what may be called, in light of earlier discussion, "international responsibility." This resolution was of course the result of diplomatic, not arbitral, decision. As elsewhere, the negotiation process leading finally to France's postwar settlements appears to have resolved, however imperfectly, most of the issues to which claims concerning deprivor objectives are addressed. The French commissions have been left with little to consider in this connection.

Still, there has been room for some interpretation. This is seen, albeit again more implicitly than explicitly, in a few of the decisions of the Czech, Romanian, and 1951 Yugoslav commissions. The cases divide into three general categories, involving deprivor demands for the protection of community power, wealth, and rectitude.

---

[106] For details, see WESTON 52–67.

One decision, rendered by the Romanian Commission, concerned a widow's claims for "emoluments due," or loss of maintenance, resulting from her deceased husband's seven-year "detention" and "forced labor" at the hands of postwar Romanian authorities because of "acts of espionage in favor of France."[107] The Commission's decision, denying compensation without explanation other than that the claim "falls outside the scope of the [1959 Romanian] Accord," was ambiguous at best. The Commission neglected to explain whether its decision was based on the view that deprivations undertaken for reasons of national security do not incur liability or, in the alternative, that loss of maintenance does not constitute "property, rights, and interests" within the meaning of Article 1(a) of the 1959 Accord.[108] Its precedential value, therefore, is virtually nil. Nevertheless, it merits notice that deprivative measures taken for reasons of "national security"—admittedly a term that is subject to wide definitional variation—appear frequently tolerated without compensation.[109]

Three cases, each decided by the Czech Commission and identical in all essentials, concerned some French debt claims against a single nationalized enterprise and repudiated by the Czech Government's "Fonds de l'Économic Nationalisée" for the avowed reason that the obligations were "unjustified from an economic point of view."[110] The Commission extended relief to each of the three claimants pursuant to Article 1(b) of the 1950 Czech Accord, but without discussing, if even considering, the permissibility of repudiating foreign-owned debt claims for the stated purpose.[111] Again, therefore, there is little precedential value to be seen for present discussion. Still, the inference is to be drawn, at least as concerns the Czech claims program, that private-debt repudiations justified by economic

---

107 FR 12 (1960).
108 Conceivably the Commission concluded that this was an "ordinary" (*i.e.*, non-deprivative) debt claim whose indemnification had to be won through other channels. *See* text at note 344 *infra.*
109 *See, e.g.*, B. WORTLEY, EXPROPRIATION IN PUBLIC INTERNATIONAL LAW 42–44, 105 (1959) [hereinafter cited as "WORTLEY"]. On the taking of property for "national-political interests," see I. FOIGHEL, NATIONALIZATION AND COMPENSATION 39, 45–47 (1964) [hereinafter cited as "FOIGHEL"].
110 FCz 96–98 (1956).
111 For relevant discussion, see text at notes 185–194, *infra.*

necessity (or a need to protect community wealth), while probably not impermissible *ab initio*, do not avoid expectation of payment. Regrettably, the dearth of international law scholarship on this discrete issue prohibits further conclusions.[112] A proper inquiry, however, would take into account, among other considerations, not only the express and implied promises involved but, as well, the severity of the economic need and the threat to a productive global economy that such measures manifestly pose.

Finally, seven decisions, six by the Czech Commission and one by the 1951 Yugoslav Commission, have dealt with deprivations aimed at producing ethical or law-conforming behavior. The six Czech decisions, all basically the same, involved claims for compensation of personal or real assets "confiscated" because the claimants had failed to declare their assets as required by the general property or income tax laws in force in Czechoslovakia.[113] The Yugoslav decision, similar in kind, involved a claim for reparation of merchandise "confiscated" because the claimant had fraudulently hidden her stock to evade fiscal laws in force in Yugoslavia.[114] In each of these cases, the commissions denied compensation, pointing out that the 1950 Czech and 1951 Yugoslav accords, respectively, did not authorize indemnification for what was called in one of the cases a "financial sanction."[115] Possibly the Czech Commission decisions were based on the theory that the deprivative sanctions did not, in the words of Article 1(b) of the 1950 Czech Accord, bear "upon reforms directed at the Czech economic structure." But given the Yugoslav decision mentioned, rendered in the absence of such language, it is fair to conclude that both commissions were saying that "confiscations" reasonably aimed at producing law-conforming behavior, at least as concerns the fiscal laws in issue, do not engage international responsibility. If so, the decisions would appear consistent with both international law and sound policy.[116] Assuming

---

[112] For general discussion concerning the consequences of debt repudiations, without consideration of their economic justification, see 2 O'CONNELL 1089–93.

[113] *See* FCz 136 (1956); 163, 218 (1957); 322, 345 (1958); 1355 (1964).

[114] *See* FY 95 (1964).

[115] FCz 136 (1956).

[116] *See, e.g.,* 2 O'CONNELL 851; WORTLEY 44. *See also* S. FRIEDMAN, EXPROPRIATION IN INTERNATIONAL LAW 1–2, 50–51 (1953).

maintenance of "simple human respect" (*i.e.*, non-discrimination) and no disproportionate destruction of other values, it is indispensable that States should have broad competence to guarantee their internal orders.

C. Claims Relating to Situations which Affect Deprivor Action

The situations (or particular contexts of confrontation) within which foreign-wealth deprivations take place are manifold. From the standpoint of a world of acts and events that most commonly challenge and influence decision-makers, however, they can be seen most frequently to concern (as in most other interactions) four basic but interdependent dimensions: space, time, institutionalization, and crisis.[117] Explicit and implicit claims relating to each of these dimensions have challenged and influenced postwar French practice in a number of different ways.

Claim That Deprivations Pursued Within the Territory of Deprivor Communities are Not Permissible or, in Any Event, Engage Legal Responsibility

Risking pedantry and some repetition, it merits notice that all the Settlement Agreements, and so the decisions rendered pursuant to them, have recognized more or less explicitly the "right" of Eastern Europe, Egypt, and Cuba to appropriate French "property, rights, and interests" within their borders[118] (excepting, of course, the Axis Powers during World War II). Even Egypt, whose 1956 daring at Suez triggered well-known retaliations and counter-actions which for France were tentatively resolved by the partially rehabilitative 1958 Zurich Accord,[119] was conceded this competence by the 1966 Egyptian Accord. Doubtless this approval has been, as it usually is, less an acknowledgment of the "principle of sovereign territoriality" than an acceptance of fact. Whatever the rationale, however, it remains that, consistent with customary prac-

---

[117] For details, see WESTON 67–75.

[118] Most explicit in this connection has been the 1948 Polish Accord. *See* Article 2. Least explicit has been the 1959 Romanian Accord. Unlike the other Settlement Agreements it contains no express geographic reference.

[119] For relevant discussion, see text at Part II, notes 86–96.

tice, the Settlement Agreements have evinced acceptance of deprivations imposed within deprivor frontiers.[120] Accordingly, except as they have embodied official protests through the incorporation of 1947 Peace Treaty provisions, the Settlement Agreements stand as proof of deprivative authority in this geographic setting—reinforced, it should be added, by provisions releasing "the [payor] State as well as all [payor State] institutions and natural or juridical persons considered as the successors-in-interest to the original [French] owners under [payor State] law . . . from all claims on the part of the French interested parties."[121] In sum, bearing in mind that some formerly French-owned wealth would likely return to France under some payor State title in the course of later resumed transaction, the Settlement Agreements have precluded virtually all possibility that the "validity" of the specified territorial measures would ever be successfully challenged.[122] Of course, it must be reemphasized that the Eastern European, Egyptian, and Cuban deprivations did not escape French expectations of payment because of their domestic setting. Again the need, if not the duty, to compensate was recognized.

[120] For indication of customary practice, see, e.g., G. FOUILLOUX, LA NATIONALISATION ET LE DROIT INTERNATIONAL PUBLIC 176–97 (1962) [hereinafter cited as "FOUILLOUX"]. See also G. WHITE, NATIONALISATION OF FOREIGN PROPERTY 32–38, 93–118 (1961).

[121] This modified quotation is taken from Article 3 of the 1950 Czech Accord. For equivalent provisions, see 1955 Bulgarian Accord, art. 4; 1967 Cuban Accord, arts. 3 and 4; 1966 Egyptian Accord, arts. 4 and 18; 1950 Hungarian Accord, art. 4; 1965 Hungarian Accord, art. 3; 1948 Polish Accord, arts. 2 and 3; 1959 Romanian Accord, art. 2; 1951 Yugoslav Accord, arts. 2 and 3; 1963 Yugoslav Accord, art. 3.

[122] In this context, by invoking either international law norms, or prescriptions unique to a more exclusive arena, "title" or "ownership" may be contested, and the extent to which territorial deprivations shall be honored or somehow endowed with "extraterritorial validity" opened to fundamental challenge. It is in this setting that are found such competing claims as are readily familiar to domestic systems and whose common concern is the extraterritorial honoring or dishonoring of the application of deprivative power—e.g., the claim that a deprivation is an "Act of State" which does (does not) require abstention from review, the claim that a deprivation by an unrecognized body-politic shall (shall not) be accorded "validity," or the claim that a deprivation contrary to "the public policy of the forum" may (may not) be denied effect. For two recent illustrations of the refusal of the French Cour de Cassation to honor French-wealth deprivations deemed "contrary" or "offensive" to French public policy, see Crédit industriel et commercial v. Cara, [1969] D. S. Jur. 350; Cie. Française de Crédit et de Banque v. S.A.R.L. Atard Frères et Autres, [1969] D. S. Jur. 351. Each of these decisions concerned Algerian nationalizations.

Claim That Deprivations Pursued Outside the Territory of Deprivor Communities are Not Permissible or, in Any Event, Engage Legal Responsibility

It has not been for the Settlement Agreements simply to be addressed to deprivations sustained within Eastern European, Egyptian, and Cuban boundaries. Except for the two Yugoslav accords, they appear to have been wholly restricted to deprivations ("peacetime" and "wartime") taken within these territories.[123] In other words, the French Government appears generally to have refused to waive claims that may have accrued because of possible attempts at the extraterritorial application of deprivative measures (meaning that, while not free to benefit from the respective settlements, French nationals who lost wealth outside these countries because of measures taken within have been free, in principle, to seek reparation through further appeal or negotiation). Of course, this is not to say that, as a matter of customary international law, extraterritorial deprivations are impermissible *ab initio* or that they always engage international responsibility, no more than it is to say that such pursuits are invariably lawful or without liability. To insist as much would be illogical, if not self-defeating from the standpoint of common interest. In refusing to waive extraterritorially based claims, France did not refuse to honor the extraterritorial application of deprivative undertakings generally, or in any event surely not to the extent of setting bad precedent for potential extraterritorial claims of her own making at some future time. Essentially these are discretionary matters, questions of interjurisdictional reciprocity, that only wider practice can answer.[124]

Indeed, the discretionary nature of the issue is demonstrated, conveniently, by the 1951 and 1963 Yugoslav accords which, as indicated, made exception to the non-waiver pattern. By Article 5(4) of the 1951 Accord and Article 4 of the 1963 Accord (incor-

---

123 Again, the 1948 Polish Accord has been most explicit in this connection. *See* Article 2. Least explicit has been the 1950 Czech Accord. For discussion of the 1950 Czech Accord in this regard, see Sarraute & Tager, *Les effets en France des nationalisations étrangères,* 79 J. DROIT INT'L 1138, 1180–84 (1952).

124 For a sensitive but still insufficiently contextual demonstration of this point, see G. WHITE, *supra* note 120, at 93–118.

porating *mutatis mutandis* Articles 3–9 of the 1951 Accord) and subject to the provisos of these articles that French-based debt claims of French-controlled Yugoslav companies were not to be considered as extinguished by Yugoslav deprivative legislation, Paris conceded that French majority and minority shareholders of "affected" Yugoslav companies were to forfeit such rights as they may have had in respect of debt claims owned by these companies, not only within Yugoslavia but outside as well. In effect, France agreed to honor Yugoslav claims to extraterritorial competence outside France. To be sure, this extraterritorial recognition concerned creditor claims only, and not all such claims at that. But one is led to ask, as has Vienot,[125] what other assets of these companies might have been appropriated beyond the French frontier? Curiously, the Yugoslav commissions have never discussed these provisions in their opinions.

Claim That "Temporary" Deprivations Engage Legal Responsibility

Except as the express incorporation of 1947 Peace Treaty provisions in the 1955 Bulgarian, 1950 Hungarian, and 1959 Romanian accords may have meant that temporary "wartime requisitions" were to be compensated with the lump sums paid,[126] none of the Settlement Agreements have provided explicitly for "temporary" (sometimes called "partial") losses. On the other hand, if the phrase "all other measures restrictive of the right of property" (or its equivalents) is to mean or include temporary loss, then almost all the Settlement Agreements have vouchsafed implicitly against such "takings."[127] Judging from the few decisions rendered by the Czech,

---

[125] *See* VIENOT 176.

[126] The 1955 Bulgarian, 1950 Hungarian, and 1959 Romanian accords were drafted without reference to this discrete issue.

[127] For language identical or nearly identical to that used above, see 1955 Bulgarian Accord, art. 1(a); 1950 Czech Accord, preamble and art. 1(b); 1950 Hungarian Accord, preamble; 1965 Hungarian Accord, preamble and art. 1; 1948 Polish Accord, "Protocole d'Application," para. 3 (*i.e.*, the 1951 Polish Protocol); 1959 Romanian Accord, art. 1(a); 1951 Yugoslav Accord, preamble and art. 1; 1963 Yugoslav Accord, art. 2. The 1967 Cuban Accord, although containing no such language, nonetheless refers to "the laws and measures promulgated by the Revolutionary Government of the Republic of Cuba." *See* Article 1. The 1966 Egyptian Accord is

Egyptian, 1965 Hungarian, and Romanian commissions, however—apparently the only commissions to have so far had occasion to consider whether temporary dispossessions warrant repair[128]—this was not the case, at least not as concerns the controlling Settlement Agreements involved. In four out of seven instances, unfortunately with little or no elaboration, the Czech, 1965 Hungarian, and Romanian commissions have rejoined in the negative, withholding relief whether the temporary loss was one of ownership or control and in one case even when the loss endured for as long as nine years.[129] In only three cases, two decided by the Czech Commission and one by the Romanian Commission, have different (but not contrary) views been expressed—one involving a "sequestration" still in effect and concerning which the claimant had already begun restitution proceedings in Czechslovakia (thus admitting the claim under Article 1(c) of the 1950 Czech Accord),[130] the others concerning a "requisition" and a "sequestration" that apparently ceased to be practical issues because the properties in question ultimately were "confiscated" or "nationalized."[131] However, in none of these three cases did the commissions even hint that the "temporary" share of the dispossessions may have figured into the valuation of the indemnities finally awarded; all three of their awards appear to have been calculated from the definitive rather than the initial seizure dates. The conclusion, it seems—at least for the Czech, 1965 Hungarian, and Romanian commissions—is that temporary losses, however lengthy and even when followed by (or matured into) "permanent" loss, do not warrant reparation. The rationale, presumably, is that title, not control, is the subject-matter of compensable loss.[132]

---

altogether silent in this respect as regards the pre-1958 "sequestrations" which concerned the Egyptian Commission. *But see* Article 9 thereof for equivalent language relating to post-1958 deprivations.

[128] This observation is accurate to the extent that certain State administration measures, potentially temporary deprivations, are not taken into account. *See* text at notes 199–216 *infra*.

[129] FCz 68 (1955); 346 (1958); 1103 (1950)/FH2d 56 (1967).

[130] Article 1(c) of the 1950 Czech Accord authorized compensation to "French interests which are now the object of restitution procedures in Czechoslovakia."

[131] FCz 186 (1957)/FR 16 (1960).

[132] For related cases, involving State administration measures and occupations and use, see text at notes 199–216 and 248–257 *infra*.

Interestingly, notwithstanding the conflictual context out of which claims arose against Egypt, the few decisions so far rendered by the Egyptian Commission evince neither inconsistent nor unfamiliar approaches to this question. Adhering closely to the guidelines set forth in the 1966 Egyptian Accord and the Egyptian Commission Constitutive Law,[133] the Commission has extended relief only when property "sequestered" at the time of Suez and "liberated" in 1958[134] has been subsequently "liquidated" either in fact[135] or, because of non-restoration in the face of restitutive demands, in effect.[136] When these conditions have not been met, relief has been denied[137]—on a number of occasions, significantly, because the property was returned to or recouped by the claimants.[138] Again, temporary loss, without more, has not been sufficient to compel payment.

There is, to be sure, support for the view that temporary dispossessions are to be tolerated without compensation, at least when they have not ripened into "permanent takings."[139] Yet from a perspective that favors a stable, growing international economy, the view is open to challenge. However short-lived, temporary deprivations do cause economic and psychological disequilibrium, so that the burden of policy proof must be on those who maintain that such deprivations should not give rise to compensatory liability. Of course, definitive judgements are impossible until all features of the immediate and worldwide deprivative contexts are taken carefully into account, including, but not limited to, the reasons for "temporary takings," their duration, and the consequences of their imposition in both absolute and relative terms. It is therefore disappointing that the French commissions appear never to have entertained such considerations in their deliberations.

133 *See* 1966 Egyptian Accord, arts. 2 and 4; Decree No. 68–103 of January 30, 1968, [1968] J.O. 1228, art. 5.

134 The quoted words are from Article 1 of the 1966 Egyptian Accord.

135 FE 4, 78 (1969). For related discussion, see text at notes 178–184 *infra.*

136 FE 11, 12, 14, 15, 18, 22, 28, 30, 33, 47, 49, 54, 58, 79, 82, 85, 86, 89, 93, 96 (1969). For related discussion, see text at notes 258–260 *infra.*

137 FE 1, 4, 6, 8, 9, 20, 23, 27, 31, 42, 43, 45, 50, 53, 58, 62, 69, 73, 78, 81, 87, 88 (1969).

138 FE 9, 13, 16, 21, 25, 48, 59, 62, 64, 95 (1969).

139 *See, e.g.,* Christie, *What Constitutes a Taking of Property Under International Law?* 38 Brit. Y. B. Int'l L. 307, 322–24 (1962). *See also* Fouilloux 169–72.

Claim That Breach of Explicit or Implicit Promises Not to Deprive Engages Special Legal Responsibility

A contemporary theme which focuses squarely upon one of the many institutions that environ and ostensibly condition the deprivation of foreign wealth (here looking upon "institutions" not simply as formal structures but also as integrated and recurring perspectives about, and ways of doing, certain things) is that foreign wealth that is hosted through "concession" or other agreements is not to be subjected to deprivation with the same freedom, if at all, that international law gives to the deprivation of foreign wealth that is received on an informal basis conditioned only by tacit understandings about domestic law and mutual self-restraint.[140] The theme contains two basic arguments: first, that States do not have the legal authority prematurely to terminate such arrangements; and second, that if termination does take place, States are liable not only for the assets they may "take" along the way but also for "specific performance" or "special damage" for the unilateral termination itself. Both of these arguments have been implicated in postwar French practice because of 12 known cases that have involved the premature termination and nationalization of a number of French concessionary interests.[141]

Consider the first argument. Although it is reported to have served as the basis of actual French diplomatic protest in one of the cases cited,[142] it seems fair to conclude that France never took it very seriously. At any rate, there is nothing in the relevant Settlement Agreements—the 1955 Bulgarian, 1948 Polish, and 1951 Yugoslav accords—to suggest as much. At most, the Settlement Agreements

---

[140] *See, e.g.*, Carlston, *Concession Agreements and Nationalization*, 52 AM. J. INT'L L. 260 (1958); Domke, *Foreign Nationalizations—Some Aspects of International Law*, 55 AM. J. INT'L L. 585 (1961); Kissam & Leach, *Sovereign Expropriation of Property and Abrogation of Concession Contracts*, 28 FORDHAM L. REV. 177 (1959); Olmstead, *Nationalization of Foreign Property Interests, Particularly Those Subject to Agreements with the State*, 32 N.Y.U.L. REV. 1122 (1957); Schwebel, *International Protection of Contractual Arrangements*, 53 PROCEEDINGS OF THE AMERICAN SOCIETY OF INTERNATIONAL LAW 266 (1959). *See also* WORTLEY 55–57.

[141] The twelve cases—involving, however, more than twelve concessionaires—include: FB 121 (1963)/FP 131 (1954), *aff'd on rehearing*, 200 (1955); 244, 261 (1956); 294, 323 (1957)/FY 174 (1955); 335 (1956); 433, 443 (1957); 523 (1958); 747 (1960).

[142] *See* FB 121 (1963).

in their principal texts or attached "annexes" have but referred by name to the concessionaires in question.[143] To be sure, it can be argued that this means no more than that France acknowledged a *fait accompli* or that she conceded that Bulgaria, Poland, and Yugoslavia had the brute power to terminate and nationalize. Recalling, however, that France appears to have protested formally (before lump sum negotiation) in one instance only and, in addition, that she gave formal releases in exchange for lump sum payment, then it is legitimate to maintain, whatever the pressures, that the key Settlement Agreements are at least evidence that States have the legal competence to terminate concession agreements in this manner. As such, of course, the Settlement Agreements are but expressions of accepted practice[144] and, in any event, of the interest that all governments share, including the French Government, in maintaining a maximum freedom of control over people, resources, and institutions that are to be found within their jurisdictions.

On the other hand, turning now to the second argument mentioned, it is of interest that each of the claimants in the cases cited, in addition to requesting (and obtaining) compensation for the nationalization of their "éléments actifs" (book assets), sought indemnification for the value of their prematurely terminated concessions as such, *i.e.*, for the right—sometimes exclusive—to profit from certain national resources and institutions for a specified time. Significantly, in all but two instances wherein the Polish Commission dismissed the requests because the "non-exploitation" of the concessions had rendered the concessions valueless,[145] the concerned commissions (including the Polish Commission in three other cases) appear to have granted the claimants' requests.[146] Unable, obviously, to require "specific performance," they authorized payment of lost

---

[143] *See* annex to 1955 Bulgarian Accord entitled "Nationalisations et Mesures Similaires Intervenues en Bulgarie," [1959] J.O. 2744; 1948 Polish Accord, art. 4, subparas. 1–4 and "Annexe" set forth at [1951] J.O. 11191–92; 1951 Yugoslav Accord, "Tableau Annexe" set forth at [1953] J.O. 6725.

[144] *See, e.g.*, FOIGHEL 156–93; FOUILLOUX 280–321; 2 O'CONNELL, 1066–80. *See also* Baldus, *State Competence to Terminate Concession Agreements with Aliens,* 53 KY. L.J. 56 (1964).

[145] *See* FP 202 (1955); 244 (1956).

[146] *See* FB 121 (1963)/FP 261 (1956); 294, 323 (1957)/FY 174 (1955); 335 (1956); 433, 443 (1957); 523 (1958); 747 (1960).

profits ("bénéfices éventuels"), with only the Polish Commission having any apparent textual justification for doing so.[147] Standing alone, of course, this fact has little importance. The point is, however, that neither these commissions nor any of the others appear to have authorized payment of lost profits in any other case.[148] In other words, at least as concerns the Bulgarian, Polish, and 1951 Yugoslav commissions, postwar French practice may be said to speak for the proposition that the premature deprivation of formally solicited foreign wealth, although not impermissible *ab initio,* compels exceptional treatment.

The proposition, however, is subject to serious debate. In the first place, recent international legal utterances notwithstanding, it finds scant support in historic practice.[149] Second, from a perspective that seeks to balance legitimate conflicting interests by promoting the greatest possible common good, it is questionable as a matter of policy. As one astute writer has observed (with a global frame of reference), the proposition "overprotects the interests of the concessionaire and his government, threatens to discourage the importing of capital, and increases the risk of crisis and fighting in the settlement of termination controversies."[150] In the context of French commission practice, in tending to overprotect, the proposition diminishes for other deserving claimants what little there is to be gotten from an already small distribution fund. The central concern should be not the automatic assumption that payment of lost profits is justified "as a matter of right" but, rather, the compensation that is necessary to assure that initial profit expectations will have been satisfied. Assuming satisfaction, it is reasonable to expect that risks of termination will not deter future investments of like nature.[151]

---

[147] *See* 1948 Polish Accord, art. 4.

[148] *See* text at notes 383–385 *infra.*

[149] For incisive proof of this observation, see Baldus, *supra* note 144. *See also* FOIGHEL 156–93; 2 O'CONNELL 1066–80. *But see* LILLICH (G.B.) 121, reporting payment of future profits to concessionaires by the British Foreign Compensation Commission.

[150] Baldus, *supra* note 144, at 75. For further clarification of this observation, see *id.* at 67–75.

[151] *See id.* at 69–70: "[T]he businessman invests abroad for profit. He is concerned with the protection of his concession expectations only as a means of ensuring a return on his money. If the terminating government pays him the equivalent of the return

Claim That Crises Marked by Conflict do Not per se Release Deprivors from Responsibility for Deprivations Imposed Incidental Thereto

As several times noted, owing to alliances made during World War II and in order to resolve matters left unsettled after the Peace Treaties of 1947, only the 1955 Bulgarian, 1950 Hungarian, and 1959 Romanian accords provided for "war damage" claims.[152] Accordingly, except upon failure to meet the pertinent eligibility requirements mentioned above and below (these being basically the same for "war damage" claimants as for other claimants), only the Bulgarian, 1950 Hungarian, and Romanian commissions have honored such claims, provided, of course, that the claimed losses were caused by World War II or by measures directed toward property during World War II.[153] Unless able to prove additional, postwar bases for recovery, "war damage" claimants coming before the

---

he anticipated, he may reasonably be expected to undertake again the same risk in another investment. If compensation can satisfy the investor's expectations of profit, it will induce him to re-invest abroad in spite of termination and can thereby maintain a flow of international investment. To achieve this goal, the level of compensation paid must satisfy this test: would the typical concessionaire whose enterprise is taken for compensation be willing to undertake the same investment with the expectation that he may be treated that way again in the future?"

[152] *See* note 86 *supra*.

[153] FB 61, 81 (1962); 94, 120–21, 132, 134 (1963); 140–43, 146, 173 (1964); 180 (1965); 203 (1968)/FH 1–17 (1952); 18–23, 31–38, 41, 42, 44–46, 48, 49, 51, 52, 61–63, 65, 66, 70, 72, 77, 82, 85, 87–93, 102, 104–105, 107–109, 111–16, 120–27, 129, 131, 134–46, 149, 154 (1953); 160, 165–66, 169–72, 174–77, 180–86, 194–96, 198–99, 201, 239–42 (1954); 248, 251–56 (1955); 261 (1954); 267, 269–70, 272, 275–77, 281–82, 290, 292, 299, 327, 331–32 (1955); 340–41 (1956); 347, 358–59 (1957)/FR 11, 13, 14, 22, 65–68, 78, 79, 81 (1960); 147, 181, 184–85, 229, 235, 255, 299, 300, 359, 362–63, 393, 396, 432, 468, 472–74, 539, 699, 765, 790–91 (1961); 969–70, 1054–55, 1100, 1212, 1356, 1504, 1716–18, 1852, 1919 (1962); 2108, 2177, 2441, 2518, 2590, 2634–35, 2987 (1963); 3476, 4052–53 (1964); 7387 (1967). *But cf.* note 96 *supra,* citing decisions rejecting "war damage" claims against Romania because the losses were inflicted after Romania withdrew from the Axis alliance.

Bulgarian Commission decision FB 203 (1968) was the result of an appeal to the *Conseil d'État*. The *Conseil* annulled an earlier decision of the Commission [FB 147 (1964)] which withheld relief for deprivation caused by wartime Bulgarian "racial laws" (*i.e.,* anti-Semitic legislation) on the grounds that such laws did not fall within the incorporated 1947 Peace Treaty provisions of the 1955 Bulgarian Accord. *Sieur Covo,* [1967] Cons. d'Ét., Section du Contentieux, No. 69,611 (unpublished mimeo.). For related discussion, see notes 245–247 and accompanying text *infra*. To same effect, see *Dame veuve Rubel,* [1958] Rec. Cons. d'Ét. 33, *annulling* FH 264 (1955). The author has been unable to locate the decision finally rendered by the 1950 Hungarian Commission in this case. However, considering that the French commissions have always executed the decisions of the *Conseil d'État*, it is probable that compensation was ultimately awarded.

other (Eastern European) commissions uniformly have failed to obtain relief.[154]

Nuances bearing upon these decisions have been and will continue to be discussed throughout this study. What matters here, however, is less the French commission decisions themselves than the fact that "war damage" claims have been put forward irrespective of whether the commissions have had jurisdiction to adjudicate them. In other words, implicit in many of the "war damage" claims has been the argument (distinct from, but related to, questions concerning the attribution of deprivative responsibility)[155] that liability for deprivations imposed by payor governments, as belligerents, does not abate because the deprivations were carried out under situations of intense conflict. In a narrow sense, at least as applied to Bulgaria, Hungary, and Romania, the thesis has merit. Because of the 1947 Peace Treaties these former Axis Powers were under international legal obligation to make the reparations transferred. Thus restricted, however, the argument begs the question: why the peace treaty obligations? Also, when applied to a wider context it is ill founded. For example, why were not Czechoslovakia, Poland, and Yugoslavia likewise required to pay for French war damage inflicted within their borders, and in particular war damage inflicted by them or their allies?[156] Or why, shifting the focus somewhat, has Egypt escaped paying reparations for damage inflicted upon French nationals in 1956 pursuant to orders of the "Governor Military General" under a proclaimed "state of siege"?[157] The point is, obviously, that belligerents may or may not be discharged from responsibility for deprivations imposed during periods of intense conflict depending not simply on the presence or absence of treaty

[154] *See* text at note 338 *infra.*

[155] *See* text at notes 85–86 and 93–96 *supra.*

[156] For decisions known to have denied compensation for damage inflicted by the particular payor country in question or its allies, the commissions usually being inexplicit on this point, see FCz 39 (1954); 116, 120 (1956)/FP 135 (1954)/FY 54 (1953); 337 (1956).

[157] *See* Egyptian Proclamation No. 5, [1956] Egyptian Official Journal No. 88(A). The 1966 Egyptian Accord, extending compensation for losses caused initially by "sequestrations" effected pursuant to Proclamation No. 5, authorized distribution only in the event that the "sequestered" interests were later "liquidated" or otherwise unrestored by the Egyptian Government. *See* 1966 Egyptian Accord, art. 4. Thus, indemnification under the 1966 Accord has been for post-conflict deprivative action, not "wartime" seizures.

commitments, but rather on the manner in which all relevant values of authority and control are allocated from context to context. To know these patterns, of course, it is necessary to consider all the complex factors that condition "the Law of War," an inquiry that is well beyond the scope of this study.[158] Surely a guiding preference, however, would be one that favors imposing heavy liability upon those who can be identified as having initiated the coercion in question.

Claim That Crises Unmarked by Conflict do Not per se Release Deprivors from Responsibility for Deprivations Imposed Incidental Thereto

As mentioned, the founding of the postwar Eastern European Peoples' Republics, Nasser's Egypt, and Castro's Cuba heralded new social orders, and patently the making of these revolutions (essentially non-conflictual from the standpoint of French involvement) spelled times of high crisis for the countries involved, provoking deprivations both major and minor along the way. However, as concerns at least the international law principle of compensation, as distinct from the speed, amount, and form thereof, it appears that these crises per se have had little if any impact. Although never explicitly determined, if even considered, at either the diplomatic or arbitral levels of postwar French practice, neither, it seems, has it ever been supposed that Eastern Europe, Egypt, or Cuba would or should be discharged from repairing losses on the grounds, recently advanced in some Third World quarters, that the deprivations (at least those of large scale) were an essential part of the fundamental reformations of these countries. All the Settlement Agreements, and hence the decisions rendered under them, have been at least testimony for the thesis that deprivative responsibility is not to be avoided because of revolutionary upheaval.

On the other hand, just as it is necessary to look to all the dynamics and trends of "wartime" deprivation to reach definitive conclusions, so also is it necessary to account for all the dynamics and trends of deprivations imposed during "peacetime" crises.

---

[158] For relevant discussion, however, see M. McDOUGAL & F. FELICIANO, *supra* note 1, at 435–519, 587–610, 809–32; J. STONE, LEGAL CONTROLS OF INTERNATIONAL CONFLICT 434–41, 451–54, 706–19 (rev. ed. 1959).

Traditional systems can foreclose genuine wide participation in the economic process and therefore preclude greater productivity and reward in the broadest sense. By tearing that system apart, however, for all the havoc that this wreaks and even to the extent of denying compensation in some instances, a more inclusive shaping and sharing of values and consequently a more enduring global stability may be ultimately realized. Still, it is not to be overlooked that French experience has not been unique in this setting, and this fact provides us with probably the best available view of what the law is and should be as a general proposition.[159]

D. Claims Relating to Deprivor Base Values

Whether, how, and to what extent foreign-wealth deprivations can or will be undertaken obviously depend on the means that deprivation-prone communities have at their disposal for effecting them. For example, a relatively well-trained labor force (skills) and a real—even imagined—ability to command grassroot loyalties (power, affection) are, with other base values, more likely than not to permit realization of deprivative policies. Perceptions of this kind are of course exceedingly relevant to legal policy. Knowing what values are actually available to would-be depriving communities enables wealth owners to predict events and thereby to anticipate or hedge against risk. In turn, this ability to anticipate, before the fact, can figure prominently into judgements about the reasonableness or legitimacy of claims (and actions) that respond to or issue after the fact. *Volenti non fit injuria.* To assume a risk is, possibly, to bar complaint.

It is both to minimize risk and to preserve freedom of future claim and counteraction that it is sometimes argued that the ability to make "full" compensation is a prerequisite to deprivative competence.[160] Fearful of setting bad precedent and constrained to

159 For more than 10 years Cuba and the United States have not been able to reach a settlement as regards the 1959–1960 Cuban deprivation of American wealth interests. On the other hand, this delay is not unusual, if only by French standards, and therefore should not be interpreted to mean any more than that agreement-making in this area is commonly a long and painful process.

160 This theme has its various and occasionally watered-down manifestations. In two recent decisions by the French *Cour de Cassation,* for example, it was said that "no legal effect can be given in France to an [Algerian] expropriation carried out

prevent the impression that they are lax in protecting their own foreign interests or those of their nationals, governments naturally are reluctant to concede that other governments are the least justified in pursuing a deprivative course unless they can offer "prompt, adequate, and effective" compensation. In any event, if France's postwar lump sum agreements are any indication, they rarely do so in as many words.

The 1958 Yugoslav Accord, however—which, it will be recalled, liberalized the terms upon which the balance due on the 1951 promise would be paid[161]—made exception to this pattern. According to the Accord's preamble, the French Government agreed to the amount and manner of lump sum payment promised—an estimated 25 percent of the actual losses suffered[162]—by "[t]aking into account Yugoslavia's capacity for payment and transfer."[163] In effect, France expressly accepted that Yugoslavia's inability to pay "prompt, adequate, and effective" compensation, distinct from her failure to do so, hardly was reason to dishonor Yugoslavia's deprivative policies as unlawful *per se*. Doubtless this acceptance was prompted partly by the French Government's desire to achieve a diplomatic *rapprochement* with Belgrade after nearly a decade of complex negotiation. Still, given the difficult plight of Yugoslavia's postwar economy and her like negotiations with other countries, the conclusion seems reasonable. Indeed, it is not unfair to draw the same conclusion, however inductively, from all the other Settlement Agreements. Considering that none approached what may be called "prompt, adequate, and effective" compensation (some even less than the initial 25 percent Yugoslav settlement),[164] that all necessitated "value-tying" arrangements and that few, if any, of the depriving countries were free of financial incapacities, then the concession to principle, if not simply to plain fact, is clear. In the case of the 1966 Egyptian settlement, indeed, there is reason to believe that the 300,000 Egyptian pounds promised by Egypt represented not an actual capital transfer but a commercial credit to be de-

---

by a foreign State without prior determination of fair compensation." *Supra* note 122 [M. Diamond transl., in 8 INT'L L. MATERIALS 1215, 1216 (1969)].

161 *See* Part II, notes 65 & 106. *See also* text at Part II, notes 78–85.
162 *See* VIENOT 177.
163 Decree No. 59–654 of May 5, 1959, [1959] J.O. 5244.
164 *See* text at Part II, notes 98–102.

ducted by France from the French share of the balance of payments between France and Egypt.[165]

In sum, postwar French practice makes abundantly clear that "the right to take" in no way depends upon "the ability to pay"— a "rule" which, although the result of diplomatic decision, can be fairly imputed, for reasons already noted, to all the distributive decisions of the French commissions. As such, Franch practice has been altogether consistent with equivalent practice elsewhere.[166] Also, recognizing the intense nationalism and ideological fervor that today abounds throughout the world, as well as the obvious critical risks that in this setting would attend insistence upon a contrary "rule," disinclination to make deprivative competence contingent upon financial capacity is wise policy.

E. Claims Relating to Deprivor Strategies

Foreign-wealth deprivations are themselves economic strategies *par excellence*. This is much emphasized by all the leading commentaries. However, perhaps because of excessive preoccupation with consequences, surprisingly little attention has been paid to the many and diverse techniques by which, through action or failure to act, wealth deprivations are themselves effected—surprising because, as the ancient debate about ends and means makes abundantly clear, how goals are pursued is usually of fundamental, if not always decisive, importance for policy recommendation and decision. In any event, a number of these instrumental techniques, classifiable in terms of most of the conventional forms of strategy that prevail between human beings (diplomatic, ideological, economic, and military) and including what has come to be known as "indirect," *"de facto,"* "surreptitious," or "creeping" expropriation, have been considered in postwar French practice and therefore necessitate review.[167]

Most conspicuous, of course, have been "peacetime" and "war-

---

[165] This belief is deduced from conversations with several French officials in and out of government.

[166] *See generally* LILLICH (U.S.) ; LILLICH (G.B.) ; LILLICH & CHRISTENSON; R. LILLICH & B. WESTON, 2 INTERNATIONAL CLAIMS: THEIR SETTLEMENT BY LUMP SUM AGREEMENTS, to be published by the Syracuse University Press.

[167] For details concerning strategies of deprivation in the global context, see WESTON 75–80.

time" measures of "confiscation," "expropriation," "nationalization," and "requisition" *stricto sensu,* archetypal deprivative techniques and examples of diplomatic strategy insofar as they can be simultaneously distinguished by their common use of acts and signs which, short of actual force, are communicated directly to target owners, usually for the purpose of extinguishing or threatening title. Apparently uncontested by the French Government in any strategic sense (excepting, of course, during World War II), it need only be reemphasized that none of these "peacetime" and "wartime" archetypes—at least none of them that actually have been covered by the Settlement Agreements—escaped French expectation of payment.[168] The literally thousands of decisions that have been rendered by the French commissions to date naturally have reflected this fact.

It will be recalled, however, that all but two of the Settlement Agreements (the 1967 Cuban and 1966 Egyptian accords) have authorized indemnification expressly for losses sustained from other than archetypal deprivative measures,[169] *i.e.,* from "toute autre mesure restrictive consécutive aux modifications apportées à la structure économique,"[170] from "mesures . . . de restriction d'un caractère similaire,"[171] from "autres mesures restrictives de caractère similaire,"[172] from "toutes autres mesures restrictives du droit de propriété,"[173] from "autres mesures de dépossession totale ou partielle,"[174] and from "autres mesures restrictives similaires."[175] Obviously, this language has left much room for interpretation and so has made possible a variety of claims whose central and common feature has concerned the prospect that certain exercises of public

---

[168] *But cf.* the *Conseil d'État* appeals cited in note 153 *supra,* indicating that there has sometimes been confusion about what archetypal measures did not escape such French expectation.

[169] The 1967 Cuban Accord, covering "French property, rights, and interests in Cuba which have been affected by the laws and measures promulgated by the Revolutionary Government of Cuba," of course may be interpreted to include *de facto* as well as *de jure* deprivative devices. *See* preamble. The few number of decisions rendered by the Cuban Commission as of this writing, however, prevent knowing whether this interpretation would be a legitimate one. The 1966 Egyptian Accord is altogether silent in these respects. *But cf.* note 127 *supra.*

[170] 1950 Czech Accord, art. 1(b).

[171] 1950 Hungarian Accord, preamble; 1965 Hungarian Accord, preamble and art. 1.

[172] 1951 Yugoslav Accord, preamble and art. 1.

[173] 1948 Polish Accord, "Protocole d'Application" of 1951, subpara. 3.

[174] 1955 Bulgarian Accord, art. 1(a).

[175] 1959 Romanian Accord, art. 1(a); 1963 Yugoslav Accord, art. 2.

power, while not "confiscations," "expropriations," "nationalizations," or "requisitions" *stricto sensu,* nevertheless might be considered the *de facto* or functional equivalents of the archetypal
measures for which compensation under the Settlement Agreements
has been required in principle. Regrettably, owing to the failure of
the French commissions always to identify and describe carefully
the deprivative measures that have concerned them, a number of
claims that have been put to the commissions seemingly in this connection defy analysis.[176] Such demands as have been illuminated,
however, have borne exclusively on the diplomatic, economic, and
military instruments of policy (typologies which because of their
sometimes redundant character do not purport to recreate the real
world in its every detail).[177] Proceeding *seriatim,* it may be assumed
that as a matter of policy preference this writer is sympathetic to
all those decisions that would discourage or safeguard against
deprivations which, irrespective of the specific modalities employed,
can be shown (singly or in combination) realistically to impair a
mutually productive flow of wealth across national boundaries.

*Claim That Certain Uses of the Diplomatic Instrument of Policy
Serve as the Functional Equivalents of Deprivations That Give
Rise to Legal Responsibility*

Supplementing their consideration of the archetypal measures
noted, some of the French commissions have had occasion to contemplate the compensability of losses wrought by "liquidations,"
"debt repudiations," and "forced sales," also diplomatic strategies
as defined above. As may be seen, not all of them have been found
to warrant reparation.

Liquidations. Seemingly using the term "liquidation" to denote
an appropriation by public authorities, without compensation, of
the profit and loss derived from the "winding up" of a business or

---

[176] *See* FCz 58 (1955); 370–93, 427 (1958); 728, 771, 871, 879, 901 (1959); 1059,
1064, 1191, 1194, 1196 (1960)/FP 561 (1964)/FR 1357, 1587 (1962); 6334 (1966);
7386 (1967).

[177] The author is unaware of any occasion in which ideological strategies of deprivation have been implicated in postwar French practice, *i.e.,* strategies which concern
the creation and dissemination of symbols, slogans, and doctrines for the purpose
of altering the perspectives of local audiences vis-à-vis foreign-wealth ownership in
a manner calculated to impair the well-being of such ownership.

estate, in fact the French commissions nowhere have defined the concept. Indeed, but for the 1966 Egyptian Accord and some isolated decisions, rarely has the device even been referred to in postwar French practice.[178] Nevertheless, it can be said that the technique has from time to time figured in the decisions of most of the French commissions.[179] More importantly, except in the case of the Polish Commission, compensation for "liquidations" is said always to have been allowed in principle.[180] In other words, the silence of the commissions about this device has not meant an absence of "liquidation claims," but rather the commissions' unquestioning acceptance that such claims should give rise to indemnification; hence, the commissions' unconcern to single out "liquidations" for special comment.

As suggested above, however, the Polish Commission has not been so indifferent. Because lump sum distribution under the unamended 1948 Polish Accord was restricted to interests damaged or divested by the Polish nationalization law of January 3, 1946,[181] and because, according to the Commission, the "restrictive measure" language of the amendatory 1951 Polish Protocol was intended to refer only to deprivations oriented to real property,[182] the Polish Commission has been obliged to be still more cautious than the other commissions about strategic matters. At any rate, it is this controlling framework that explains the Polish Commission's rejection of claims based on company liquidations unrelated to the 1946 nationalization law or to real property interests.[183] Were it not for the 1948 Accord and the 1951 Protocol, doubtless the Com-

---

[178] See 1966 Egyptian Accord, art. 4.

[179] Interview with Dervieu, in Paris, June 28, 1969. For decisions taken under the 1966 Egyptian Accord and awarding compensation expressly for "liquidations," see FE 4, 11, 82 (1969). To like effect, see FCz 68 (1955).

[180] Interview with Dervieu, in Paris, June 28, 1969. Cf. FY 312 (1956) wherein the 1951 Yugoslav Commission denied relief to a claimant insurance company which, although paid by Yugoslavia for the "liquidation" of its insurance business, nonetheless charged the Yugoslav authorities with such "abusive and false" behavior as to prevent it from realizing all its assets. The claimant, the Commission observed, was unable to support this charge with any "legal and precise" evidence. The Commission also noted that there was no evidence that the Yugoslav Government had acted in a discriminatory manner against other foreign companies similarly situated.

[181] See 1948 Polish Accord, preamble and art. 3.

[182] See text at note 173 supra.

[183] FP 3, 4, 7, 12, 20, 21, 24 (1952); 34, 35, 57, 69 (1953); 106 (1954); 168 (1955); 499 (1961).

mission would have reached the same sensible conclusions as the other French commissions, conclusions which appear consistent with customary practice generally.[184]

Debt Repudiations. Likewise in keeping with customary international practice have been several cases in which the Bulgarian, Czech, and 1950 Hungarian commissions uniformly have extended relief for "debt repudiations."[185] Most of these cases have involved the "extinction" of bank deposit and other creditor accounts previously "blocked,"[186] while others have concerned the governmental discharge of secured and unsecured private obligations[187] and the formal cancellation of public debts guaranteed by international arbitral award[188] and international agreement.[189] Save to point out that none of the Controlling Texts have been explicit about "debt repudiations," it need only be added that the commissions have insisted on proof of actual debt "taking" (express or implied) as a precondition of eligibility in these cases.[190] Hence the refusal of the Bulgarian Commission to extend relief for "debt suspensions"[191] (except in two cases where the concerned obligations, assumed by Bulgaria under its 1947 Peace Treaty, had been so long suspended as to amount to debt repudiations).[192] Hence also the refusals of the Bulgarian and other commissions to extend relief for mere non-payment[193] (except in one case where the unpaid debt was due from a domestic "expropriation proceeding" which had assured the payment of bonds to effectuate an urban renewal).[194]

Forced Sales. French commission decisions concerning "forced sales" (*ventes forcées*) have been few in number. Nevertheless, they

---

[184] *See, e.g.,* 2 O'CONNELL 842–43; WORTLEY 55, 111.

[185] *See, e.g.,* 2 O'CONNELL 1080–94. *See also* 8 M. WHITEMAN, DIGEST OF INTERNATIONAL LAW 933–69 (1967).

[186] *See* note 223 and accompanying text *infra.*

[187] *See* FCz 96–98 (1956)/FH 178 (1953).

[188] *See* FB 101 (1963).

[189] *See* FB 120, 129 (1963).

[190] For relevant discussion, see text at note 271 *infra.*

[191] FB 12, 30–32 (1961); 106, 120 (1963). *Compare* these decisions *with* 2 O'CONNELL 1090: "The rule against repudiation must also contemplate virtual repudiation, where the abstract obligation remains but non-payment has persisted for an unreasonable time and without adequate economic justification."

[192] FB 101 (1963); 196 (1965).

[193] *See* text at notes 415–437 *infra. Compare* these decisions *with* 2 O'CONNELL, *supra* note 191.

[194] FB 101 (1963).

appear to have kept pace with general international practice.[195] Limited to the Bulgarian, Romanian, and 1951 Yugoslav commissions, they divide into three categories. First, one decision by the Romanian Commission and another by the 1951 Yugoslav Commission have involved what may be described as *ad hoc* compulsory transfers to public authorities without a *quid pro quo*.[196] As might be supposed, given that these kinds of measures are really no different than their more institutionalized archetypes, the commissions allowed indemnification. In the second category, *i.e.*, sales by public authorities ostensibly for non-enterprisory purposes, is to be found but one case, concerning a Bulgarian "tax sale" purportedly effected to collect on a levy of 398,000 levas, previously reduced from 1,928,000 levas.[197] Concurring in the claimant's judgement that the size of this reduction demonstrated "the uncertainty of the taxation," the Bulgarian Commission imputed bad faith to the Bulgarians and granted compensation. Lacking further information, it is of course impossible to know whether the Commission's otherwise sensible conclusion was justified. Nevertheless, without derogating from the fundamental interest that all States share in promoting the optimum functioning of their own internal orders, it illustrates vividly that deprivor objectives can fundamentally affect legal decision. Finally, there is to be found a decision rendered by the 1951 Yugoslav Commission concerning a private sale made under threat of deprivation.[198] Although the sale was "publicly supervised" and despite its having resulted in "dommages importants," the Commission withheld indemnification. Given that this decision seems on its face open to question, it is hardly sufficient for the Commission to have said only that a contrary outcome would have been unfair to other Yugoslav Commission claimants. Obviously, even mere threats of deprivation can sometimes work as effectively as any other technique to bring about deprivation in fact. On the other hand, if after careful assessment the Commission found the claimant to have

---

[195] *See, e.g.,* Christie, *supra* note 139, at 324–29. *See also* WORTLEY 1–2. *See generally* Karasik, *Problems of Compensation and Restitution in Germany and Austria,* 16 LAW & CONTEMP. PROB. 448 (1951). For additional relevant decisions in postwar French practice, see text at notes 345–351 *infra.*

[196] FR 558 (1961)/FY 336 (1956).

[197] FB 96 (1963). For related discussion, see text at notes 225–240 *infra.*

[198] FY 104 (1954).

realized proportionately more from the sale than other claimants were to receive from lump sum distribution then the decision would be understandable.

Claim That Certain Uses of the Economic Instrument of Policy Serve as the Functional Equivalents of Deprivations That Give Rise to Legal Responsibility

Public exercises of economic power, regardless if they actually serve in particular instances as the functional equivalents of archetypal deprivations, can be conveniently, although not rigidly, grouped according to the techniques that governments commonly employ to affect not wealth ownership as such, but (1) participation in, (2) use of, and (3) benefit or yield from wealth processes and values. All three of these strategic categories have been considered by the French commissions, mainly the Eastern European commissions.

MEASURES AFFECTING PARTICIPATION IN WEALTH PROCESS

Only the Czech, 1965 Hungarian, Polish, and Romanian commissions appear so far to have rendered decisions that fall within this category. Of these commissions, the Czech and Polish have been the most active.

On a number of occasions, 15 in all, the now inoperative Czech Commission was asked to grant relief for "property, rights, and interests" placed under Czech "national administration," the apparent practical effect of which, although left wholly unexplained by the Commission, was to remove the claimants from participation in the wealth activities to which they were then specialized. That is, the Commission was asked to equate loss of proprietary control with loss of wealth ownership. Over-all, due mainly to insufficient discussion, the Commission's response remains ambiguous. In four cases, it accepted the equation without explanation, pinpointing the loss apparently as of the date of the order placing the property under "national administration."[199] In another case, also without comment, it did not.[200] And in four others, a subsequent

[199] FCz 22 (1954); 82 (1956); 165 (1957); 402 (1958).
[200] FCz 415 (1958).

"liquidation," "expropriation," and "nationalization" rendered the question moot.[201] In short, only in the remaining six of this cluster of decisions did the Commission undertake to explain itself, and then only inferentially. It accepted or rejected the equation depending on the claimants' ability to demonstrate either the existence of pending "restitution proceedings" in Czechoslovakia[202] (in accordance with Article 1(c) of the 1950 Czech Accord) or the fact or likelihood that proprietary control would never be restored,[203] as the three cases involving a subsequent "liquidation," "expropriation," and "nationalization" tend to demonstrate. Regrettably, the Commission gave no hint whether the rationale that emerges from these decisions was equally at work in the first four cases mentioned, thus leaving the matter in a rather ambiguous state. In the one unexplained case where relief was denied,[204] it is of course possible that the relevant "national administration" measure was not one "bearing upon reforms directed at the Czech economic structure" as required by the 1950 Czech Accord.[205]

Nine similar cases are to be found among the rulings of the all-but-defunct Polish Commission. They divide into two groups, two cases involving measures of "administration forcée"[206] and seven cases concerning the "provisionary administration" of abandoned or ex-German property.[207] Unfortunately, the full significance of the first two decisions cannot be reported. Although seemingly satisfied that an "administration forcée" was the functional equivalent of a deprivation that gave rise to compensation under the 1948 Polish Accord and 1951 Polish Protocol, the Commission denied

---

201 FCz 19 (1954); 68 (1955); 155, 174 (1957).

202 See FCz 99 (1956); 164 (1957). Both claims were declared "recevable."

203 See FCz 39 (1954), declared "recevable" because "restitution" had been denied by the Czech authorities; 84 (1956), declared "recevable" because the Czech government had communicated to the French Foreign Ministry that the claimants should be indemnified under the 1950 settlement terms; 417, 627 (1958), declared "irrecevable" because there was no evidence of "confiscation"; and 1103 (1960), declared "recevable" because of continued "occupation" of the premises by Czech authorities from 1945 to 1960.

204 Case cited note 200 supra.

205 See 1950 Czech Accord, art. 1(b).

206 See FP 14 (1952); 49 (1953).

207 See FP 44, 56, 63, 71, 89 (1953); 103 (1954). See also FP 73 (1953), rev'd on rehearing, FP 502 (1961).

relief because the claims, having accrued after the entry into force of the 1948 Accord, were not scheduled for lump sum relief.[208] Accordingly, it was unnecessary for the Commission to clarify its conception of "administration forcée." Whether its perspective was at variance with the "national administration" decisions rendered by the Czech Commission therefore must be left unresolved. In contrast, however, the "provisionary administration" cases are easily understood. Uniformly refusing compensation because the administered property was subject to possible restoration through authorized appeal to appropriate Polish offices, the Commission held that these measures did not constitute the equivalent of deprivations that gave rise to indemnification under the Polish settlement. Withholding relief in the absence of some further dispossessive act on the part of the Polish authorities,[209] these decisions are reminiscent of the Czech "national administration" cases already considered.

Finally, one case decided by the 1965 Hungarian Commission and one by the Romanian Commission should be noted. While factually different from one another as well as from the preceding cases, each concerned actions affecting not wealth ownership as such but participation in the wealth process. Thus, in the Hungarian Commission case, compensation was asked for agricultural lands which, although not nationalized, were being "managed" by the "municipal counsel" of a Hungarian village. Observing that this management was being carried out "without an accounting" to the claimant, the Commission granted relief, commenting that the lands "were thus practically confiscated" and that "this kind of expropriation can be considered as within the terms of the 14 May 1965 Accord."[210] The Romanian Commission decision, even if consistent, was cryptic by contrast. Without elaboration, the Commission granted compensation for "withdrawal of the license to which [the licensee] was incumbent for the sale of petroleum products."[211]

Summarizing, French commission decisions concerning the functional equivalency of measures that would deny participation in the

---

[208] For discussion concerning this time factor, see text at note 339 *infra*.

[209] *See, e.g.*, FP 502 (1961), *reversing* FP 73 (1953) because the property under administration had been subjected to formal transfer to the Polish State.

[210] FH2d 72 (1968).

[211] FR 82 (1960).

wealth process appear, at first glance, contradictory. Without further detail, it is difficult to reconcile the Czech and Polish commission State administration cases with the 1965 Hungarian and Romanian decisions noted. However, reading between the lines, a certain consistency is discernible. Borrowing from the counterpart experience of the United States Foreign Claims Settlement Commission, it is reasonable to assume that the Czech "national administration" measures were regarded by the Czech Commission, as they were by the FCSC, "as . . . temporary action[s] to be terminated after the [Czech] Government . . . ascertained whether . . . [the] property should be returned to the original owners, or confiscated, nationalized or otherwise disposed of."[212] For this reason, the Czech Commission probably determined, in keeping with its temporary deprivation decisions[213] and again like the FCSC, that only "in those cases where it is established that a national administrator was appointed specifically to liquidate a business . . . [would] such action . . . be considered as a taking."[214] The same logic was doubtless at work in respect of the Polish "provisionary administration" measures which, it will be recalled, did not of themselves deny title, but rather allowed owners of abandoned property to seek restitution from the Polish authorities.[215] In short, State administration measures seem to have been viewed generally as temporary in character, subject to withdrawal or later substitution by "permanent" deprivative actions. The Hungarian and Romanian measures, on the other hand, appear to have been looked upon as definitive in character, leaving the claimants not only without opportunity to participate in their enterprises, but without recourse to constituted authorities and therefore without effective title as well. In other words, measures that impair only proprietary control have not been regarded by the French commissions as the functional equivalents

212 FOREIGN CLAIMS SETTLEMENT COMMISSION OF THE UNITED STATES, FOURTEENTH SEMIANNUAL REPORT TO THE CONGRESS FOR THE PERIOD ENDING JUNE 30, 1961, Panel Opinion No. 6, Jan. 18, 1960, at 134.

213 See text at notes 126–139 supra.

214 Opinion cited note 212 supra.

215 For evidence that this logic was at work as regards American "provisionary administration" claims against Poland, see FOREIGN CLAIMS SETTLEMENT COMMISSION OF THE UNITED STATES, DECISIONS AND ANNOTATIONS 510–11 (1968).

of archetypal deprivations. For reasons earlier discussed, this view raises serious policy questions.[216]

MEASURES AFFECTING USE OF WEALTH VALUES

Including even the Cuban and Egyptian commissions which, it will be recalled, had no "restrictive measure" language to go by, all the French commissions and notably the Bulgarian and Czech commissions have been faced with claims asserting the equivalency of measures that affect access to, or exploitation of, wealth values— *i.e.*, "the means of production" (land, labor, capital, entrepreneurial talent). Except for one case, all have been of a kind.

The one exceptional case, decided by the Czech Commission, received excessively short shrift and therefore ambiguous treatment. Supplementing a number of disparate demands, the claimant sought compensation equal to four million Czech crowns for "prejudice" caused in the form of "the loss of his business" because of "prohibitions imposed by the Czechoslovak Government on the importation and manufacture of chemical and pharmaceutical products." Abjuring express interpretation of the 1950 Czech Accord's "restrictive measure" language and without explanation other than that the claim fell outside the limits of the 1950 settlement, the Commission withheld relief.[217]

The majority of decisions, about 100 to date, have concerned what are popularly known as "exchange control" measures—here, the "blocking" or "freezing" usually of non-resident bank deposit and other creditor accounts as a matter of general (*i.e.*, "non-discriminatory") governmental policy. Just as the aforementioned State administration measures have denied participation in the wealth process, these measures, by proscribing the free transfer of foreign-owned assets, have denied access to wealth values upon which wealth processes are built. Again claimants have sought to equate these measures with those acts for which compensation, in principle, has been authorized. In every instance, save when the

---

[216] *See* text accompanying note 139 *supra*.

[217] FCz 728 (1959). A further, but clearly secondary, reason for rejecting the claim was that the "prejudice" was sustained after the entry into force of the 1950 Czech Accord. Thus, even if the substance of the claim were to have succeeded, compensation would have been withheld. For discussion concerning this time factor, see text at note 339 *infra*.

cases have turned less (if at all) upon the "exchange control" measures effected than upon the formal or informal "extinction" or
"expropriation" of the accounts in question, the commissions have
refused to do so. Consistent with customary international practice,[218]
they have contended that the "blocking" or "freezing" of assets as
a matter of general monetary policy "does not deprive the claimant
of his property"[219] since it concerns only the non-transferability of
assets which does not prevent the accounts from being used in the
"blocking" countries.[220] As stated by the *Conseil d'État* in a case
on appeal from the Bulgarian Commission, "the prohibition against
transferring sums outside Bulgaria cannot be regarded as equivalent
to a confiscation giving right to benefit from the Franco-Bulgarian
accord of 28 July 1955."[221] Thus, only when the accounts have been
shown extinguished or otherwise disposed of, as in a Czech Commission case wherein the accounts were found to have been not simply
"blocked" but "also intransmissible,"[222] have contrary judgments
been reached;[223] and then, of course, because of the debt "taking,"
not the "blocking" or "freezing" order.[224]

In sum, just as the French commissions have denied the func-

---

[218] *See, e.g.,* A. NUSSBAUM, MONEY IN THE LAW, NATIONAL AND INTERNATIONAL
446–61 (rev. ed. 1950); 2 O'CONNELL 1100–101; Mann, *Money in Public International
Law*, 96 RECUEIL DES COURS (Hague Academy of International Law) 7, 37–74
(I-1959). *See also* WORTLEY 46–47.

[219] *Quoting* FCz 3 (1953).

[220] FB 28, 35, 36, 38–40, 47 (1961); 58, 66 (1962); 92, 95, 100–102, 110, 116, 122,
126 (1963); 139, 145, 152–53, 163 (1964); 179, 188, 190–91, 196 (1965); 200 (1966)/
FCz 2, 3, 12 (1953); 84, 110 (1956); 151–52, 155, 167, 204, 206, 219–21 (1957);
259, 261–62, 321, 346, 348, 351–53, 396–98, 412, 427, 624 (1958); 727, 729, 795, 799,
871–72 (1959); 1314 (1961)/FE 16 (1969)/FH 178 (1954)/FH2d 43, 51 (1967)/FP
222 (1956)/FR 2178 (1963)/FY 55, 56 (1953); 273, 278 (1956)/405–406, 440–42,
444 (1957); 528 (1958); 606 (1959)/FY2d 5, 12–14, 26 (1965); 41 (1966); 68–70
(1968). In FCz 346 (1958), the Czech Commission observed that the claimants
"have the right to the free disposition of the [bank] books within the limits imposed concerning the transfer of currency." In FY2d 41 (1966), the 1963 Yugoslav
Commission denied relief notwithstanding that the claimant's passbook had been
retained by the Yugoslav authorities, presumably (but dubiously) because a receipt
had been given therefor.

[221] *Sieur Mura-Michel,* [1967] Cons. d'Ét., Section du Contentieux, No. 70,408
(unpublished mimeo.), on appeal from FB 200 (1966).

[222] FCz 84 (1956). It has to be conceded, however, that the distinctive meaning
of "intransmissible" is not altogether clear.

[223] *See* FB 46, 48, 49, 83, 90 (1962); 116, 122 (1963); 172 (1964); 185, 188
(1965)/FC 5, 8 (1969)/FCz 11, 12 (1953); 84 (1956); 155 (1957).

[224] For related "debt claims" discussion, see text at notes 185–194 *supra* and notes
271–272, 415–437 *infra.*

tional equivalency of measures directed at participation in wealth processes, so have they denied the functional equivalency of measures directed at use of wealth values. There are, of course, eminently sound reasons for the exchange control holdings, at least in the apparent absence of complaints about discrimination. In a world of demonstrably unequal currencies, it is basic that States should be given broad competence to manage their monetary systems along lines that they perceive to be in their productive interest. On the other hand, from a perspective that would maximize the free flow of international trade and investment by taking into account the mid-century growth of treaty and other transnational efforts which aim to stabilize the manifest interdependence of national economies, refusals to challenge the unfettered exercise of exchange control policies, however consistent with customary trends, must be called increasingly into question. From the same perspective, the exceptional Czech Commission decision noted is subject to possible censure.

MEASURES AFFECTING BENEFIT OR YIELD FROM
WEALTH PROCESSES AND VALUES

As of this writing, only the Bulgarian, Czech, 1950 Hungarian, Romanian, and 1951 Yugoslav commissions appear to have entertained cases that fall within this category. They divide into two distinct groups, the first concerning taxation and similar fiscal measures, the second concerning monetary devaluation (which, like taxation and other economic devices, can effectively impair, in whole or in part, the benefit or yield from wealth processes and values).

Except in one curious decision wherein the Bulgarian Commission denied relief for loss resulting from the imposition of an anti-Semitic tax,[225] the fiscal measure cases, decided by the Bulgarian, Czech, Polish, and 1951 Yugoslav commissions, have held no mysteries—at least not in any cumulative sense. Together, including the questionable Bulgarian Commission decision, they have formed a consistent whole. Again in keeping with customary practice,[226] the com-

---

[225] See FB 125 (1963).
[226] See, e.g., S. FRIEDMAN, supra note 116, at 2–3; M. WHITEMAN, supra note 185,

missions have held that, as a general rule, taxation and similar fiscal measures are not to be considered as the functional equivalents of archetypal deprivative techniques. Thus the now inoperative Czech Commission refused to grant relief, in one case, for an amount paid as a general property and capital gains tax ("impôt sur la fortune"),[227] and, in another case, for securities transferred in payment of general income and capital gains taxes,[228] expressly contending in the first instance that a tax measure "does not constitute a measure of nationalization or expropriation." Identical logic appears to have been at work among some of the other commissions: in two refusals of the Polish Commission, one concerning a claim for the return of property taxes paid,[229] the other for forfeited exemptions;[230] in two decisions of the Romanian Commission, one withholding compensation for the occupation of premises to secure payment of land taxes,[231] the other refusing reimbursement for an alleged "forced deposit" required to cover transportation debts incurred by the claimant before leaving Romania;[232] and in two orders of the 1951 Yugoslav Commission, one disallowing relief for sums paid pursuant to a general price support program,[233] the other preventing recoupment of amounts forfeited for a "tax on war benefits."[234]

It would of course be incorrect to conclude from these few decisions that all taxation and similar fiscal measures have been considered exempt from liability. In the first place, as three decisions of the Bulgarian Commission make clear, the commissions that were charged to apply provisions of the 1947 Peace Treaties (*i.e.*, the Bulgarian, 1950 Hungarian, and Romanian commissions) have had

---

at 507–39; WORTLEY 45–46. *See generally* Dalimier, *Droit Fiscal International Français—Généralités*, 3 JURIS-CLASSEUR DE DROIT INTERNATIONAL, Fasc. 301.

[227] FCz 10 (1953).

[228] FCz 1355 (1964).

[229] FP 72 (1953).

[230] FP 98 (1953). The Polish Commission rejected the claim because the forfeited exemptions did not pertain to "municipalized land." Although it is not clear why, apparently this fact was sufficient to place the claim outside the protection afforded by the 1951 Polish Protocol.

[231] FR 1354 (1962).

[232] FR 1919 (1962). This refusal was appealed unsuccessfully to the *Conseil d'État. Sieur Biazotti,* [1967] Cons. d'Ét., Section du Contentieux, No. 59,939 (unpublished mimeo.).

[233] FY 95 (1954).

[234] FY 117 (1954). For related discussion, see text at notes 238–239 *infra*.

to grant relief in respect of "war tax" measures.[235] Further, the commissions have been unwilling to reject claims when the levies at issue could be deemed "excessive." Hence the Bulgarian Commission, on two occasions, has extended relief for taxes levied on shares held in already nationalized enterprises.[236] Likewise, the Polish Commission has granted compensation, in one case, because the taxes levied (payment of which was a condition precedent to the restitution of property placed under "provisionary administration") were "of a sum of much greater value" than the property itself.[237] Thus, too, in a case involving a "seizure" by Yugoslav authorities of a claimant's factory in order to enforce a "[delinquent taxes] judgment of the fourth commercial tribunal of Belgrade," the 1951 Yugoslav Commission granted an award for amounts forfeited in excess of taxes levied.[238] Finally, it appears that the commissions— more precisely, the Bulgarian and 1951 Yugoslav commissions— have been willing to question the stated purposes of a fiscal measure. Thus, in the Yugoslav tax seizure case just cited, the 1951 Yugoslav Commission rejected the claimant's contention that "the seizure was used as an excuse by the Yugoslav authorities to seize his enterprise" (meaning, of course, that the instant tax measure pursuant to which the "seizure" was made was not itself seen to give rise to compensatory obligation).[239] On the other hand, precisely opposite results were reached, it will be recalled, in the decision earlier discussed wherein the Bulgarian Commission, because of "the uncertainty of the taxation," imputed bad faith to the Bulgarians and granted compensation for what it called a "forced sale."[240]

Turning, finally, to the French commission decisions that have concerned the alleged equivalence of monetary devaluations, again we find a consistency with customary international practice.[241] Echoing the same rationale that appears to have prevailed in the fiscal measure cases just considered, the Bulgarian, 1950 Hungarian,

[235] See FB 100, 120 (1963); 155 (1964).
[236] FB 116, 122 (1963).
[237] FP 247 (1956).
[238] Case cited note 234 supra.
[239] Id. However, the Commission did agree that "the seizure of [the claimant's] business falls within the category of restrictive measures set forth in the accord of 14 April 1951."
[240] See note 197 and accompanying text supra.
[241] See, e.g., 2 O'CONNELL 1098–1100, 1104–105; WORTLEY 47–50.

Romanian, and 1951 Yugoslav commissions have in every instance denied relief on the grounds that the monetary devaluations, however injurious to some, were not, without proof of discriminatory or other ulterior motive, to be considered as functional equivalents of deprivative measures that give rise to compensatory treatment.[242] As stated by the Romanian Commission in two cases returned from appeal to the *Conseil d'État*:[243]

> . . . the Commission . . . verifies that as of August 1947 the value of the lei had fallen practically to zero and that, consequently, the monetary reform law of 15 August 1947 must have been enacted to account for this situation and to render old leis without value; that if, at the same time, this law gave to each natural and juridical person, whether Romanian or foreign national, the opportunity to exchange his old leis up to the amount of 150 stabilized leis, this was in order to give to each [person] an immediate indispensable minimum to prevent the collapse of the country's economic life; that this provision thus appears, in fact, not as a spoliation but, to the

[242] FB 102 (1963)/FH 31, 47, 130 (1953); 178 (1954); 266 (1955)/FR 238, 259, 584, 699 (1961); 974, 1031, 1700, 1505, 1854, 1919 (1962); 2492, 2635 (1963); 4514, 4903 (1965)/FY 95 (1954); 203 (1955); 248, 250–51, 318 (1956). Romanian Commission decision FR 1919 was in this connection affirmed on appeal by the *Conseil d'État*. See *Sieur Biazotti*, [1967] Cons. d'Ét., Section du Contentieux, No. 59,939 (unpublished mimeo.). *See also* note 243 *infra* for two other of the Romanian Commission decisions that were appealed to the *Conseil d'État*.

[243] FR 4131 (1964); 4514 (1965). The first of these cases had been decided by the Romanian Commission in 1961. See FR 116. The *Conseil d'État* annulled this decision and returned the case to the Commission on the ground that the Commission had not taken adequately into consideration an interpretation of the Minister of Foreign Affairs concerning the Romanian monetary reform law of August 15, 1947. *Dame Keim*, [1963] Cons. d'Ét. 464. The second of these cases followed a more intricate course, having been appealed to, and returned by, the *Conseil d'État* on two separate occasions. The first time, the *Conseil* annulled the Romanian Commission's decision (FR 187) on the ground that the Commission had exceeded its powers by not obtaining the advice of the Quai d'Orsay as regards the effect of the 1947 monetary reform law upon debt claims held by French nationals against Romania. *Sieur Pioton ès-qualité de liquidateur de la Société industrielle des pétroles roumains*, [1962] Cons. d'Ét. 142. For related discussion, see Part II, note 256 and accompanying text. The second time, on appeal from the Commission's reconsideration of the case [FR 2309 (1963)], the *Conseil* returned the case for rehearing on grounds virtually identical to those set forth in *Dame Keim, supra*. *Société industrielle des pétroles roumains*, [1963] Cons. d'Ét., Section du Contentieux, No. 60,539 (unpublished mimeo.). See the abbreviated annotation of this decision at [1963] Cons. d'Ét. 933, wherein it is reported correctly that the French Foreign Ministry, as well as the *Conseil d'État*, were willing to admit of the possibility that the 1947 monetary reform law could fall within the "restrictive measure" language of the 1959 Romanian Accord.

contrary, as a measure favorable to holders of old leis, since these leis had by then lost all value; that, consequently, the monetary reform law of 15 August 1947 cannot be invoked to claim an indemnity under the Franco-Romanian accord of 9 February 1959."[244]

As indicated, these fiscal and devaluation measure decisions can be said to have been generally consistent with customary international practice. More importantly, given their implied recognition of the need for maintaining stable fiscal and monetary orders while at the same time assuring non-discrimination in international trade and investment, the majority of them appear to have been motivated by enlightened policy considerations. How then does one reconcile the above-mentioned and arguably reprehensible Bulgarian Commission decision to withhold relief for loss resulting from an anti-Semitic tax?[245] Judging from another Bulgarian Commission case decided initially on the same grounds (*i.e.*, that Bulgarian "racial legislation" did not fall within the incorporated 1947 Peace Treaty provisions of the 1955 Bulgarian Accord), but later reversed following appeal to the *Conseil d'État*,[246] probably it is not "good law."[247]

Claim That Certain Uses of the Military Instrument of Policy Serve as the Functional Equivalents of Deprivations That Give Rise to Legal Responsibility

Force, or physical power, in its most mild or severe forms, can serve prescriptive as well as its more commonly recognized applicative functions; it can constitute as well as reinforce decision. Ex-

---

[244] *Quoting* FR 4131 (1964).

[245] Case cited note 225 *supra*.

[246] *See* FB 202 and 203 (1968). This case, concerning, *inter alia,* property damages sustained as a result of the application of Bulgarian "racial laws," was first decided by the Bulgarian Commission in 1964. *See* FB 146. The claimant, having already received compensation from Bulgaria subject to his reservation that such compensation was inadequate, sought relief for amounts he considered still due. The Commission withheld this additional relief on the grounds that the Bulgarian authorities had assumed the obligation to make all these reparations, that they were doing so in accordance with their own internal procedures, and that, for this reason, the damages fell outside the 1955 settlement terms. The *Conseil d'État* annulled this decision on the grounds that the Commission should have taken these additional requested amounts into account in making its over-all award. *Sieur Covo,* [1967] Cons. d'Ét., Section du Contentieux, No. 69,611 (unpublished mimeo.). For related discussion, see note 153 and accompanying text *supra.*

[247] However, the case appears never to have been appealed to the *Conseil d'État*.

clusive of many possibly relevant but insufficiently explained Bulgarian, 1950 Hungarian, and Romanian commission "war damage" cases, a number of decisions rendered by the Cuban, Czech, 1965 Hungarian, Polish, Romanian, and 1951 Yugoslav commissions have involved this prescriptive use. Concerning claimants who sought indemnification for "peacetime" losses that appear to have been unprescribed in any formal sense, once again the cases divide into three groups.

Occupations or Use. On several occasions, claimants have tried to obtain awards for losses resulting from the occupation or use of their property. The Czech Commission, in three instances, refused these requests, implicitly contending that the mere occupation or use of premises by public officials, without more, could not be considered functionally equivalent to measures for which compensation was authorized under the 1950 Czech Accord.[248] In the absence of "a legal act or regulation" or "a contract" or "a judicial decision,"[249] the argument that "rents"[250] or other "indemnities"[251] are required for this kind of deprivative conduct simply had "no juridical existence."[252] Although it did not say so, presumably the Commission was motivated by Article 1(b) of the 1950 Czech Accord which, it will be recalled, limited compensation for "restrictive measures" only to those measures bearing upon reforms directed at the economic structure of Czechoslovakia. At any rate, three other decisions, one by the 1965 Hungarian Commission, one by the Polish Commission, and one by the 1951 Yugoslav Commission—with none of these commissions being similarly circumscribed—tend to confirm this view. Thus the 1965 Hungarian Commission granted compensation in respect of an unnationalized building "occupied" by persons acting under authority of a Budapest "town council" (seemingly to make the best of scarce housing facilities)—or, in the Commission's words, for "requisition by occupation and not nationalization."[253] To like effect, the 1951 Yugoslav Commission allowed recovery for "occupation of . . . [the claimant's] commercial buildings for army

248 FCz 24 (1954); 78, 79 (1956).
249 FCz 78 (1956).
250 FCz 24 (1954); 78 (1956).
251 FCz 79 (1956).
252 FCz 78 (1956).
253 FH2d 56 (1967).

stores, and as a consequence, assignation [*attribution*] of the merchandise to the Yugoslav authorities" because "this can be considered the result of a true expropriation according to the 14 April 1951 accord."[254] The Polish Commission decision, more prolix than most, is especially illustrative:[255]

> Whereas [the claimant transport company] was obliged to . . . abandon all its installations upon the arrival of the Germans in Danzig;
>
> Whereas, after the return of the Polish troops . . . in 1944, the Polish Government took possession of the said installations; that despite two Polish tribunal decisions replacing them into the private sector and returning them to the claimant *société*, the latter has never been able to obtain the restitution;
>
> Whereas in reply to the requests of [the claimant] to be authorized to resume its activity and use of its installations, the Polish Government responded by demurrer, alleging that similar kinds of [existing] enterprises . . . were sufficient to assure the needs of Franco-Polish commerce;
>
> Whereas cargo and transport enterprises similar to [the claimant] have all been nationalized and in fact function . . . with the installations of the claimant *société*;
>
> Whereas it results from these diverse elements that if no nationalization measure has been taken as regards the interested *société*, it has been dispossessed in effect of its materiel for the benefit of a nationalized enterprise; [therefore] it is possible to consider [the claimant] as having been made the object of a restrictive property measure in the sense of the protocol of 7 September 1951.

In short, barring limitative treaty provisions, the French commissions appear to have been predisposed to equate unprescribed occupation or use with archetypal deprivative measures. Of course, given the few decisions involved, the presence of judicial verdicts in the Polish Commission case, and the possibly contradictory posture of the Czech Commission, this conclusion is a tenuous one. Assuming it is accurate, however, the predisposition may be said to be in keeping not only with customary international legal thinking,[256] but also

---

254 FY 95 (1954).
255 FP 100 (1953).
256 *See, e.g., Walter Fletcher Smith* v. *Compañia Urbanizadora del Parque y Playa de Marañao* (United States v. Cuba), 2 U.N.R.I.A.A. 913 (1929); Lena Goldfields

with the mainstream of progressive human rights decision and policy that has swelled since the close of World War II.[257]

Detentions. On four known occasions, claimants have sought indemnification for the detention, or non-restoration, of property previously taken as "enemy property" or for other reasons. They have succeeded in every instance, in each case, however, because of prior restorative commitments made. Thus, in one case the Czech Commission ruled that "the repeated refusal" of the Czech authorities to make restitution "notwithstanding the numerous official representations" of the French Government "constituted in fact, despite the absence of an explicit confiscation decision, a measure of spoliation giving rise to an indemnity under paragraph (c) of article 1 of the [1950 Czech] accord."[258] Three Polish Commission decisions, including the one quoted in the preceding paragraph, had no treaty promise to go by. Instead, they relied, at least in part, on municipal tribunal decisions which had earlier called for the return of the claimants' property.[259] At any rate, it takes no pedant's footnotes to see that these commission rulings were sensible. Recalling the horizontal structure of the international legal order, it is essential that effect be given to municipal and other decisions that are consistent with enlightened world order policies, as *arguendo* were the precedent decisions involved in these cases. A *sine qua non* of a productive and widely distributive global wealth process is stability of expectation, and this stability, in turn, depends upon confidence in judicial undertakings.[260]

Expulsions. French commission claimants have on 18 known occasions, once before the Cuban Commission, 7 times before the 1951

Arbitration [1930], set forth in the Appendix to Nussbaum, *The Arbitration Between the Lena Goldfields, Ltd., and the Soviet Government,* 36 CORNELL L. Q. 31, 42 (1950). *See also* 2 O'CONNELL 842–43; 2 M. WHITEMAN, DAMAGES IN INTERNATIONAL LAW 941–44, 1376–85 (1937).

[257] For an indication of some recent progressive thinking from a policy-oriented perspective, see McDougal, Lasswell, & Chen, *Human Rights and World Public Order: A Framework for Policy-Oriented Inquiry,* 63 AM. J. INT'L L. 237 (1969).

[258] FCz 116 (1956). Article 1(c) of 1950 Czech Accord promised indemnification to "French interests which are now the object of restitution procedures in Czechoslovakia."

[259] FP 100 (1953); 110 (1954); 384 (1958).

[260] As demonstrated by an earlier cited Bulgarian Commission decision, the French commissions have been concerned about this stability in terms of giving effect not only to precedent "restitution" decisions, but as well to prior "indemnification" decisions. *See* note 194 and accompanying text *supra.*

Yugoslav Commission, and 10 times before the Romanian Commission, sought distributive relief for "abandonment and forfeiture" of property resulting from deportative "expulsion."[261] The Cuban Commission decision, rejecting the claim, is ambiguous. However, because the Commission took the trouble to point out that the 1967 Cuban Accord was intended to cover only governmental deprivative measures, it appears likely that when "the claimant hastily left Havana on 29 November 1961" she did so of her own volition.[262] Regrettably, the cumulative impact of the Romanian and 1951 Yugoslav commission decisions is not much clearer. Notwithstanding that the 1959 Romanian and 1951 Yugoslav accords contained virtually identical "restrictive measure" language,[263] the Romanian Commission uniformly granted, and the 1951 Yugoslav Commission systematically denied, these requests.[264] For this reason, and because the commissions were undisposed to elaborate their reasoning, one is at pains to discern accommodating rationales. Reading between the lines, however, it can be inferred that the Romanian Commission decisions represent the prevailing rule of postwar French practice in this connection, an inference that is drawn from the fact that the 1951 Yugoslav Commission decisions, unlike their Romanian counterparts which concerned the "forfeiture" of corporeal assets, involved debt claims which presumably had never been subjected to actual "extinction."[265] Assuming this conclusion is accu-

---

[261] A legal distinction is sometimes drawn in international practice between "deportation" and "expulsion," the former ostensibly referring to the removal of persons whose initial entry is "illegal," the latter to the termination of "legal" entry and the freedom to remain. For present purposes, however, the term "expulsion" is used in purely a descriptive sense.

[262] FC 4 (1968).

[263] See 1959 Romanian Accord, art. 1(a); 1951 Yugoslav Accord, preamble and art. 2.

[264] FR 38 (1960); 114, 181, 306, 364 (1961); 1549, 1893 (1962); 2373, 2492 (1963); 6305 (1966)/FY 206–11 (1955); 436 (1957).

[265] This presumption is reflected in one of the 1951 Yugoslav Commission cases, appealed to the Conseil d'État. See Sieur Campion, [1960] Cons. d'Ét. 30, affirming FY 436 (1957). The claimant sought indemnification for "emoluments" alleged due from his former employer, an agency of the Yugoslav Government, but uncollected owing to the claimant's "expulsion" from Yugoslavia. In addition to noting that the "expulsion" was "by the German authorities" and that the non-payment was due not to a "restrictive measure" but to the "reorganization" of the governmental agency in question, each of which facts were sufficient to reject the appeal, the Conseil observed that the debt claim had not been repudiated by the Yugoslav Government. For relevant comment, see text at notes 271–272 infra.

rate, again French perspectives may be seen as consistent with customary practice[266] and, for obvious reasons, sound policy. Coercive strategies must always be required to shoulder the burden of proof when it comes to legitimizing actions that would derogate from individual human security and peaceful world order.

F. Claims Relating to Outcomes of Deprivation

Central to outcomes-oriented inquiry in the comprehensive global context (or decisional arena) within which foreign-wealth deprivations take place is the identification of the wealth and other value losses that actually obtain in concrete cases for the purpose of explaining and appraising both the character and legitimacy of protective response—diplomatic, military, or otherwise—that invariably follows.[267] In the more limited decisional context within which the French commissions have operated, however, these prospective concerns (distinct from the task of value loss identification, considered below) have been moot, they having been resolved at the pre-settlement stage of deprivor-deprivee interaction. They are, therefore, beyond the scope of this study, although it merits recollection that France, like other countries since World War II, has chosen more a persuasive than a coercive stance toward the protection of her deprived nationals (save initially in the case of Egypt at the time of Suez). However, other issues germane to this outcome phase of inquiry, resolved at the diplomatic level and clarified at the arbitral level, have been implicated in the decisions of the French Commissions, i.e., issues of "loss-in-fact" and "cause-in-fact."

Claim That Legal Responsibility is Engaged Without Loss-in-Fact or Proof of Loss

Before it is possible to know who is entitled under what circumstances to what relief for what losses, it is axiomatic that there be

---

266 See 2 O'CONNELL 765–70; 1 SIBERT 620–27. See also 1 M. WHITEMAN, DAMAGES IN INTERNATIONAL LAW 418–82 (1937); Revised Draft on International Responsibility of the State for Injuries Caused in its Territory to the Person or Property of Aliens, in 2 YB. INT'L L. COMM'N 46, 47 (I.L.C. Doc. A/CN.4/34/Add.1, 1961).

267 For indication of the variety of wealth and other value losses that can obtain in concrete cases, see WESTON 80–98. For indication of the variety of protective response that invariably follows, see id. at 117–65.

shown a loss in fact. At least this is the logical assumption upon which all the Settlement Agreements have been premised. Nevertheless, exclusive of cases in which the French commissions have found particular measures to result in no *compensable* loss (*e.g.*, temporary and alleged *de facto* "takings"), a large number of cases have arisen even when claimants have known or had reason to know that they suffered no deprivation whatsoever, doubtless because of genuine misunderstandings in most instances.[268] At all times, as might be supposed, the commissions have declared the petitions "irrecevable." The cases divide into three general categories.

Most predictable, first, are the literally scores of cases in which the commissions have found the claimants altogether in error about the fact of loss, at any time.[269] Many of these cases have involved facts which demonstrate that at the time of alleged deprivation the claimants lacked ownership of, and so the capacity to lose title to, the wealth ostensibly forfeited.[270] Others have involved public and private debt claims held still to be viable either because the debts had not been extinguished as believed[271] or, in the case of private debt claims (many of them bondholder claims), because the obligations had been assumed by the nationalized or otherwise deprived debtors—in either of which events the claims have been treated as "ordinary" commercial debt claims, or "payements courants," whose settlement was to be covered (if at all) by alternative arrangements outside French commission jurisdiction.[272] In still other cases, the

---

[268] *See, e.g.*, FH2d 44 (1967) wherein the 1965 Hungarian Commission, in rejecting a claim for lack of sufficient proofs, stated that the claimant's "good faith is not in question."

[269] *See* FB 7, 21, 41 (1961); 59, 66, 70, 75, 82, 88, 89 (1962); 94, 100, 107–108, 120, 126, 130 (1963); 144, 160, 164 (1964); 182, 184–85, 189, 196 (1965); 200 (1966)/ FCz 3, 11 (1953); 56, 58, 113 (1956); 179–81 (1957); 263, 319–20, 363, 416, 441– 610, 626, 628, 631–46 (1958); 679–80, 686–88, 722–25, 731–32, 771–72, 788, 790, 812–24, 830, 833–67, 871, 885–86, 907–53, 955, 957–62 (1959)/FE 4, 8, 29, 52, 66 (1969)/FH 60 (1953); 278, 287 (1955); TV533–63, TV585–95, TV634, TV647–51, TV702, TV705, TV713 (1956)/FH2d 1, 2, 13 (1967); 62 (1968)/FP 4, 5, 8, 10, 13, 23, 24, 26–29, 39, 41, 46, 52, 54, 60, 67, 95 (1953); 109, 112, 163 (1954); 178, 192, 199 (1955); 226, 262 (1956); 302 (1957); 364 (1958); 483 (1960); 529–30 (1962)/FR 1354, 1440, 1850 (1962); 2308, 2781, 2949 (1963); 4510, 4643, 5063–64, 5547–52 (1965); 6467, 6788 (1966)/FY 57, 58, 61, 71, 72 (1953); 100 (1954); 178, 181, 200, 206–11, 275, 318–19, 328, 330 (1956); 395–97, 400, 406–407, 436, 440 (1957); 527–29 (1958); 750, 853 (1960); 862–63 (1962)/FY2d 56 (1966); 67 (1967). *See also* the cases cited at note 14 *supra*.

[270] *See* note 14 *supra*.

[271] *See, e.g.*, text at notes 218–224 *supra*.

[272] *See* FB 7 (1961); 59, 75, 82, 88 (1962); 100, 107–108, 120, 130 (1963); 164

properties in question have been found "repatriated" and "voluntarily withdrawn" from the country[273] or retained by friends and relations.[274]

Next are cases in which the commissions have found no loss because the claimants, according to the commissions, had already been fully repaired by the deprivor governments or others through restitution, indemnification, or other payment.[275] Four examples are representative: a Bulgarian Commission case wherein a creditor claimant was found to have been reimbursed by the nationalized debtor;[276] a Czech Commission case in which it was found that the claimant, whose land had been surrendered pursuant to a 1948 agrarian reform law, had in 1949 received "a selling price of 258,000 Czech crowns";[277] two Egyptian Commission cases in which it was found that the claimants' "sequestered" estates had been returned to them;[278] and a Romanian Commission case wherein it was shown that the claimant had been earlier indemnified by the Polish Commission.[279] Two related groups of cases, the first involving voluntary sales to the German State or German nationals during World War II, the second involving prior partial payments by the Egyptian Government, were decided mainly on other grounds.[280]

Finally, but less commonplace, are cases wherein the Bulgarian, Cuban, 1950 Hungarian, Polish, Romanian, and 1951 Yugoslav commissions have found no loss because the concerned property

(1964); 182, 184–85, 189, 196, 200 (1966)/FCz 3 (1953); 180–81 (1957); 441–610, 631–46 (1958); 679–80, 686–88, 722–25, 731–32, 771, 788, 812–24, 833–67, 885–86, 907–53, 955, 957–62 (1959)/FH 278, 287 (1955)/FH2d 2 (1967)/FP 4, 5, 8, 10, 13, 24, 26, 27, 29, 39, 41, 46, 52, 54, 67, 95 (1953); 109, 112, 163 (1954); 178, 192, 199 (1955); 226 (1956); 483 (1960); 529–30 (1962)/FR 1440 (1962); 5064 (1965)/ FY 58, 61 (1953); 100 (1954); 397, 400, 406, 436 (1957); 527–29 (1958); 853 (1960); 863 (1962).

273 *See* FB 94, 134 (1963).

274 *See* FE 4, 8 (1969).

275 *See* FB 13 (1961); 64, 66, 75 (1962); 102, 126 (1963); 146, 160, 162, 164 (1964)/FC 1 (1968)/FCz 56, 58, 68 (1955); 179 (1957); 320, 348, 363, 402, 416 (1958); 770, 789 (1959)/FE 8, 9, 16, 59, 62, 64 (1969)/FH 260 (1954); TV663–99, TV702–08, TV711, TV713 (1956)/FH2d 34, 53 (1967); 72 (1968)/FP 31, 61, 89 (1963)/FR 3, 77 (1960); 356, 544 (1961); 2711 (1963); 3477 (1964); 5064 (1965); 7306, 7311 (1967)/FY 175 (1955); 321 (1956)/FY2d 29 (1965); 41 (1966); 66 (1967).

276 FB 164 (1964).

277 FCz 348 (1958).

278 FE 9, 71 (1969).

279 FR 544 (1961), citing FP 369 (1958).

280 Regarding the German transfer cases, see text at notes 345–351 *infra*. Regarding the Egyptian partial payment cases, see text at notes 352–356 *infra*.

was shown to be without monetary value at the time of claimed deprivation.[281] Illustrative is a case in which the Bulgarian Commission observed that a deposit of 14.32 levas, "closed" upon nationalization of the depository bank, was worthless owing to the devaluation of the French franc.[282] Likewise illustrative is a case in which the Cuban Commission found "that the claimant knows that since 30 July 1962 her business had no activity . . . , that an inventory made then demonstrated assets less than the debts she had to pay . . . , and that in these conditions she could not be considered as having been affected [*i.e.*, deprived] by the laws and regulations of the Cuban Government since 1 January 1959."[283] The logic is obvious. Absent worth there can be no loss, at least not in "property" terms or in terms of alienability. That other values may have been lost along the way has been a matter about which the French commissions generally have been indifferent.[284]

The commissions have not stopped here, however. Consistent with their Controlling Texts, in particular their Rules,[285] they have many times refused to grant compensation because the claimants have failed, as an evidentiary matter, to prove the fact of loss[286] or, in a

---

[281] *See* FB 3 (1960); 156, 165, 167 (1964); 183 (1965)/FC 3 (1968)/FH 71 (1953)/FP 202 (1955), *affirming* 131 (1954); 244 (1956); 355 (1957); 521 (1962)/ FR 7, 40 (1960); 357, 359 (1961); 1240 (1962); 2418, 2493–94, 3227 (1963); 3351, 3745, 3747, 4135 [*affirming* 37 (1960)] (1964); 4901, 5070, 5547–52 (1965); 6198 (1966); 7136, 7218, 7220, 7224 (1967)/FY 313 (1956); 405 (1957).

[282] FB 156 (1964).

[283] FC 3 (1968).

[284] *See* text at notes 369–376 *infra*.

[285] *See* text at Part II, notes 234–240.

[286] FB 23–25, 29, 30, 33, 37, 38 (1961); 50, 62, 84 (1962); 94, 97, 98, 113–15, 120 (1963); 144, 147, 163 (1964)/FC 4 (1968)/FCz 8, 11, 12 (1953); 50, 63 (1955); 104, 131, 141 (1956); 180–81, 185, 221 (1957); 326, 350, 370–93, 422, 427, 627, 647–49 (1958); 679–80, 687–88, 771, 871, 885–86, 901, 994–95 (1959); 1059, 1064, 1191, 1194–96 (1960); 1350 (1963); 1355 (1964)/FE 88 (1969)/FH 67, 150–52 (1953); 173, 257–58 (1954); 349, 351 (1957); TV729, TV732, TV739 (1956)/FH2d 13, 24, 27, 33, 43, 44 (1967); 72 (1968)/FP 67, 74 (1953); 104, 107, 120–21, 125, 134, 156–58 (1964); 199 (1955); 293, 297, 316 (1957); 367, 383, 386, 400 (1958); 409–10 (1959); 523 (1962), *affirming* 474 (1960); 529–30, 532–35, 538 (1962); 545 (1963)/FR 307, 310 (1961); 973, 1029, 1312, 1919, 2051 (1962); 3345, 4384 (1964); 4645, 5248, 5545–46, 5589, 5716, 6023–24 (1965); 6168–71, 6304, 6678–79, 6786, 6914–16, 7013 (1966); 7125, 7135, 7212, 7297–98 (1967)/FY 204 (1955); 240, 243, 253, 255, 315, 318–19, 324, 329, 331 (1956); 342, 402, 415, 426, 437 (1957); 516, 521 (1958); 746 (1959)/FY2d 21, 32, 33 (1965); 35, 38, 40, 53, 57 (1966). Bulgarian Commission FB 144, *supra*, was affirmed without supplementary discussion by the *Conseil d'État*. *See Dame Arié*, [1965] Cons. d'Ét., Section du Contentieux, No. 64,555 (unpublished mimeo.). So also was Romanian Commission decision FR 1919 in like

few cases, the existence of value.[287] In short, the burden of proving loss and worth has been upon the claimants; but not, be it noted, to the point of exalting form over substance. On numerous occasions, demonstrating both their recognition of the difficulties of proof and their flexible procedures, the commissions have gone far—oftentimes at their own initiative—to give claimants, if not always the benefit of the doubt, at least liberal opportunity to prove their case.[288] Thus, in one case, the Czech Commission agreed to indemnify notwithstanding that the claimant "does not prove the confiscation of her personal effects" because "information available to the Commission leads it to admit that the claimant was the owner of some furnishings confiscated in 1948 at the home of the claimant and her husband."[289] Thus, in two other cases, rather than deny recovery for lack of proof of the worth of a nationalized enterprise, the Romanian Commission considered it "suitable to rely on the information furnished by the Government of the Romanian Peoples' Republic."[290]

In short, because of diplomatic decisions earlier made, the French commissions have held that loss or proof of loss is, as it should be, a condition precedent to the engagement of international responsibility.[291] In so doing, they have been indifferent about whether the claims have borne upon "wartime" or "peacetime" deprivation.

Claim That a Wealth Loss Which is Not, or is Not Proven to be, the Outcome of Deprivative Conduct Nonetheless Engages Legal Responsibility

As Edwin Borchard is reported to have said, "[e]very man whose property rights are diminished thinks that there has been a 'confiscation.' "[292] French commission claimants have been no exception.

---

manner. See *Sieur Biazotti*, [1967] Cons. d'Ét., Section du Contentieux, No. 59,939 (unpublished mimeo.).

[287] See FH TV733 (1956)/FP 202 (1955), *affirming* 131 (1954)/FR 3094 (1963); 4773 (1965), *enforcing* 366–67 (1961); 6564, 6916 (1966)/FY 405 (1957).

[288] In other words, in the absence of sufficient proofs, the commissions have not infrequently deferred final decision until after the claimants have tried to amass supporting evidence to justify their petitions.

[289] FCz 693 (1959).

[290] FR 3095–96 (1963).

[291] For indication of like approaches in Great Britain and the United States, see LILLICH (G.B.) 9–13; LILLICH & CHRISTENSON 52–67.

[292] *Quoted in* Witenberg, *La protection de la propriété immobilière des Étrangers*, 55 J. DROIT INT'L 566, 579 (1928).

Accordingly, the question of "cause-in-fact"—*i.e.*, whether a loss is in whole or in part the outcome of activity for which accused parties may be held responsible—is a matter about which the French commissions have had to be concerned. Approaching "peacetime" and "wartime" deprivative claims with equal strictness, their decisions have been commonsense, predictable, and uniform. Supplementing decisions wherein they have denied relief for third-government seizures[293] and for deprivative measures not expressly covered by the Settlement Agreements,[294] the commissions have refused to grant compensation whenever the losses complained of were caused by other than governmental conduct: *e.g.*, "natural" causes and disasters,[295] company "disappearances" and liquidations owing to wartime circumstances,[296] voluntary dissolutions and liquidations,[297] voluntary mergers,[298] private leasehold evictions[299] and job dismissals,[300] voluntary absences or departures from the country,[301] currency convertibility complications,[302] and even appropriation pursuant to international agreement.[303] Again, the burden of proof has been

[293] *See* text at notes 89–96 *supra*.

[294] Egyptian and Polish commission claimants (the latter prior to the entry into force of the 1951 Polish Protocol) have sometimes sought recovery for losses not caused by the specific deprivative measures referred to in the 1966 Egyptian and 1948 Polish accords; to wit, Egyptian Proclamation No. 5 of November 1, 1956, and the Polish nationalization law of January 3, 1946. *See* 1966 Egyptian Accord, arts. 1 & 4; 1948 Polish Accord, preamble and art. 3. In each instance the commissions have denied relief. FE 1, 3, 7, 82, 92 (1969)/FP 34 (1953); 317 (1957); 350, 393 (1958). The later Polish Commission decisions cited appear to have involved claims that failed also to meet the terms of the 1951 Polish Protocol.

[295] *Landslide:* FB 87 (1962). *Fire:* FCz 59 (1955)/FP 271 (1957). *Flooding:* FY 318 (1956). *Train derailment:* FB 15–20 (1961).

[296] FP 53, 66, 87, 90, 91 (1953); 177 (1955)/FY 606 (1959). *But see* FP 566 (1965), granting compensation for "back interest" suspended because of World War II. The holding was in execution of a decision of the *Conseil d'État* to which the case had been appealed. *See Sieur Devien*, [1965] Rec. Cons. d'Ét. 239.

[297] FB 79 (1962)/FH TV533–63, TV585–95, TV712, TV725, TV772 (1956)/FP 55 (1953)/FR 900 (1962); 2441 (1963); 4135–36, 4255–56 (1964); 5720 (1965); 6198, 6564 (1966); 7135, 7312 (1967)/FY 527–29 (1958); 853 (1960).

[298] FH TV508–32, TV534–63, TV585–95, TV640–46, TV702, TV705, TV711, TV716, TV722, TV724, TV726, TV728 (1956)/FP 67 (1953).

[299] FR 1652 (1962).

[300] FR 900, 1652 (1962)/FY2d 30 (1965).

[301] FB 144 (1964)/FC 4 (1968)/FR 1651–52, 1790 (1962); 2986 (1963); 4510 (1965). Bulgarian Commission decision FB 144 was affirmed without added discussion by the *Conseil d'État*. *See Dame Arié*, [1965] Cons. d'Ét., Section du Contentieux, No. 64,555 (unpublished mimeo.).

[302] FE 71 (1969)/FR 1505 (1962).

[303] FY 314 (1956) wherein the claimant was denied relief for 23 bars of gold, first

on the claimants. Failure to prove "cause-in-fact" has uniformly resulted in rejection of the claim.[304] In short, true to basic State Responsibility principles, the French commissions have not held payor governments responsible for losses not caused by them.

3. SITUATIONS AFFECTING CLAIMANT ELIGIBILITY

Just as the situations (or particular contexts of confrontation) within which international claims accrue can fundamentally condition claimant eligibility, so also can the situations within which international claims are brought for resolution prove dispositive. Also as before, these situations can be many and diverse, and for this reason demanding of an analytical framework that makes for precise identification and discrete comparison. Accordingly, it is again convenient to look to the basic and interdependent situational dimensions with which, as already indicated, decision-makers are commonly required to deal: space, time, institutionalization, and crisis.

Space

Among the variety of spatial features that serve both to characterize decisional contexts and to influence the disposition of claims, only one appears to have been clearly implicated in postwar French practice: the physical location of the claimant at the time of claim presentation or adjudication. It is of course common to many legal systems—more precisely, to many decisional arrangements within given legal systems—that claimants be physically present or available if they expect to receive favorable treatment. Such has not been the case for French commission claimants, however, and not

---

seized in France by the German occupation authorities and after the war turned over to Yugoslavia by the Tripartite Commission created by the Paris agreement on war damage indemnities.

[304] FB 52–54, 85, 86 (1962); 145 (1964)/FCz 11, 14 (1953); 61 (1955); 86 (1956); 649, 652 (1958)/FE 1, 3, 7 (1969)/FH 60 (1953)/FR 1440 (1962); 2986 (1963)/FY 405 (1957). To these decisions may be added several others which, although rendered without clear explanation, appear to have involved a failure to prove cause-in-fact. See FP 163 (1954)/FR 3 (1960); 543–44 (1961); 1919 (1962); 4641, 5064 (1965). Romanian Commission decision FR 1919 was affirmed on appeal to the *Conseil d'État*, but without supplementary explanation. *Sieur Biazotti*, [1967] Cons. d'Ét., Section du Contentieux, No. 59,939 (unpublished mimeo.).

simply in the sense that they have been free to be represented by designated proxies.[305] Although all claimants, substituted as well as original, have been at liberty to appear before the commissions prior to the "final examination" or "judgment" of their claims,[306] none have been obliged to do so. This may be inferred not only from the Rules of the Bulgarian, Cuban, two Hungarian, and Romanian commissions which, unlike the remaining Commission Rules, expressly have authorized French foreign residents to present ("addresser") their claims to local French consulates, legations, or embassies,[307] but as well from commission decisions granting awards notwithstanding the claimants' foreign addresses.[308] Even the Egyptian Commission which, it will be recalled, has been obliged to condition eligibility upon proof of legal French residence,[309] has not insisted upon physical presence either before the Commission or in France.[310]

Time

As above, only one feature of postwar French practice appears to have emerged in this situational connection. Evincing concern to prevent the presentation of stale claims, about which the Settlement Agreements have been completely silent, all the French Commission Constitutive Laws and Rules have required that claims be filed "at risk of forfeiture . . . no later than three months after the publication [or "promulgation"] of [their Constitutive Laws], except in case of *force majeure*"[311] (thereby reillustrating, parenthet-

---

[305] In this connection, see text at notes 9–12 *supra*. *See also* text at Part II, notes 251–254.

[306] *See* Part II, note 254.

[307] *See* Part II, note 236 and accompanying text.

[308] *See* cases cited at note 66 *supra*.

[309] *See* text at notes 65–70 *supra*.

[310] *See* FE 2, 3, 33 (1969).

[311] *See* text at Part II, note 166. Unlike United States practice, but following the practice in Great Britain, the French Commissions have not prescribed these time limits themselves, this task having been performed, as seen, by executive or parliamentary decree. For equivalent American and British practice in this regard, see, respectively, LILLICH & CHRISTENSON 106 and LILLICH (G.B.) 9–10. It may also be noted that the law constituting the 1961 German Commission (as to which see Part I, note 10) allowed four months from its "publication" for the filing of claims without any provision for the filing of late claims on the basis of *force majeure*. *See* Decree No. 63–359 of April 9, 1963, [1963] J.O. 3367, art. 4. However, a *force majeure*

ically, the French Government's prerogative role in setting eligibility standards no less stringent than those called for in the Settlement Agreements). In short, although the designated cut-off has proved impossibly abrupt in some instances, with the result that 18-month and 6-month extensions were granted as required,[312] as a general rule tardy claims have been declared ineligible for relief. Failure to meet the deadlines finally established usually has resulted in "forfeiture."[313] Consistent with their Controlling Texts, the commissions have admitted tardy claims only when they have been found to involve a case of *force majeure*.[314] Because the commissions have

---

provision was included in Article 1 of the Commission's unpublished Rules. These Rules are available upon request at the Commission's Secretariat, 31, Rue Dumont d'Urville, Paris XVI.

[312] *See* the three "Avis" granting 18-month extensions to Czech, Polish, and 1951 Yugoslav commission claimants in [1952] J.O. 8740, 5067 and 11688. *See also* Decree No. 60–488 of May 4, 1960, [1960] J.O. 4867, granting 6-month extensions to Bulgarian and Romanian commission claimants.

[313] FB 109 (1963); 144 (1964)/FCz 49 (1955); 153 (1957); 260, 399, 628, 653 (1958); 688, 733, 982 (1959); 1322 (1961); 1326, 1332 (1962)/FH 100, 106 (1953); 250 (1954); 297 (1955); TV487–506, TV596 (1956)/FP 25 (1952); 40–42, 47, 78, 79 (1953); 162 (1954); 191, 193, 197, 201, 212–13 (1955); 217 (1956); 289, 302 (1957); 365, 372, 385, 387, 396 (1958); 479 (1960); 514 (1961); 523 (1962)/FR 8, 9, 28, 29 (1960); 301 (1961); 895, 1793–94 (1962); 2237, 2377, 2847 (1963); 3346, 3475 (1964); 4770, 5866–67 (1965); 6168–69, 6303, 6427, 6467, 6913 (1966); 7213, 7298 (1967)/FY 48 (1953); 186–88, 235–36, 321 (1956); 420, 438–39 (1957); 519 (1958); 750, 852 (1960); 854, 856, 858, 861 (1961)/FY2d 37, 43, 44, 58 (1966). Two of the above-cited decisions were affirmed on appeal by the *Conseil d'État. See Dame Arié,* [1965] Cons. d'Ét., Section du Contentieux, No. 64,555 (unpublished mimeo.), *affirming* FB 144 (1964); *Sieur Steinberg,* [1963] Cons. d'Ét., Section du Contentieux, No. 59,621 (unpublished mimeo.), *affirming* FR 1793 (1962). Another of the above-cited denials, FP 514 (1961), was rendered in accordance with a ruling of the *Conseil d'État* to which the case had been appealed earlier. The *Conseil* had annulled the Polish Commission's earlier decision on the grounds that the Commission had neglected to explain its reasons for denying a plea of *force majeure. See Dame Landau,* [1960] Rec. Cons. d'Ét. 199.

To be assimilated with the above decisions, of course, are decisions in which the 1963 Yugoslav Commission, charged to apply the 1963 Yugoslav Accord, has declared inadmissible petitions that have been addressed to claims covered by the earlier 1951 Yugoslav Accord. *See* FY2d 4, 17–19, 30, 31, 34 (1965); 37, 41, 43, 44, 53, 54, 58 (1966); 64 (1967). *But see Sieur Julliard,* note 417 *infra.* Although no such decisions appear to have been rendered by the 1965 Hungarian Commission, charged to apply the 1965 Hungarian Accord, presumably the same results would obtain in respect of petitions that would be addressed to claims covered by the 1950 Hungarian Accord.

[314] FB 61 (1962); 107–108 (1963); 162 (1964)/FCz 1 (1952); 35, 36 (1954); 84, 90, 95, 114 (1956); 204 (1957); 263, 325 (1958); 830, 954 (1959); 1191 (1960); 1350 (1963); 1355 (1964)/FE 79, 85 (1969)/FH 242 (1954); 299, 328 (1955); 340 (1956); 346 (1957)/FH2d 57 (1967)/FP 1 (1952); 215 (1955); 413 (1959); 506 (1961); 520 (1962)/FR 1355 (1962); 2634, 2708–709, 3004, 3262 (1963); 4308, 4424 (1964); 4774 (1965); 6306, 6427 (1966)/FY 81 (1953); 95, 126–28 (1954);

ordinarily been disinclined to disclose the bases of their findings, their meaning of "force majeure" must remain impressionistic: ignorance or late notice about the fact of claim accrual or claim inheritance, usually under circumstances beyond the control of the claimant involved;[315] delay in the official publication of the location of commission headquarters to which claims had to be addressed;[316] non-receipt of procedural details requested of the French Foreign Ministry and the commission secretariats;[317] residence abroad (in one case foreign imprisonment) preventing notification of requisite procedural information;[318] "misunderstanding" about commission procedures;[319] prior filings or communications with inappropriate offices within the French Foreign Ministry;[320] negligence on the part of a French foreign legation in transmitting a filing to Paris;[321] confusion of individual shareholders about their authority to present claims in the face of filings earlier made on behalf of all shareholders;[322] difficulty in obtaining necessary proofs because of wartime anti-Semitic spoliations;[323] fear that a claim filing might cause investigations dangerous to relatives still living in Communist territory;[324] death or illness of the claimant;[325] and death or illness in the family.[326] Not considered as *forces majeures* have been: simple ignorance of Settlement Agreement and other controlling provisions;[327] confusion about the state of one's proprietary interests in the wake of World War II;[328] difficulties in obtaining information (due mainly to wartime destruction) helpful to substantiating a

---

175, 178, 185 (1955); 325, 328 (1956); 418, 421, 424 (1957); 509, 523 (1958); 746 (1959); 748–49, 752 (1960)/FY2d 23 (1965).

[315] FH 346 (1957)/FR 2708 (1963); 6306 (1966)/FY 175 (1955); 325 (1956)/FY2d 23 (1965).

[316] FCz 1 (1952)/FP 1 (1952).

[317] FCz 35 (1954); 84 (1956)/FH 340 (1956)/FY 424 (1957).

[318] FCz 95 (1956)/FR 3004 (1963)/FY 328 (1956).

[319] FCz 114 (1956).

[320] FCz 263 (1958)/FP 215 (1955); 506 (1961)/FY 95 (1964); 185 (1955); 749 (1960).

[321] FR 2634 (1963).

[322] FY 126–28 (1954).

[323] FY 523 (1958). *But cf.* text at note 329 *infra.*

[324] FR 6427 (1966).

[325] FB 107–108 (1963). *But cf.* text at note 333 *infra.*

[326] FCz 36 (1954); 90 (1956); 1350 (1963); 1355 (1964)/FP 520 (1962)/FY 746 (1959). *Cf.* text at note 334 *infra.*

[327] FR 3475 (1964); 6303, 6913 (1966).

[328] FY 858 (1961).

claim;[329] delayed notification of the rejection of an appeal for reparation made within the payor country;[330] mistaken reliances that timely initial filings validated later severable filings[331] or that filings by co-owners constituted constructive waivers of the time limitation;[332] negligence on the part of a designated proxy;[333] and claimant illness or illness in the family not inhibiting of claimant initiative.[334] Obviously, insofar as it is revealed by the above citations, this decisional pattern raises questions about uniformity and equity. On balance, however, it is fair to say, as has the 1963 Yugoslav Commission, that the commissions have tried to rule on these matters "dans un sentiment de bienveillante équité [de] la situation particulière."[335]

Institutionalization

Like spatial and temporal situations, institutional features of claim process can serve to circumscribe, even to deny altogether, the redress that claimants seek. Virtually all of these features as they have borne on postwar French practice—*e.g.*, the composition of the French commissions, their rules of procedure, the right to judicial

---

329 FCz 49 (1955)/FP 365 (1958). *But cf.* text at note 323 *supra*.

330 FCz 1322 (1961). The Czech Commission reasoned that the claimant could have petitioned the Commission notwithstanding her appeal because Article 1(c) of the 1950 Accord expressly authorized compensation for French interests then actually involved in "procédures en restitution" in Czechoslovakia. The Commission's decision was affirmed on appeal by the *Conseil d'État. Affaire Dame Haeffele,* [1963] Cons. d'Ét., Section du Contentieux, No. 55,963 (unpublished mimeo.).

331 FP 520, 523 (1962)/FY 861 (1961).

332 FR 895 (1962). *Cf.* FB 162 (1964) wherein the Bulgarian Commission admitted a late filing because the claim concerned the identical issue already put to the Commission by the claimant's co-owner, a situation that did not obtain in the abovecited Romanian Commission decision.

333 FR 5867 (1965).

334 FR 3346 (1964); 4513 (1965)/FY 858 (1961). *Cf.* note 326 *supra*.

335 FY2d 23 (1965). For the Egyptian Commission, an interesting question is raised by the "événements de mai" of May 1968, when the outward calm of France was shattered by the general strike and student revolt that was ultimately to help bring about the removal of President De Gaulle. It was during this time that the due date for filing claims with the Egyptian Commission matured. Although as of this writing the Egyptian Commission has yet to indicate whether this "petite révolution" would excuse a late filing, judging from the French commissions already noted it seems likely that it will be considered a *force majeure*. At least this approach would be consistent with the 1963 Yugoslav Commission's expressed predilection for ruling on these matters "in a spirit of benevolent equity."

review by the *Conseil d'État*—already have been considered. One in particular deserves special reemphasis, however, partly because the commissions have had to take it into account on literally scores of occasions and partly because the very frequency of its accounting bears implications that are important to appraisal; to wit, the allocation of competence to grant relief in respect of specific kinds of claims.

That is, without legal capacity to play the benefactor, no decision-maker can be expected to give satisfaction. The proposition is elementary; indeed, so much so that one can only wonder how so many French commission claimants can have managed to overlook it (excepting, of course, where there has been room for genuine misunderstanding owing to the ambiguity of the Controlling Texts). Yet in fact they have—in three similar but distinct situations—and in each instance, for lack of sufficient competence, the commissions have had to refrain from making awards. To understand fully the jurisdictional frame with which French commission claimants have had to deal, albeit at the risk of some repetition, each of these situations are quickly reviewed. However, because the many negative decisions themselves add little if anything either to this appreciation or to the authoritativeness of the observations that follow, economy dictates that they not be cited. It need but be pointed out that only the Cuban Commission, owing to its still short life-span, has yet to be concerned with this problem.

First are cases in which competence has been lacking because the Settlement Agreements have been altogether silent about the claims raised, *i.e.*: certain of the "ordinary" (non-deprivative) debt claims brought before the Bulgarian, Romanian, and 1963 Yugoslav commissions;[336] all "ordinary" debt claims addressed to the 1965 Hungarian, Polish, and 1951 Yugoslav commissions;[337] "wartime" deprivation claims presented to the Czech, 1965 Hungarian, Polish,

---

[336] The 1955 Bulgarian, 1959 Romanian, and 1963 Yugoslav settlements each provided for the indemnification of certain expressly named "ordinary" debt claims. *See* 1955 Bulgarian Accord, art. 1(c); 1959 Romanian Accord, art. 1(c) and (d); 1963 Yugoslav Accord, art. 1. Nonetheless, a number of Bulgarian, Romanian, and 1963 Yugoslav commission claimants have sought compensation for "ordinary" debts nowhere mentioned in these Settlement Agreements.

[337] Neither the 1965 Hungarian Accord nor the 1948 Polish and 1951 Yugoslav accords contain any language referring to "ordinary" debt claims.

THE PROCESS OF CLAIM

and two Yugoslav commissions;[338] and all post-settlement deprivation claims put to any one of the commissions.[339] Lump sum distributions being juridically impossible in these instances, obviously
the claimants have been left to their own devices, sometimes to
pursue alternative channels opened for them,[340] otherwise to appeal
directly to the foreign authorities involved or to await the diplomatic
intervention of the Quai d'Orsay.[341]

Second are cases in which competence has been lacking because
the Settlement Agreements, although accounting for the claims
raised, have required that they be resolved through other settlement
processes, *i.e.*: certain of the "ordinary" debt claims brought before
the Czech and 1950 Hungarian commissions;[342] and post-1958
"sequestration" claims addressed to the Egyptian Commission.[343]
To recover, claimants have had to proceed strictly in accordance
with the alternatives prescribed, or risk forfeiture.

Finally, there are cases in which competence has been lacking
not because the Settlement Agreements have failed to provide indemnification for the claims raised, but because the French Government, in exercise of its diplomatically prescribed prerogative to
distribute the lump sums according to its own dictates, had removed
the claims from commission determination, *i.e.*, certain of the
"ordinary" debt claims brought to the Bulgarian and Romanian

---

[338] For reasons already mentioned several times, the 1950 Czech, 1965 Hungarian,
1948 Polish, and two Yugoslav accords made no provision for "war damages."

[339] Not infrequently claimants have sought indemnification for alleged deprivations
sustained after the signing or entry into force of the Settlement Agreements, notwithstanding that the Settlement Agreements have been addressed expressly to claims
arisen before settlement.

[340] *See* text at Part II, notes 124–129, 154–158. *See also* Part I, note 10.

[341] *See,* for example, the 1964 Czech Protocol (Part II, note 55), the 1964 Egyptian
Accord (Part II, note 56), the 1951 Polish Accord (Part II, note 62), and the 1958
Yugoslav Accord (Part II, note 65).

[342] *See* 1950 Czech Accord, Additional Protocol No. 1, para. 2, wherein certain
"ordinary" debt claims were stated to be outside the 1950 settlement because already
regulated by the Commercial Agreement and Monetary Settlement Between France
and Czechoslovakia of July 26, 1946 (Decree of November 9, 1946, [1946] J.O.
2645) ; 1950 Hungarian Accord, art. 5, wherein certain "financial questions" (*i.e.*,
"ordinary" debt claims) were referred to "the agreements of 29 December 1949."
The author has been unable to locate copies of these 1949 agreements.

[343] *See* Decree No. 68–103 of January 30, 1968, art. 5, [1968] J.O. 1228, the
Egyptian Commission Constitutive Law which limits indemnification to unrestored
pre-1958 "sequestration" losses.

commissions.[344] In this setting, by virtue of French Foreign Ministry edicts, the claimants have had to resort to "la répartition administrative."

In sum, claimants many times have been denied commission beneficence for no reason other than that institutional arrangements have made commission distribution impossible. To the extent that they have overlooked this brute fact, whether out of simple confusion or otherwise, they of course have suffered needless expense and bother; more importantly, a loss in precious time. In turn, depending on the requirements of the forum that has had distributive competence (if any such), this waste can have resulted in the complete forfeiture of their claims. Assuming, reasonably, that out of the many claimants involved at least half would not have undertaken to petition the commissions had they but read the Controlling Texts, one must wonder about the adequacy of notice on the part of the French Government.

Crisis

Except as post-settlement *forces majeures* may be said to constitute crisis features that influence the disposition of claims,[345] only one critical dimension of postwar French practice appears to have had any impact at this schematic juncture. It illustrates again the distributive prerogatives of the French Government. Thus, whereas the 1950 Czech, 1950 Hungarian, 1948 Polish, and 1951 Yugoslav accords were silent on the subject, the Constitutive Laws of the now inactive (or virtually inactive) commissions that were charged to apply these agreements were drafted so as to penalize claimants who, during World War II, profited from property transfers to the German State or to German nationals.[346] On several occasions, because persons claiming deprivation at the hands of Czechoslovakia, Hungary, Poland, or Yugoslavia had transferred their "affected interests" to the German State or to German nationals, the Czech, 1950 Hungarian, Polish, and 1951 Yugoslav commissions had to take these provisions into account. In each case,

---

[344] *See* Part II, note 156 and accompanying text.
[345] For relevant discussion, see notes 311–335 *supra.*
[346] *See* text at Part II, following notes 167 & 170.

the claimants having established their right to present their claims (*i.e.*, their retroactive ownership) by virtue of a prior French nullification of their German assignments,[347] the key problem, assuming proof of deprivation, was to determine if the transfer had been made under "duress." If so, indemnification was allowed in principle.[348] If not (*i.e.*, if the sale were shown to have been voluntary), the award was reduced in an amount equal to the purchase price paid by the Germans, the French *Trésor* collecting the disallowed amount in lieu of the claimant for distribution among the other claimants—a process which, because of the amounts involved, sometimes had the effect of foreclosing recovery altogether.[349] To

---

[347] See "Ordonnance" No. 45-1224 of June 9, 1945, [1945] J.O. 3379.

[348] See FCz 174, 192-94 (1957); 1349 (1963); 1370 (1965)/FP 257 (1956); 343, 408 (1957)/FY 76 (1953). The principal criterion for establishing "duress" or "constraint" was the interposition of "German managers" prior to transfer. See text at Part II, following note 171. In one 1950 Hungarian Commission case where "duress" was established, FH 300 (1955), the claim was rejected because the property in question had been appropriated by Soviet and not Hungarian authorities as alleged. In two decisions rendered on appeal from the Polish Commission, the *Conseil d'État* held that, notwithstanding a prior finding of "duress" by the *Tribunal civil de la Seine* in connection with a German "sale" made by certain shareholders of a French company, the Commission nonetheless was obliged to undertake its own investigation of this matter in respect to all the company's shareholders. Presuming duress from the limited civil tribunal holding, the *Conseil* reasoned, prevented the Commission's decision from having the authority of "la chose jugée." *Sieur Pioton, ès-qualité de liquidateur de la Société des Usines de fabrication de tubes et forges de Sosnowice,* [1964] Cons. d'Ét., Section du Contentieux, No. 55,620 (unpublished mimeo.); *Sieur Pioton, ès-qualité de liquidateur de la Société des charbonnages, mines et usines de Sosnowice et de représentant de ses actionnaires ou de ses créanciers,* [1964] Rec. Cons. d'Ét. 458. For further relevant discussion, see note 349 *infra.*

[349] See FCz 139 (1956), *rev'd in part, Banque des Pays-Bas de l'Europe Centrale,* [1959] Rec. Cons. d'Ét. 672, *modified on rehearing,* 1344 (1962), *aff'd sub nom., Commissaire du government près de la Commission de répartition de l'indemnité tchécoslovaque,* [1964] Cons. d'Ét., Section du Contentieux, No. 58,667 (unpublished mimeo.); 140 (1956); 149 (1956), *aff'd, Société financière et industrielle des pétroles,* [1958] Rec. Cons. d'Ét. 133, *vacated on other grounds,* [1961] Rec. Cons. d'Ét. 311, *modified on other grounds on rehearing,* 1331 (1962), *aff'd sub nom., Société financière et industrielle des pétroles et Commissaire du gouvernement près de la Commission de répartition de l'indemnité tchécoslovaques,* [1964] Rec. Cons. d'Ét. 233. In reversing FCz 139 in part, the *Conseil d'État* dismissed the Czech Commission's application of the French *Ordonnance* of June 9, 1945, pursuant to which French transfers to the German State and to German nationals had been nullified and in accordance with which French transferors were required to turn over their receipts to the French *Trésor.* This application being a matter for the "ordre judiciaire," the *Conseil* observed, the Commission could not apply the *Ordonnance* "without exceeding the limits of its competence." *Banque des Pays-Bas de l'Europe Centrale,* [1959] Rec. Cons. d'Ét. 672. Nevertheless, the *Conseil* affirmed that the Commission was right to assume an obligation to make its own independent investi-

reward claimants for having exploited World War II to self-advantage, the commissions reasoned, would be "contrary to justice and even to morality," considering especially that there were "persons who refused to sell their property to the Germans."[350] Indeed, so much did this point of view prevail that indemnification was sometimes withheld even when duress was proved, the rationale being that the claimants already had received a *quid pro quo* from their German purchasers.[351] Simply put, claimants who benefited from World War II were not now to be shown special favor.

4. CLAIMANT BASE VALUES

Just as possession of certain base values (means for producing desired outcomes) is basic to successfully influencing decision-makers generally, so has possession of certain base values been basic to successfully influencing the French commissions specifically. Most comprehensively, of course, these have included all the integrants heretofore and hereinafter noted that have been necessary to obtain favorable judgment. Two items, however, unique to the

---

gation about the actuality of "duress" and that Article 3 of Additional Protocol No. 1 to the 1950 Czech Accord, which mentioned the claimant's ceded property by name as among the French properties believed to have been "spoliated" by the Germans, did not dispense with that duty. For an explication of this latter holding, see Gervais, *Revue de Jurisprudence Française en Matière Internationale*, 76 REV. DE DROIT PUB. ET DE SCI. POLITIQUE 870, 877–81 (1960). The author of this article contends that the naming of the claimant's ceded property in Article 3 of Additional Protocol No. I was only suggestive and that, in any event, because of Article 7 of the 1950 Accord —giving France exclusive competence in the matter of claims distribution—it could not be considered as binding on the Czech Commission in this connection. For a similar holding, see note 348 *supra*.

For Polish Commission cases wherein no "duress" was found, see FP 240 (1956); 355 (1958), *rev'd in part, Société anonyme de l'industrie textile*, [1964] Rec. Cons. d'Ét. 360, *modified on rehearing*, 584 (1967); 510–12 (1961). In reversing FP 240 in part, the *Conseil d'État* held that the Polish Commission had exceeded its competence in determining, pursuant to the *Ordonnance* of June 9, 1945, the amounts that the claimant was required to turn over to the French *Trésor*. This task, it observed, was a matter for the "ordre judiciaire." The decision was thus in keeping with its earlier decision, *Banque des Pays-Bas de l'Europe Centrale, supra*. For Yugoslav Commission cases wherein no "duress" was found, see FY 189–91, 193–99 (1955).

[350] FCz 1349 (1963), *modifying* FCz 191 (1957), *rev'd in part on other grounds, Union européenne industrielle financière*, [1963] Cons. d'Ét., Section du Contentieux, No. 61,371 (unpublished mimeo.). To like effect, see FP 257 (1956); 343, 408 (1957).

[351] *See* FCz 174, 192–94 (1957); 1349 (1963).

Egyptian claims program and each quickly dealt with, require mention at this point, not only because they implicate this phase of claim process but, as well, because they demonstrate that it is sometimes as much what claimants possess relative to one another as what they do or do not have in absolute terms that is important for decision. Neither of them to be found in the 1966 Egyptian Accord, each illustrates once again the prerogative role of the French Government in the matter of lump sum distribution.

Thus, quoting from the Egyptian Commission Constitutive Law, claimants wanting to share in the 1966 Egyptian lump sum "can have [already] recovered for their assets put under sequestration only property representing less than 20 percent of the value of the patrimony declared [by them] at the *service des biens et intérêts privés*."[352] Further, they "cannot have benefited from a transfer of an amount equal to or more than 1,000 Egyptian pounds, within the framework of article 4, paragraph (a), of the accord on transfers of 22 August 1958."[353] Accordingly, already in about 28 percent of the cases decided as of this writing, the Egyptian Commission has denied relief (1) to all claimants who, by whatever means, have secured, in money or in kind, more than 80 percent of the self-declared value of their non-restored, sequestered property,[354] and (2) to all claimants who, regardless of the quantum of their loss, have received more than 1,000 Egyptian pounds.[355] The rationale for these limitations apparently is to be found in the fact that an estimated nine hundred claimants are expected to share in the 300,000 Egyptian pound indemnity;[356] or, as they say in France, "to strip Peter to clothe Paul."

---

[352] Decree No. 68–103 of January 30, 1968, art. 5(d), [1968] J.O. 1228. The word "property" is translated from the word "biens," a term which under French law includes both corporeal and incorporeal wealth.

[353] *Id.*, art. 5(e). The transfer agreement referred to is to be found at [1958] J.O. 7925. Attached to, and made a part of the 1958 Zurich Accord (as to which, see Part II, note 34), its Article 4, paragraph (a) reads as follows: "Assets of natural persons referred to at articles 2 and 3 [*i.e.*, French persons whose property had been liquidated by Egypt and who were no longer authorized to reside in Egypt] shall be placed, within the limit of 5,000 Egyptian pounds per householder, in the accounts of non-residents and transferred pursuant to the payment Agreement."

[354] FE 13, 25, 29, 63, 67, 68, 70–72, 74, 76, 80, 83, 90, 91 (1969).

[355] FE 17, 19, 24, 26, 32, 34, 51, 56, 61, 77, 84, 98 (1969).

[356] Interview with Dervieu, in Paris, July 2, 1969.

5. Claimant Strategies

It is of course endemic to any claims process, formal or informal, that claimants must follow certain procedures if they expect to realize their objectives. At any rate, as the discussion should by now have made abundantly clear, such has been the obligation of postwar French commission claimants. Although simple letters rather than official forms are all that have been required to register claims, without timely application, without sufficient proofs of nationality, residence or title, without reasoned argument—in short, without observing all the registration and post-registration procedures that have been near uniformly required by the Statutory Instruments and Commission Rules, ordinarily no claimant can have expected to receive favorable treatment.

All of these registration and post-registration rules of procedure have already been noted.[357] Deserving special mention, however, mainly because they are the only pre-registration procedures that have been *expressly* required of French commission claimants,[358] are two stipulations that were set forth in the Egyptian Commission Constitutive Law, to wit, that indemnification would be restricted to claimants who shall have:

> (i) presented to the *service des biens et intérêts privés du minis-tère des affaires étrangères* between 1 October 1956 and 22 August 1958 a declaration of their assets put under sequestration in Egypt,[359] [and]
>
> (ii) made a request for removal of sequestration according to the

---

[357] *See generally* Part II, Section 3.

[358] The word "expressly" is used advisedly. In cases where claimants have sought indemnification because their property was placed under State administration (as in Czechoslovakia and Poland), the commissions have been unwilling to grant compensation unless the claimants were unsuccessful in obtaining restitution from the foreign authorities involved. For relevant discussion, see, *e.g.,* text at notes 202–203 *supra*. It is also to be noted that Article 1(c) of the 1950 Czech Accord, which authorized compensation to French interests already involved in "procédures en restitution" in Czechoslovakia, gave explicit although indirect approval to the use of pre-registration rehabilitative remedies.

[359] Decree No. 68–103 of January 30, 1968, art. 5(a), [1968] J.O. 1228. The reason for referring to October 1, 1956, is unclear, this date preceding by one month the day upon which French assets actually were "sequestered" by Egypt (November 1, 1956). The date August 22, 1958, is of course the date of signature of the 1958 Zurich Accord.

provisions of Article 2 of Protocol No. II annexed to the General Agreement of 22 August 1958.[360]

The first of these preconditions, nowhere to be found in the 1966 Egyptian Accord and therefore demonstrating again the French Government's prerogative role, has so far prevented only one claimant from sharing in the Egyptian Commission's lump sum distributions.[361] The second, however, originally set forth in the 1966 Egyptian Accord,[362] has proved dispositive on a number of occasions. Enforcing the stipulation, the Egyptian Commission has refused compensation, except in one instance thus far, to all claimants who have neglected to demand the restoration of their property as provided.[363] The one exception, a case in which the Commission refused to penalize a claimant for not having demanded restoration because he "acquired French nationality only after the expiration of the time authorized to request the . . . removal [of sequestration],"[364] makes clear that the Commission, strictly construing Protocol No. II to the 1958 Accord,[365] will condone application of this restriction in the future only against claimants who were French nationals before the end of the period allowed for restorative demand.[366]

6. OUTCOMES OF CLAIM

Faced with a claim proven to be eligible in all the respects thus far mentioned, it has remained for the French commissions to decide whether, on final analysis, reparation might be warranted for the particular kinds of losses actually sustained by their claimants (*i.e.*, whether the nature of the losses *per se* might justify any com-

---

[360] *Id.*, art. 5(c). The relevant provisions read as follows: "(a) French owners of property and titles put under sequestration by Egyptian authorities, or their trustees, shall address to the General Sequestration, directly or through an intermediary, within a year from the effective date of the General Agreement, a claim requesting a lifting of sequestration. (b) This claim will be made by registered letter with receipt and will be drawn up by an agent having power of attorney."

[361] *See* FE 87 (1969).

[362] *See* 1966 Egyptian Accord, arts. 2 and 4.

[363] FE 6, 8, 20, 23, 27, 31, 33, 42, 43, 45, 50, 53, 58, 62, 69, 73, 81, 88 (1969).

[364] FE 4 (1969).

[365] *See* note 360 *supra*.

[366] This construction is consistent with the nationality requirements of the Egyptian claims program. *See* text at note 33 *supra*.

pensation at all) and, if so, the measure of relief to be awarded. These are questions that of course hold considerable interest for lawyers and other students of the global economic process; however, not simply because the stability of international economic transaction depends upon knowledge about what and to what extent "property, rights, and interests" are protectable under international law. When seen as part of that wider synthesis we call the "Law of International Claims" (and "State Responsibility"), the answers to these questions, as earlier indicated, serve to qualify not only the character but, as well, the legitimacy of the protective responses that in the wider context invariably follow.[367]

A. Compensability of the Loss Per Se

With minor variation, all the Settlement Agreements have referred indiscriminately to "French interests" or to "biens, droits et intérêts français" (French property, rights, and interests) as the subject-matter of loss for which compensation should be given in principle.[368] Doubtless reflecting an attempt to clarify a confusion between forms or objects of wealth, on the one hand, and the interests or rights that are exercised over them, on the other—a confusion which contemporary civil law inherits from Rome and from which the common law is not immune—nonetheless this language has left much for interpretation. The remaining Controlling Texts, however, were to give it no greater precision. Accordingly, it has been for the French commissions, cognizant of French law, to give it meaning, to determine for themselves whether

---

[367] These answers are the same ones referred to earlier in the discussion concerning outcomes of the process of deprivation. See text at note 267 supra. They are dealt with here, however, because they constitute in fact the end results of the process of postwar French claim. A comprehensive analysis of the global process of deprivation of course would take these answers into account when trying to assess worldwide trends at the outcome stage of deprivative interaction. For details concerning the nature of the protective responses that emerge in the wider global context, see WESTON 117–65.

[368] See 1955 Bulgarian Accord, preamble and art. 1(a); 1967 Cuban Accord, preamble and art. 1; 1950 Czech Accord, preamble and art. 4; 1966 Egyptian Accord, arts. 1 and 4; 1950 Hungarian Accord, preamble; 1965 Hungarian Accord, preamble and art. 1; 1959 Romanian Accord, art. 1(a); 1951 Yugoslav Accord, preamble and art. 1; 1963 Yugoslav Accord, preamble and art. 2. The preamble and Articles 2 and 3 of the 1948 Polish Accord, as well as the text of its amendatory 1951 Protocol, refer simply to "French interests."

it was intended to refer to all or to only some kinds of wealth and wealth interest.

It has to be said at the outset, however, that on a number of occasions the commissions have been asked to grant compensation not for the loss of wealth itself, but for the loss of other values upon which the production, conservation, distribution, and consumption of wealth depend (*e.g.*, well-being, skill, enlightenment, power, respect, rectitude, affection):[369] (1) in the many State administration, exchange control, invasionary occupation, and similar cases wherein claimants have sought to safeguard against loss of proprietary control (power);[370] (2) in cases wherein the Czech, Egyptian, Romanian, and 1951 Yugoslav commissions have been asked to indemnify for loss of "clientèle," or future income based on goodwill (affection);[371] (3) in a 1965 Hungarian Commission case wherein relief was sought for loss of principal tenant status (respect);[372] (4) in a case wherein the Romanian Commission was asked to make an award for "physical and moral damages suffered by the claimant himself and members of his family" (well-being and/or rectitude);[373] and finally, (5) in a 1951 Yugoslav Commission case wherein the claimant sought compensation for loss of his employment as "manager" of a nationalized factory (well-being, power, respect).[374] In sum, the French commissions have from time to time been asked to attach a meaning to "biens, droits et intérêts français" that extends beyond the notion of property, or wealth, *stricto sensu*. Only in the first two of these groups of cases, however, have they agreed to do so; in the first group, only when loss of proprietary control has appeared permanent or irreversible; and

---

[369] For an indication of the nature and potential severity of these cognate losses in the wider global context, see WESTON 80–98.

[370] See *generally* text at notes 199–216, 248–257 *supra*.

[371] See FCz 109, 130 (1956)/FR 1358 (1962)/FY 103 (1954); 329 (1956); 855 (1961). The Egyptian Commission decisions do not reflect this fact. However, the author is advised that many of the Commission's decisions have involved consideration of "goodwill." See text at note 375 *infra*. For related and seemingly contradictory decisions involving claims for loss of "fonds de commerce," a concept that may include "goodwill," see note 387 and accompanying text *infra*. For relevant discussion on this point, see note 388 and accompanying text *infra*.

[372] See FH2d 38 (1967).

[373] See FR 694 (1961). See *also* FR 12 (1960) wherein a widow, unsuccessful possibly on other grounds, sought indemnification for loss of maintenance. For discussion concerning this case, see text at notes 107–109 *supra*.

[374] See FY 117 (1954).

in the second group, only in the instance of the Egyptian Commission where the majority of claimants have been small-time merchants "who [had] few assets besides goodwill."[375] Generally, non-wealth value losses have been treated as "dommages éventuels" (in contrast to "dommages certains") and therefore, in the commissions' collective opinion, so speculative or incapable of measurement as to preclude lump sum protection. Otherwise, unless for lack of sufficient funds to go about, it is difficult to explain why the Bulgarian, 1950 Hungarian, and Romanian commissions, although not asked to do so in so many words, have made no supplementary provision for anti-Semitic deprivations in Bulgaria, Hungary, and Romania which, in inflicting losses in "simple human respect," obviously worked injury to more than one "French interest."[376]

In other words, the French commissions have tended to read "French property, rights, and interests" not serially, but coordinately—*i.e.*, without the commas, as "French property rights and interests." On the other hand, in restricting compensation mainly to wealth losses *stricto sensu*, a posture that is not altogether in keeping with what is said to be customary practice,[377] the commissions have not gone so far as to consider every wealth loss as equally deserving of reparation. Distinctions are to be seen, most efficiently, in terms of (1) the corporeal and incorporeal wealth objects involved, and (2) the interests that attach to them. It is of course to be recognized that this demarcation is adopted without purporting to eliminate the conceptual redundancies that manifestly exist between so-called incorporeal things, on the one hand, and rights or interests in wealth, on the other.[378]

[375] Interview with Dervieu, in Paris, June 11, 1969. Postwar French practice thus may be seen to be somewhat at variance with American practice in this regard, and substantially at variance with British practice. *See* LILLICH (G.B.) 120.

[376] For details concerning these cases, see note 153 and notes 245–247 and accompanying text *supra*.

[377] *See, e.g.,* 2 O'CONNELL 1209, wherein the author sets forth a number of international tribunal decisions tending to grant reparation, in the presence of "international wrongs," for "impairement of livelihood," "loss of bread-winner," and "mental suffering." *See generally* M. WHITEMAN, *supra* note 266.

[378] Thus Wortley writes: "For the purposes of expropriation in its international aspects it is best to think of property as a 'thing', but not solely as a material or tangible thing (for what, indeed, is material in a world of commerce that deals with electricity, wireless waves, radioactive emanations and cosmic rays?), but as a 'thing' in the sense adopted by Pollock, that is, 'some possible matter of rights and duties conceived as a whole and apart from all others'. In modern Anglo-American legal

Compensability of Wealth Objects

CORPOREAL OBJECTS

Considering the vast number of award-winning claims for loss of corporeal wealth (using this term in a descriptive sense), only pedantry would justify documenting *ad infinitum* the many and diverse kinds of tangible losses that the French commissions have deemed reparable. Suffice it to say that these losses have concerned all kinds of corporeal property—"movable" and "immovable," "real" and "personal" (land and land growth, buildings and other structures, agricultural and industrial machinery, animal and rolling stock, commercial and domestic furnishings, crops and merchandise, personal effects)—and that in no known instance have the commissions denied relief by reason of the character of the tangible "thing" involved alone. Consistent with comparative and customary practice, seemingly all kinds of corporeal wealth have been considered "protectable," although, as shall be seen, not all rights or interests in them.[379]

INCORPOREAL OBJECTS

Compensation for loss of incorporeal wealth (again descriptively speaking) appears to have been less widely available. In dealing with this question, however—if by "incorporeal wealth" is meant, departing somewhat from French convention, rather the abstract entities that men are capable of owning in whole or in part[380] than the divisible ownership interests or interests less than ownership

---

thinking, 'things' which are the objects of ownership also include all varieties of rights and claims that can be lawfully transferred, or disposed of, or for that matter expropriated. Thus, under the term 'property' are included choses in action, that is, stocks, shares, bills of exchange, cheques, promissory notes, debentures, copyrights, patents and concessions, and also debts which amount to little more than rights or claims to sue, as well as contingent and defeasible interests which may never mature, but which are saleable or mortgageable; also treated as property are beneficial interests in trust funds which may be defeated by a conveyance of a legal estate to a *bona fide* purchaser for value. There is, indeed, no limit to the varieties of things which man's ingenuity can treat as property." WORTLEY 8–9 (footnotes omitted). For details from a common law perspective concerning French law "property" conceptions, including recognition of "the logically unsatisfactory character of the distinction between real rights (less than ownership) and incorporeal things," see F. LAWSON, A. ANTON, & L. BROWN, *supra* note 72, at 87–136.

[379] *See, e.g.,* FOIGHEL 214–19; S. FRIEDMAN, *supra* note 116, at 146–47; WORTLEY 8–12. *See also* M. WHITEMAN, *supra* note 256, at 956–1022, 1435–1547.

[380] *E.g.,* copyrights, patents, and trademarks.

(*démembrements de la propriété*) that men exercise over wealth[381]—the French commissions have been regrettably inexplicit. In writing their opinions, usually they have neglected to identify precisely, if at all, the wealth objects that have been the subject-matter of claim, and this neglect, of course, makes generalizations hazardous. Still, judging from the remarkable decisional uniformity that has generally prevailed among the commissions in the absence of express textual directives, it is reasonable to conclude that all the commissions have been disinclined in this setting, as in their decisions concerning non-wealth value losses, to make awards whenever the lost incorporeal object has in their opinion amounted to a "dommage éventuel" (*i.e.*, a speculative loss incapable of measurement).[382] Thus have the Czech, Polish, Romanian, and 1951 Yugoslav commissions each consistently denied relief, except in cases involving the premature termination of concessions,[383] for loss of future earnings or profits.[384] Thus has the Bulgarian Commission declined to indemnify for the loss of "minérai 'probable' " (*i.e.*, unextracted and unverified minerals) under a prematurely terminated mining concession.[385] Thus has the 1951 Yugoslav Commission denied relief for loss of a credit that it determined to be "uncertain and aleatory."[386] And thus also have the Polish, Romanian, and 1951 Yugoslav commissions refused to compensate for loss of "fonds de commerce,"[387] a French law conception which "is best translated as 'business', for like a business, it is a unit for practical but not for legal purposes. Its essential element is 'goodwill', the probability that it will keep its customers, but it is usually regarded as including also many other elements, such as name, patents, trade-marks, premises, plant, and even stock in trade."[388]

---

[381] *E.g.*, credits, easements, and inheritances.

[382] In customary international practice, this speculative status is sometimes referred to as "the remoteness of damage." *See* 2 O'CONNELL 1207–208.

[383] For discussion concerning the treatment accorded deprived concessionary interests, see text at notes 140–151 *supra*.

[384] FCz 130 (1956)/FP 103 (1954); 261 (1956)/FR 359, 465, 538, 694 (1961); 6805 (1966)/FY 749 (1960).

[385] FB 121 (1963).

[386] FY 747 (1960).

[387] FP 584 (1967)/FR 1358, 1579, 1853 (1962)/FY 104, 117 (1954); 254–55, 329, 335 (1956); 430, 434 (1957); 749 (1960); 873 (1961). *But cf.* note 389 and accompanying text *infra*.

[388] F. LAWSON, A. ANTON, & L. BROWN, *supra* note 72, at 98. The authors write,

However, because of contrary decisions rendered by the *Conseil d'État* in respect of two of the Romanian and one of the Yugoslav commission rulings, it appears that on final analysis the loss of *fonds de commerce* is to be viewed as within the meaning of "French property, rights and interests" and, therefore, compensable in post-war French practice.[389]

Compensability of Wealth Interests

CO-OWNERSHIP INTERESTS

The compensability of deprived co-ownership interests—here meaning all forms of common or joint ownership exclusive of those held in commercial and non-commercial legal entities—was nowhere expressly detailed in the Settlement Agreements (or any of the other Controlling Texts). Any suggestion that these interests were to be indemnified therefore has had to be deduced, if not from

---

subsequently, that "[t]his term, which is sometimes mistranslated as goodwill, has no precise equivalent in English, for it embraces both the tangible and intangible assets of a business, including tools, equipment, materials, stock, goodwill, trade marks and patents, business-name, and the lease of the place of business together with the right to its renewal. . . . To some extent the *fonds de commerce* is regarded as an entity distinct from the elements which compose it. . . . To speak in English of owning or selling 'a business' comes very close to the French concept." *Id.* at 343. For a detailed but not inconsistent analysis of *fonds de commerce* by a well-known French authority, see G. RIPERT, *supra* note 72, at 231–88. *See also* Lehmann, *Le fonds de commerce en droit international privé*, 6 JURIS-CLASSEUR DE DROIT INT'L, Fasc. 562.

[389] Decisions FR 1853 (1962), FY 335 (1956), and FY 873 (1961) were appealed to the *Conseil d'État* and in each case annulled. *See*, respectively, *Sieur Verglas*, [1964] Cons. d'Ét., Section du Contentieux, No. 59,696 (unpublished mimeo.); *Sieur Couhadoux*, [1962] Rec. Cons. d'Ét. 629; and *Société orientale d'oxygène et d'acétylène dissous (S.O.D.A.D.)*, [1965] Rec. Cons. d'Ét. 163. Each of these decisions was rendered on identical grounds. Quoting from the most recent, *Société orientale*, the *Conseil* observed "that it results clearly from . . . [the] text [of the 1951 Yugoslav Accord], considering the generality of the terms employed, that it allows indemnification for the privation of all patrimonial elements and, in particular, in the case of an industrial or commercial enterprise, the total value of the said enterprise, including all the material property, securities, liquid assets, credits and incorporeal rights calculable in money and constituting the capital of the enterprise." Despite this unequivocal language, however, it is not altogether clear that compensation for loss of *fonds de commerce* is always to be granted in French practice. For example, Polish Commission decision FP 584 (*supra* note 387), denying compensation for loss of *fonds de commerce*, was but a reaffirmation of an earlier ruling involving the same case. *See* FP 355 (1958). This earlier decision was annulled by the *Conseil d'État* and returned to the Polish Commission, but without comment on this question, notwithstanding that one of the reasons for the "annulation" was the fact that FP 355 had been based on erroneous expert advice in respect of valuation. *See Société anonyme de l'industrie textile*, [1964] Rec. Cons. d'Ét. 360.

some non-textual indices of diplomatic expectation, strictly from the general language of these agreements. At any rate, except for the Cuban and Egyptian commissions which because of their youth have yet to consider the matter, this is what the French commissions seem to have done, extending protection as they have to many claimants (mainly spouses and co-heirs) who in varying ratio have held joint and severable, but neither co-contractual nor joint stock, ownership in appropriated property of one sort or another[390]—again a pattern that appears consistent with comparative and customary practice.[391]

In sum, one searches in vain for any decision in which compensation has been withheld by reason of co-ownership alone. However, at least two negative decisions merit comment, one by the Bulgarian Commission and the other by the 1965 Hungarian Commission, each of them demonstrating that rote adherence to legal technicalities that surround co-ownership in the presence of the French nationality rule can bring about preclusive and, in this writer's view, absurd results. The Bulgarian Commission decision concerned a claim for loss of community property (*communauté de biens*) held by the claimant, at all key times a French national, and her husband, a Spaniard. The Commission denied relief on the grounds that Spanish law, the law ordinarily "governing" the community property by virtue of the husband's nationality, made the claimant's community

---

[390] *See* FB 48, 67, 68, 75 (1962); 94, 101, 104, 111, 127 (1963); 140–43, 147–51, 163, 166, 173 (1964); 180 (1965)/FCz 24 (1954); 52, 54, 58 (1955); 78, 79, 84, 87, 90, 114–15, 145 (1956); 160, 164–65, 185–86, 190, 202, 204, 219 (1957); 258, 405, 418, 650 (1958); 680, 793, 954, 994–95 (1959); 1103 (1960); 1350 (1963)/FH 18, 122, 129, 138 (1953); 185, 201 (1954); 251–52, 261, 269, 271, 275–77 (1956)/FH2d 12, 14, 16, 17, 23, 27, 28, 33, 37, 39, 45, 47, 49, 52, 54 (1967); 61, 64, 69–72 (1968)/FP 105, 108, 136, 138–39, 147, 154 (1954); 169, 187–89, 207, 214 (1955); 221–22, 232 (1956); 286–87, 295, 322 (1957); 328, 357, 362, 364, 383, 401 (1958); 406, 415, 423, 436–37, 450, 452 (1959); 461, 463, 468, 473, 478 (1960); 499, 502 (1961); 520 (1962); 548 (1964); 578 (1966)/FR 70 (1960); 209, 229, 235, 292, 299, 300, 359, 363, 392, 397, 400, 428, 465, 468, 504, 580, 762 (1961); 816, 894, 946, 1007, 1028, 1125, 1341, 1353, 1355, 1439, 1577, 1650, 1714, 1717, 1893, 1912–14, 1983–84, 2023 (1962); 2217, 2242, 2372, 2491, 2518, 2590, 2873, 2924, 2926–27, 2948, 3004, 3138, 3227 (1963); 3597, 4013, 4052–53, 4130, 4308, 4424 (1964); 4512, 4773, 5250 (1965); 6805, 7014, 7029 (1966); 7387 (1967)/FY 69 (1953); 91 (1954); 233, 242, 252, 311, 330, 334 (1956); 341, 343, 392 (1957); 513, 523 (1958); 605, 746 (1959); 748 (1960); 857 (1961)/FY2d 39, 47–50 (1966); 60 (1967); 71 (1968).

[391] This pattern is more implicitly than explicitly to be found among the scholarly commentaries. *See,* in particular, LILLICH (G.B.) 24–59; LILLICH (U.S.) 71–101; LILLICH & CHRISTENSON 7–25, 40–51.

interest, despite her own French nationality, Spanish-owned and therefore outside the protection afforded by the 1955 Bulgarian Accord.[392] The 1965 Hungarian Commission decision concerned a claim for loss of a building owned half by the claimant, again at all key times a French national, and half by two Hungarian companies. Because at the time of nationalization the building had been registered in the local "land office" in the name of the two Hungarian companies, the Commission held that the building was Hungarian-owned and consequently outside the protection given by the 1965 Hungarian Accord.[393] From the standpoint of "private international law" (or "conflict of laws"), one of course wants to know more about the facts in these cases. On their face, however, one is led to ask what conceivable French or other policy interests could possibly have been served by these results? Regrettably, bearing in mind the uniformity of decision that has prevailed among the commissions, probably the same results would have obtained among the other commissions given the same or similar facts.

SHAREHOLDER INTERESTS

Only one of the French commissions, the Egyptian Commission, has yet to deal with the compensability of deprived shareholder interests—here meaning all forms of common or joint ownership in commercial and non-commercial legal entities (including "stockholder" interests, *stricto sensu*). Again this is a result of the but recent functioning of the Egyptian Commission. But not entirely. Most if not all deprived stockholder interests, it will be recalled, were to be compensated in accordance with the 1964 Egyptian Accord[394]—not the 1966 Egyptian Accord—and this arrangement, in turn, meant that lump sum distribution for these interests was to proceed along different lines (*i.e.,* according to "la répartition administrative").[395] The point merits recollection not only because it reclarifies the operation of the Egyptian Commission or because it highlights that stockholder interests deprived in Egypt were not to go uncompensated, but as well because it is a reminder that

392 FB 128 (1963).
393 FH2d 36 (1967).
394 *See* Part II, note 56.
395 *See* text at Part II, notes 67–72.

creditor claims need not have been the only claims relegated to administrative distribution in postwar French practice. Of course, the fact that stockholder interests have not been eligible to share in Egyptian Commission distributions tells one nothing about how the Egyptian Commission might approach compensating other deprived shareholder interests (including other stockholder interests, if any). Since the Commission has yet to rule on the matter, however, and since none of its Controlling Texts offer any guidance, the answer to this question cannot be given at this time.

On the other hand, most of the other French commissions have dealt with the issue, albeit with varying precision and to varying degree (*e.g.*, the Cuban Commission thus far in one case only).[396] To understand their decisions, largely but not entirely the result of explicit or implicit directives contained in their Settlement Agreements and Statutory Instruments,[397] it is helpful to distinguish between "direct" and "indirect" shareholder claims—*i.e.*, claims based on shares held in the target entity and claims based on shares held in an intermediary entity which, in turn, maintains a share interest in the target entity.[398] In so doing, however, it is important to recognize that in no known instance have the commissions withheld compensation because the wealth interest has been *per se* shareholder in character.

[396] *See* text at note 412 *infra.* It appears also that, as of this writing, the 1965 Hungarian and 1963 Yugoslav commissions have been almost wholly if not completely inactive in this regard, presumably because of the nature of the deprivative measures actually undertaken during the periods covered by the 1965 Hungarian and 1963 Yugoslav accords. At any rate, the author is unaware of any formal restriction against the presentation of shareholder claims to these commissions. Indeed, the 1963 Yugoslav Accord explicitly mentions shareholder interests among its provisions. *See* note 397 *infra.*

[397] Only five of the Settlement Agreements were drafted to include explicit reference to shareholder interests, although it is not clear, in their translation, whether the references are exclusively to stockholder interests, *stricto sensu*, or to all kinds of shareholder interests, including what can loosely be called partnership interests. See 1955 Bulgarian Accord, art. 5 (referring to "actionnaire"); 1948 Polish Accord, art. 4 (referring to "participation"); 1959 Romanian Accord, art. 3 (referring to "actionnaire"); 1951 Yugoslav Accord, art. 5 (referring to "participation"); 1963 Yugoslav Accord, art. 2 (referring to "participation"). As shall be seen, the commissions have been indifferent about this potential distinction. The complete silence of the other Settlement Agreements regarding shareholder interests was indirectly overcome by the laws pursuant to which the Cuban, Czech, and two Hungarian commissions were constituted. *See* text at Part II, note 167.

[398] The same distinction has been made in postwar American and British practice. *See* Lillich (U.S.) 90–94; Lillich (G.B.) 40–52.

Consider, first, direct shareholder interests. Provided that the actual target of deprivation, distinct from the proprietary interests in it, could properly be designated a French or deprivor-State entity, and that if French or French-controlled it was not itself to act as primary claimant,[399] the commissions have had little or no difficulty in extending aliquot protection:[400] occasionally to non-stock interests in *associations* and in what may be loosely called partnerships (*sociétés en nom collectif* and *sociétés en commandite simple*); and in literally thousands of cases to both majority and minority stock interests—"active" and "inactive," "common" and "privileged"—in *sociétés anonymes* or *sociétés en commandite par actions*.[401] When, however, the direct interest (stock or non-stock) has attached to a target entity that has owed its legal existence to a third State, not a frequent occurrence, the commissions have each time refused to make an award.[402] Precisely why they have ruled in this manner is not very clear, and regrettably so. Considering that the Settlement Agreements have been silent or ambiguous on the point and that the French Commission Constitutive Laws have implied that claims based on direct share ownership in third-State targets were to be compensated,[403] the preclusive French nationality rule invoked by the commissions is plainly inadequate as an explanation. Probably at work, taking into account the rationale that lies behind the virtually identical results that have obtained in postwar British practice,[404] has been the traditional formalistic notion,

[399] *See* text at Part II, note 167.

[400] Direct shareholder (mainly "stockholder") claims have constituted by far the bulk of the cumulative work of the French commissions, so much so that the decisions of the commissions in this connection are frequently to be found in multiple mimeograph form, modified only to fit the facts of each case. For example, the Romanian Commission alone has awarded compensation to deprived stockholders in over 7,000 instances as of this writing. To cite each of these decisions would of course be uneconomical. Further, believing that the discussion and references which follow fulfill adequately the purpose of documentation, it is unnecessary.

[401] For discussion concerning the nature of these various kinds of "moral persons" under French law, see F. LAWSON, A. ANTON, & L. BROWN, *supra* note 72, at 47–57, 345–55. For lengthy consideration, limited to commercial companies (*sociétés*), see G. RIPERT, *supra* note 72, at 289–717.

[402] *See* FB 76 (1962)/FCz 692, 812, 976 (1959)/FH 275, 280, 284, 298 (1955); TV709, TV715, TV758–70 (1958); TV773–74 (1959)/FR 3478 (1964); 5385, 5870 (1965); 7219, 7303 (1967)/FY 1 (1953); 108–11 (1954); 315 (1956).

[403] *See* text at Part II, note 167.

[404] *See* LILLICH (G.B.) 42–47.

recently buttressed by *Barcelona Traction*,[405] that a shareholder interest is not protectable until there is no possibility that the "primary claim" of the third-State target can be satisfied, and even then not until appropriate arrangements have been made between the States capable of espousing the claims involved.[406] This perspective, however, is scarcely sensitive to present-day realities. Further, a better, more sensible approach is possible. As Lillich has remarked, the traditional view "presupposes a degree of cooperation between claimant countries which is simply nonexistent . . . [and moreover] provides an excellent opportunity for a taking state to avoid paying just compensation for the foreign property it has nationalized . . . . A simple solution . . . is to reverse the presumption, i.e., to allow such claims unless the third state already has entered into an agreement *expressly covering* their interests."[407]

French commission decisions concerning the protectability of deprived indirect shareholder interests, vastly fewer but about as consistent as the foregoing, are both paradoxical and questionable. Thus, whenever the stock or non-stock interest has attached to a deprivor-State intermediary, so far a circumstance with which apparently only the Bulgarian Commission has had to deal, protection has been extended[408]—a resolution that is not a little curious considering that such indirect interests are at least formally more removed than the non-compensable share interests that are held directly in third-State enterprises.[409] Conversely, whenever the share interest has attached to a third-State intermediary, a circumstance that has faced the Bulgarian, Czech, 1950 Hungarian, Polish, and Romanian commissions, compensation has been withheld,[410] evi-

---

405 [1970] I.C.J. 3 (Second Phase).

406 For indication that at least the 1951 Yugoslav Commission has assumed these arrangements to be necessary, see FY 102 (1954); 855 (1961).

407 LILLICH (G.B.) 45. Lillich goes on to point out that "Annex A(g) of the United States-Polish Agreement of 1960, codifying this presumption, specifically allows all such claims except those 'which are compensable through any other international agreement to which Poland is a party.'" *Id.* 45–46.

408 *See* FB 100 (1963); 184–85, 189 (1965).

409 For like holdings in Great Britain, see LILLICH (G.B.) 48–49.

410 FCz 1325 (1961); 1327 (1962); 1355 (1964)/FB 34 (1961)/FH 291 (1955)/FP 99 (1953); 210 (1955)/FR 434 (1961); 3721–22, 3724, 3742, 4259 (1964). Czech Commission decision FCz 1325 was the result of numerous appeals to the *Conseil d'État*. For details, explaining the reasoning behind it, see note 26 *supra*. Polish Commission decision FP 210 was affirmed on appeal without added comment. *Société*

dently notwithstanding the amount of French control involved[411] and again, presumably, out of concern for that illusive interstate cooperation which could avoid double recovery. A possible exception, a case in which the Cuban Commission granted relief, regrettably defies firm classification because the Commission neglected to identify the nationality of the intermediary.[412] If Cuban, obviously the decision joins the first group of Bulgarian decisions mentioned above. If a third-State entity, however, the decision represents a significant departure from standard French practice, and arguably a salutary one. Too great a reluctance to "pierce the corporate veil" can lead to absurd results, as indeed it has in at least one of the negative decisions cited.[413] A decision of the Bulgarian Commission, it concerned a French stockholder of an intermediary company whose Swiss *siège* prompted the stockholder to request relief from the Swiss Government under the lump sum agreement between Switzerland and Bulgaria of November 26, 1964.[414] Because the intermediary was 65 percent French-owned, 30 percent Bulgarian-owned, and only 5 percent Swiss-owned, the Swiss, on a "substantial interest" theory of corporate nationality, rejected the claim. None of these facts appear to have made much impression upon the Bulgarian Commission, however. Adhering rigidly to a *siège social* theory of corporate nationality, it refused relief and thereby left the stockholder (and the intermediary company) without recourse. Along the way, it demonstrated vividly the illusiveness of interstate cooperation in this area and at the same time gave outlet to confiscatory ambitions.

CREDITOR INTERESTS

A great number of "creditor claims," also known as "contract claims" or "debt claims," have been brought before the French commissions: claims for principal or interest due on public and private bond issues; claims for sums owing on unblocked cash and

---

Celtex, [1961] Rec. Cons. d'Ét. 24. Romanian Commission decision FR 434 was affirmed on appeal to the *Conseil d'État. Époux Cassel,* [1963] Cons. d'Ét., Section du Contentieux, No. 55,697 (unpublished mimeo.).

[411] *See, e.g.,* FB 34 (1961), discussed in the text at note 413 *infra.*

[412] *See* FC 2 (1968).

[413] *See* FB 34 (1961).

[414] Botschaft nr. 6749, 8.2.55.

credit accounts; claims for amounts due on employment, pension, sales, rental, and licensing agreements; and so forth. The vast majority of these creditor claims, deprivative and "ordinary," have been ruled to be outside the reach of commission protection. In major part these denials have been due to one or both of two distinct but overlapping reasons: first, to the creditor claims having been omitted from the Settlement Agreements or, if covered, to their having been relegated to "la répartition administrative"—in which events, as earlier recounted, the commissions have lacked the competence to grant the distributions requested;[415] and second, to the absence or non-proof of any actual debt or debtor "taking" (*i.e.*, any manifest refusal to pay or inability to recover)—in which events, again as noted, the claims have been treated as ordinary commercial debts, or "payements courants," whose settlement has been or might be covered by alternative regimes likewise outside French commission jurisdiction.[416] Among all the commissions, indeed, only the 1963 Yugoslav Commission has been in any way relieved from invoking these rationales, it having been uniquely free, it will be recalled, to indemnify "*all* debt claims [deprivative and "ordinary"] existing prior to 15 May 1945" and held by French nationals "against Yugoslav natural or juridical persons or the Yugoslav State."[417]

These rationales (or eligibility preconditions) are of course among the many already noted that have served to preclude recovery for deprivation claims generally. In fact, with modest exception to be noted below, these and the other prerequisites generally applicable

---

[415] For relevant discussion, see text at notes 336–344 *supra*.

[416] For relevant discussion, see text at notes 268–304 *supra*.

[417] 1963 Yugoslav Accord, art. 2. For relevant discussion, see text at Part II, notes 124–129, 154–158. In accordance with Article 2 of the 1963 Accord, the 1963 Yugoslav Commission as of this writing has authorized indemnification of "ordinary" debt claims (mainly commercial contract claims) in five different cases. See FY2d 36, 53–55 (1966); 67 (1967). It has disallowed indemnification in two cases without explanation. See FY2d 7, 16 (1965).

A *Conseil d'État* ruling concerning a Yugoslav Commission decision which this writer has been unable to locate also deserves mention, demonstrating as it does that certain deprivative debt claims are to enjoy a special advantage over other kinds of deprivation claims under the 1963 Accord. According to the *Conseil*, the Commission rejected a creditor claim that was based on a deprivation measure taken against the debtor because the deprivation was effected at a time preceding the period covered by the 1963 Accord in respect of deprivation claims—*i.e.*, April 14, 1951 (the signature date of the 1951 Accord) to July 12, 1963 (the signature date of the

appear to be the only restrictions that have been placed upon what may be called primary creditor claims (*i.e.*, claims based on credits owned by the actual targets of deprivation). But as some of the commission decisions demonstrate, even if jurisdictional competence were present, even if "extinction" were proved, and even if all the other general eligibility requirements were met, protection of secondary creditor claims (*i.e.*, claims based on credits owned by the creditors of the actual targets of deprivation) has by no means been guaranteed. This is seen in at least four instances, the first two unique to the claims programs involved.

First, according to the "Protocole Additionnel No. 1" to the 1950 Czech Accord, compensation under the Czech claims program was to be extended "[t]o credits held, for whatever reason, against Czechoslovak companies by [French nationals] who at the same time hold at least a 50 percent participation in these same companies."[418] The language is not necessarily limitative, especially when read in conjunction with Article 2 of the 1950 Accord which provides that "all French interests affected" by Czech deprivative measures were to be covered by the settlement. Except in nine cases, however, doubtless moved by the principle *expressio unius est exclusio alterius* but in any event bolstered by the *Conseil d'État*, the Czech Commission rendered a restrictive rather than broad interpretation, granting relief only to secondary creditors who could show at least 50 percent ownership of the appropriated Czech firms in question,[419] denying compensation when they could not.[420]

1963 Accord). Indeed, it appears that the debtor "taking" was effected during the period covered by the 1951 settlement. Accordingly, it is not illogical that the Commission should have rejected the claim as apparently it did. Probably it treated the claim much as it would any tardy claim unexcused by a *force majeure* (in which connection see note 313 *supra*). The *Conseil d'État* annulled the Commission's decision, however, contending that since the deprivative debt claim had accrued prior to May 15, 1945, it should have been entitled to the benefits allowed by the above-quoted second paragraph of Article 2 of the 1963 Accord. See *Sieur Julliard*, [1966] Cons. d'Ét., Section du Contentieux, No. 67,684 (unpublished mimeo.).

[418] 1950 Czech Accord, "Protocole Additionnel No. 1," para. 1(b).

[419] FCz 9 (1953); 64, 80, 85, 114, 120, 126 (1956); 155, 175 (1957).

[420] FCz 4, 9 (1953); 29 (1954); 55, 72–76 (1955); 91, 93–94, 103–109, 111–13, 124–25, 131–35, 142 (1956); 150, 156, 179, 197, 206 (1957); 260, 366, 370–93, 402, 420, 427, 622, 626 (1958); 681, 701, 728–29, 793, 883, 885–86, 901, 993–94 (1959); 1059, 1064, 1125, 1194–96 (1960); 1287 (1961). In rejecting an appeal arising out of decision FCz 420, the *Conseil d'État* confirmed that French debt claims held against nationalized firms could be indemnified only if the claimants owned at least 50

The sole exceptions, if in fact they can be called exceptions, are six cases in which the Commission granted relief for deposit accounts actually appropriated by the Czech authorities upon the nationalization of the various debtor banks,[421] and three cases in which it authorized indemnification for some debts "repudiated" by the Czech "Fonds de l'Économie Nationalisée" following the nationalization of a Czech debtor firm.[422] Doubtless the Commission looked upon these creditor claims as primary rather than secondary in character.

Next, under the 1951 and 1963 Yugoslav claims programs protection could be extended, per Article 5 of the 1951 Accord (incorporated by reference into the 1963 Accord),[423] to creditor interests held against deprived Yugoslav companies by "French . . . persons holding majority participation [therein]"[424] and to "French . . . persons holding credits against [deprived] companies subject to Yugoslav law with French majority participation."[425] The language is ambiguous in its apparent redundancy, leaving at issue whether compensation might be had for debt claims held by minority shareholders against French-controlled Yugoslav companies. Further, like the 1950 Czech settlement, it is susceptible of liberal rather than narrow construction—*i.e.,* as authorizing indemnification not only to the secondary creditors named, but as well, for example, to postwar creditors holding claims against deprived Yugoslav individuals or against deprived Yugoslav companies with French minority participation. Judging from two cases decided by the 1951 Commission, each relevant to the first issue mentioned, creditor claims held by minority French shareholders against French-controlled Yugoslav companies have been deemed admissible.[426]

---

percent of the capital of the firms in question. *Société des Laboratoires de Reuilly,* [1962] Rec. Cons. d'Ét. 629.

421 FCz 57, 60–61 (1955); 80 (1956); 346 (1958); 692 (1959). Most of these cases involved the "confiscation" of German reichsmark accounts. In decision FCz 57, the Commission awarded compensation because the claimant's deposit had been transferred to the Czech Fund for Reconstruction and this transfer meant that the claimant "lost the right freely to dispose of her deposit." For related decisions, see notes 185–194, 217–224 and accompanying text *supra.*

422 FCz 96–88 (1956). For relevant discussion, see text at notes 185–194 *supra.*

423 *See* 1963 Yugoslav Accord, art. 4, incorporating *"mutatis mutandis . . .* Articles 3 to 9 inclusive of the Franco-Yugoslav Accord of 14 April 1951."

424 1951 Yugoslav Accord, art. 5(2).

425 *Id.* art. 5(3).

426 *See* FY 116, 123 (1954).

Whether the provisions are to be broadly or narrowly construed, on the other hand, is a question that must remain unanswered, there being no known instance in which a secondary creditor claim has been raised by persons not mentioned in the Yugoslav accords. Of course, the absence of any known claims of this kind may of itself be indicative that a restrictive interpretation has obtained. If so, it would be consistent with the above-noted approach of the Czech Commission.

Third, two negative decisions rendered by the Polish Commission make clear that, at least under the Polish claims program, creditors holding claims against French debtor firms have had to show that the deprived French debtor itself has not sought redress for, or "taken charge of," the debts in question.[427] Reminiscent of the "primary rights" accorded French companies against their shareholders, presumably this precondition has borne upon all the claims programs— at least where, as was true in the case of the Polish nationalizations, only the property and not the existence of debtors has been adversely affected.[428] At any rate, there is nothing in the various Controlling Texts to suggest otherwise.

Fourth, one Polish Commission decision disallowed relief because the creditor had earlier "reserved direct recourse" against the injured but existing debtor firm involved (again a French firm).[429] Common sense dictates that the same results would obtain among the other commissions given like circumstances and reservations.

One last item bears consideration, alluded to above and applicable to primary and secondary creditor interests alike. As mentioned in passing, secondary creditor claims brought under the Czech and two Yugoslav accords, to the extent that they have been honored at all, have had to be held against nationalized or otherwise taken *Czechoslovak* and *Yugoslav* companies, respectively.[430] Similarly, all creditor claims brought under Article 2 of the 1963 Yugoslav Accord and existing before 15 May 1945 have had to be held "against *Yugoslav* natural or juridical persons or the *Yugoslav* State."[431] Except to this limited extent, however, neither the Settlement Agreements nor any of the other Controlling Texts have conditioned

---

427 *See* FP 37 (1953); 265 (1965). The quotation is from the first of these decisions.
428 *See* 1948 Polish Accord, art. 2.
429 FP 46 (1953).
430 *See* text at notes 418 & 424–425 *supra*. (Emphases added.)
431 Emphases added.

creditor claim indemnification expressly upon the debtor being a
national of the payor State—or, for that matter, France. Indeed,
in only one known case, decided by the 1963 Yugoslav Commission
pursuant to Article 2 of the 1963 Yugoslav Accord, has a creditor
been denied relief because of debtor nationality, *i.e.*, a primary
creditor claim held by a nationalized French *société anonyme*
against a Hungarian company.[432] This general silence suggests, of
course, that indemnification of creditor claims held against French
or third-State debtors generally has been allowed. At any rate, judging from the Polish Commission decisions just reported,[433] the only
decisions known to involve French debtors and each withholding
relief clearly on other grounds, this seems a fair conclusion as concerns debt claims held against French nationals. As for debt claims
held against third-State nationals, on the other hand, none but the
unsuccessful 1963 Yugoslav Commission case mentioned being known
to have arisen as of this writing, the answer is unclear. However,
recalling the pattern that has been established vis-à-vis shareholder interests and bearing in mind that each of the payor governments in each settlement obtained a release of French claims
against only themselves and their nationals, it is unlikely that
such claims have been deemed eligible for relief.[434] Regrettably,
owing as much to the elliptic quality of the commissions' opinions as
to the dearth of claims of this kind, conclusions must now remain
tentative.

In summary, then, but for the minor exceptions noted, virtually
all kinds of deprivative debt claims—primary and secondary, secured and unsecured—have had standing before the French commissions. With little or no express guidance from the Settlement
Agreements or other Controlling Texts,[435] the commissions have

[432] FY 64 (1967).

[433] *See* text at notes 427–429 *supra*.

[434] One other decision, again rendered by the Polish Commission, tends to confirm this view. *See* FP 22 (1952). The Commission rejected a secondary creditor
claim held against a company created under Polish law but having its *siège* outside
Polish territory. On the other hand, in light of Article 2 of the 1948 Polish Accord,
it may be that the debtor company never was nationalized and therefore the debt
claim itself never abrogated.

[435] Except for the 1950 Czech and two Yugoslav accords already noted, only the
1955 Bulgarian and 1959 Romanian accords were drafted with express reference to
debt claims, and then only in the most cursory way. *See* 1955 Bulgarian Accord,
art. 5; 1959 Romanian Accord, art. 3. The other Controlling Texts have been altogether silent in this regard.

adopted generally a liberal rather than a narrow approach toward the repair of these interests, granting compensation whenever pre-conditions applicable to all deprived wealth interests have allowed.[436] Save arguably under the Czech and two Yugoslav claims programs, none appear to have been foreclosed by reason of creditor status *per se*. In this respect, postwar French practice may be seen to have contributed markedly to a current tendency to compensate deprived creditor interests, particularly secondary creditor interests, that in equivalent American and British experience has grown more reluctantly or gradually.[437] From a perspective which maintains that it is possible to assure simultaneously increased confidence and stability in international economic transaction on the one hand, and progressive idiosyncratic development of national economic orders on the other, this trend is a salutary one—at least within the industrially advanced world where one can presume a minimum capacity to pay.

MISCELLANEOUS INTERESTS

As may be rightly supposed, claims bearing upon harm done to single proprietorship, co-ownership, shareholder, and creditor interests have constituted by far the bulk of the work of the French commissions, especially the first and third of these. On a few occasions, however, the commissions have had opportunity to consider claims concerning harm done to at least two other kinds of wealth interests, and since comprehensiveness can be a virtue they

---

[436] *See* FB 46 (1961); 48, 49, 82, 83, 90 (1962); 100, 107–108, 116, 120–22, 125, 129 (1963); 172 (1964); 182, 184–85, 188–89, 192, 196 (1965); 200 (1966)/FC 5, 8 (1969)/FCz 9 (1953); 64 (1955); 80, 85, 114, 120, 126 (1956); 155, 175 (1957)/FE 28, 30, 33 (1969)/FH TV771 (1959), referring to 2,178 claimants, many but not all of whom were creditor claimants; TV775 (1959)/FP 9, 11, 16–18 (1952); 28–30, 32, 33, 36, 48, 50–52, 54, 58, 62, 64, 68, 76, 84, 87, 88, 99 (1953); 108, 112–14, 124, 127–28, 136, 145 (1954); 166, 168, 190, 209 (1955); 220, 222, 224, 227, 236, 239, 256, 264–65 (1956); 272, 294, 322–23 (1957); 336, 357, 366 (1958); 488 (1960); 566 (1965); 571 (1966)/FR 15, 16 (1960); 117, 237, 256, 310–11, 352–53, 358–59, 431, 465, 538, 587, 694, 696, 763 (1961); 896, 972, 1030–31, 1101, 1237, 1309, 1360, 1441, 1505, 1579, 1719, 1790, 1811, 1854 (1962); 2638, 3227 (1963); 3866, 4258 (1964); 4514, 4779, 4903, 4907, 5250, 5386 (1965); 6788, 6805 (1966); 7126, 7299 (1967)/FY 89 (1953); 116, 123 (1954); 237, 241, 313 (1956); 421, 427 (1957); 520, 527–29 (1958); 606 (1959); 747 (1960); 855 (1961); 863 (1962)/FY2d 24 (1965); 36 (1966); 64 (1967).

[437] *See* LILLICH (G.B.) 76–104; Note, *The Jurisprudence of the Foreign Claims Settlement Commission of the United States: Creditor Claims*, 16 SYRACUSE L. REV. 809 (1965).

merit review. Regrettably, owing to their isolated character and again to the terseness of the commissions' opinions, little more than a report is possible.

Usufructuary Interests. Claimants seeking compensation for loss of usufructs, or "usufruits"—a civil law conception not unlike the common law's life tenancy—have come before the French commissions thus far on three known occasions, each time asserting interests in real property and each time before a different commission. Without express guidance from their Controlling Texts, one of the commissions (the Romanian Commission) extended protection;[438] the two others (the 1950 Hungarian and 1951 Yugoslav commissions) did not.[439] The apparent contradiction is not explained. However, the distinguishing factor appears to have been the French nationality rule. Thus, in the Romanian Commission case the real property owner was a French national, whereas in the Hungarian and Yugoslav commission cases the real property owners were foreign nationals. In other words, postwar French practice appears to say, albeit on the basis of slim evidence, that usufructuaries will be protected only if the full owner has French nationality.

Third-Party Beneficial Interests. Although there have been many French commission cases involving insurance and other contracts, apparently (and surprisingly) only one of these cases has thus far produced a third-party beneficial interest claim, in this one case by reason of the nationalization of an insurance company.[440] Cryptically, the Romanian Commission rejected the claim "en raison de son caractère et de son imprécision."[441] Obviously, little if anything can be drawn from this statement.

B. The Measure and Mode of Compensation

In order to understand properly the measure and mode of French commission distributions, it has to be recalled that decisions were reached earlier at the diplomatic level that something less than "full compensation" was to be paid for deprivations sustained by

---

[438] FR 430 (1961).
[439] FH 267 (1955)/FY 249 (1954).
[440] *See* FR 1811 (1962).
[441] *Id.*

French nationals.[442] Of course, the fact that these decisions were rendered by diplomats instead of judges (or commissioners) does not make them any less decisions or any less noteworthy. Rather, it serves to remind us that these decisions resulted from many more and more widely diverse conditioning factors than are ordinarily to be found in highly structured decisional arenas, and that it is for this reason that one finds the argument that the decisions were ones of socioeconomic and political expediency—*i.e.*, political and not legal decisions. The jurisprudential knife cuts both ways, however. For just as some will say that a decision to accept less than "prompt, adequate and effective" compensation is a political decision, so will others say that a decision to make any payment is a political decision. Accordingly, to insist that these diplomatically rendered, partial compensation decisions were not legal decisions is to engage in self-defeatism. For however few the supportive controls, a need to indemnify was acknowledged, and this acknowledgment is not something that recipient countries are likely to forget or ignore. Whatever one may like to say is the international law norm, a norm is only an illusion of law—or duty or obligation—without the effective pressures to back it up.

In any event, the fact is that France did accede to partial lump sum compensation. Add to this the fact that the operating expenses of the French commissions—including honoraria to commission members, salaries to personnel, fees to expert witnesses, and materiel costs—have had to be drawn from the lump sums transferred,[443] and it is obvious that it has been wholly beyond the capacity of the French commissions to award eligible claimants anything approaching "full compensation." In short, a percentage recovery, subject to monetary fluctuations over the distribution years, has been the best to be won, ranging from as high as 60.6 percent of the "nominal value" of "recognized claims" in the case of the Czech claims program to as low as 4.59 percent of the "nominal value" of "recognized claims" in the case of the Bulgarian claims program.[444]

442 *See* text at Part II, notes 98–102.
443 *See* text at Part II, preceding note 180.
444 Letter from Jean-François Dervieu, Deputy Director of the *Service des Biens et Intérêts Privés*, January 22, 1970. The same correspondent advises that equivalent official figures for the inoperative 1950 Hungarian and Polish commissions are 87 and 25 percent, respectively. According to the "Secrétaire" of the former 1950 Hungarian

To allow for equitable percentage distribution, however, the commissions appear to have worked hard at achieving a realistic evaluation of the claimants' actual losses (and non-deprivative debt claims under the 1963 Yugoslav claims program). Such efforts are of course instructive; but not only because valuation is necessary to reaching conclusions about the amount of compensation that should be awarded in particular cases and contexts. They are note-worthy also because when juxtaposed with like efforts worldwide they help to articulate and refine the generally accepted, but still too speculative, "just," "adequate," or "appropriate" compensation standard.[445]

Regrettably, however, in all but a few of their opinions the French commissions have been either reluctant or unconcerned to announce their valuation criteria and methods, and when they have their explanations have been fragmentary at best.[446] Accordingly, without access to the individual "dossiers" that would clarify these matters, little more can be said than that the commissions, with the aid of expert background reports often prepared at their request,[447]

Commission, however, the first of these figures, notwithstanding its publication in the *Journal Officiel*—[1960] J.O. 7994—is inaccurate, having been based on French franc figures that did not account for postwar currency conversions. The actual percentage distribution, it is said, was "much lower." Interview with Branche, in Paris, July 10, 1969. French Government disclosure policies prevent publication of the percentage distribution figures of the commissions still operating.

[445] For constructive efforts along these lines, see Note, *Real Property Valuation for Foreign Wealth Deprivations*, 54 Iowa L. Rev. 89 (1968).

[446] The decisions of the *Conseil d'État* in this connection have not shed much greater light on the problem. Mostly they have been addressed to the correction of procedural oversights and errors (previously noted herein), the *Conseil* being tech-nically without authority to annul judgments of "fact." See *Société anonyme Finan-cière et Industrielle des Pétroles*, [1963] Cons. d'Ét., Section du Contentieux, Nos. 55,399 & 55,400 (unpublished mimeo.); *Société anonyme de l'industrie textile*, [1964] Rec. Cons. d'Ét. 360; *Banque de Paris et des Pays-Bas*, [1965] Cons. d'Ét., Section du Contentieux, No. 61,500 (unpublished mimeo.); *Société orientale d'oxygène et d'acéty-lène dissous (S.O.D.A.D.)*, [1965] Rec. Cons. d'Ét. 163; *Sieur Devien*, [1965] Rec. Cons. d'Ét. 239; *Union européenne industrielle et financière*, [1965] Cons. d'Ét., Section du Contentieux, No. 61,371 (unpublished mimeo.); *Compagnie de Saint-Gobain*, [1966] Cons. d'Ét., Section du Contentieux, No. 65,450 (unpublished mimeo.); *Sieur Mura-Michel*, [1967] Cons. d'Ét., Section du Contentieux, No. 70,408 (unpublished mimeo.); *Sieur Block*, [1968] Cons. d'Ét., Section du Contentieux, No. 71,499 (unpublished mimeo.).

[447] As might be supposed, these expert reports have sometimes been requested because the commissions have on occasion been skeptical about the valuations pre-sented by the individual claimants. See, *e.g.*, FC 2 (1968) wherein the Cuban Com-mission was disinclined to accept the claimant's "accounting practices."

appear generally to have striven for a distribution based on the "net market" or "going concern" value extant ordinarily at the time of loss.[448] When market quotations have been known, as in the case of many stockholder claims, usually these quotations (or, in their absence, "nominal values") have sufficed. Alternatively, and sometimes additionally, depending on the nature of the claim involved, the commissions have taken into account such other factors as: purchase prices paid; construction and reconstruction costs; inventories; assessments made for insurance, probate, and tax purposes; annual report and balance sheet statements; comparisons with similarly situated property and equivalent auction sales; asset composition, quality, and location; *ex parte* declarations and estimates by French and other nationals (official and unofficial) familiar with the wealth in question; and so forth. Also, adjustments have been made for such other factors as: capital appreciation and depreciation; prior recoupments; exchange rate and price fluctuations (usually based on the payor State's "gross price index"); monetary devaluations; outstanding debts and other encumbrances (public and private); war damage (where appropriate); and, generally, economic conditions prevailing at the time of loss. Using the rate of exchange available at the time of claim accrual, ordinarily the determined value has been computed in the foreign currency to which the claim has been specialized and then converted into French francs (except in the case of the Polish Commission which converted first into United States dollars and then into French francs).

To the foregoing can be added, with confidence, but four further remarks. First, "wartime" and "peacetime" deprivation claims have at all times stood on an equal compensatory footing, with no distributive preference being given to one or the other.[449] Next, claims have been dismissed because of their *de minimis* value only in the case of the Romanian claims program.[450] Third, claimants have at

---

[448] In the case of wartime losses, sometimes because of evidentiary difficulties, the commissions have based their valuations as of a date either before or after World War II, whichever has seemed the most convenient or least distortive. Interview with Dervieu, in Paris, June 27, 1969.

[449] *See, e.g.,* Letter No. 244 from Charles Lucet, on behalf of the Minister of Foreign Affairs, to the *commissaire du gouvernement,* March 8, 1962, interpreting the 1955 Bulgarian Accord (unpublished mimeo.).

[450] *See* FR 974 (1962); 4777, 4947, 5069, 5721 (1965); 6430–31 (1966); 7134, 7232, 7388 (1967). In each of these exceptional cases the Romanian Commission

all times been required to accept payment in French francs.[451] And, last but not least, interest never has been allowed from the time of claim accrual or any other time.[452]

---

refused to grant relief because currency depreciations and conversions had led to miniscule valuations. The same approach is to be found in equivalent British practice. *See* LILLICH (G.B.) 127. It may be noted that on at least one occasion a prestigious French business journal roundly criticized these Romanian *de minimis* rulings: "It is, properly speaking, scandalous. From this mountain of red tape comes the impression that the francs given by Romania were in large part devoured by French bureaucrats. For ten years the money had devalued to the profit of the *Trésor Publique* who had possession of the funds without the least interest, while the victims, restricted to dispose of the titles that they had been told were worthless, are soothed with false hopes." *Le Moniteur économique et financier,* June 6, 1969, at 3, col. 4.

[451] Interview with Dervieu, in Paris, June 27, 1969.

[452] *Id.* For related pertinent discussion, see Part III, note 11 and accompanying text.

Part IV

Appraisal and Conclusion

Convinced though one may be, and appropriately so, that the post-war French *commissions spéciales de répartition* can be regarded as decision-making agents of the international legal order, the fact remains that from their inception they have been instruments of the French legal order, and generally looked upon as such by persons both in and out of government who have had occasion to deal with them.[1] This fact, of course, is grounds for caution to any foreign observer, in particular any common law lawyer, who would seek to appraise the work of these commissions, operationally or juris-prudentially. Especially is this true where criticism is involved. The French commissions, strictly speaking not constituents of the *ordre administratif*, are nonetheless the offspring in part of an administrative tradition which, forged under the Monarchy and Napoleon, is held in such high esteem today as to have been heavily borrowed from in the formation and development of the European Community and other international governmental institutions. Indeed, the design within which the commissions have functioned itself may be seen as a corrective, as it was intended to be, of some of the weaknesses of this great tradition, most notably in its provision for restricting the discretionary exercise of governmental power, not simply by incorporating "la notion d'arbitrage" in the first place, but as well by

---

[1] One gets the impression from talking with many persons who are familiar with postwar French international claims practice that few look upon the French commissions as having much, if any, international jurisprudential significance. Of course, there are notable exceptions: *e.g.*, Monsieur André Ernest-Picard, Director of the *Association Nationale des Porteurs Français de Valeurs Mobilières* (as to which, see Part II, note 19); Monsieur Henri Glaser, Secretary General of the *Association Pour la Sauvegarde et l'Expansion des Biens et Intérêts Français à l'Étranger* (as to which, see Part II, note 16); Monsieur Jacques Piguet, President and Director General of the *Office Juridique Français et International* (a private organization informally tied to the *Association* immediately preceding); and, perhaps most importantly, the Director and Deputy Director of the *Service des Biens et Intérêts Privés* of the French Foreign Ministry.

requiring the commissions to give reasons for their decisions and by having these decisions subjected to review for *excés de pouvoir* by the *Conseil d'État*.[2] Nevertheless, one can make criticisms, although they are to be seen more in the procedures that the commissions have followed (or been obliged to follow) than in the content of what they have done.

Most conspicuous is the extraordinary secrecy that has surrounded French commission practice, as evidenced by the difficulties that this writer has encountered in attempting to obtain documentation that would shed light on the French commission decisions.[3] Of course, criticism based on this kind of evidence always can be dismissed as personal pique. The problem is, however, that many Frenchmen, in defense of their own interests or the interests of their clients, would register the same general complaint. In particular, they point to the refusal of the commissions, or whoever, to publish the commission decisions. Indeed, it is even hard to know precisely who has been responsible for this refusal. It is, in any event, lamentable. From a jurisprudential perspective, obviously this kind of secrecy inhibits the rapid development of the "Law of International Claims" (and "State Responsibility"), not to mention French law itself. Also, by preventing the decisions from entering into the lists of worldwide case and controversy, it allows to continue unchecked the flow of ambiguous and insufficiently reasoned opinions that have so marked French commission practice. Perhaps more important, however, the refusal has worked practical hardships, as evidenced by the many rejected claims that doubtless never would have been brought to the commissions had the commission decisions been published for all to observe,[4] a condition that has taken its toll not only in the unnecessary time and money that has been expended by the claimants but, also, in the prolongation of commission functioning which, for reasons to be noted, can hardly be considered desirable. Furthermore, no matter how successful the *Conseil d'État* has been in preventing abuses, it scarcely needs saying that there is

---

[2] For discussion concerning the reasons for the establishment of the French commissions, see text at Part II, notes 26–31.

[3] *See* text at Part I, notes 14–16.

[4] *See*, in particular, text at Part III, notes 336–344.

much to be said for holding public bodies publicly accountable.[5] In short, it is difficult to agree with the three reasons officially advanced for non-publication. Preservation of claimant privacy, the first, is easily assured by withholding names. The second, retaining the greatest possible flexibility for future commission decision-making is, as a procedural matter, damning on its face. And protection of diplomatic maneuverability in future lump sum negotiation, the third, is questionable in light of the publication of the Settlement Agreements and the apparent consistency that French commission practice has shared with comparative and customary international claims practice.[6]

Also subject to criticism, on practical if not jurisprudential grounds, and especially in view of the delays that marked the commencement of some of the distribution programs, is the considerable time that the French commissions have required to complete their business, averaging 8 to 10 years each. In some cases, as might be supposed, this drawn-out state of affairs is explained by the large number and diversity of petitions that have had to be processed. The 1950 Hungarian claims program, for example, begun in July 1952 and concluded about 8 years later in August 1960, involved consideration of some 3,200 petitions.[7] The explanation, however, is only a partial one. Thus, begun in March 1960 and concluded more

---

[5] It should be added that a reading of the French commission decisions reveals no grounds for believing that the commissions have had anything to hide.

[6] For similar, to some extent identical, justifications in equivalent British practice, see LILLICH (G.B.) 15. Probably the real reason for the French secretiveness, notwithstanding similar attitudes in Great Britain, is to be found in what Ardagh describes as the "climate of mistrust" that has for so long pervaded the French social character. Over the years, he writes, "[a] Frenchman grew up to look on his neighbour as potentially a selfish and hostile rival who might try to do him down, and laws and privileges existed to protect him against this. Those he could really rely on were limited to his family. . . . Though the Frenchman would also join vigorously in association with fellow-members of his own trade or social group, this was more for mutual self-defence than out of real sentiment or civic duty." J. ARDAGH, THE NEW FRENCH REVOLUTION 439 (1968). But as Ardagh goes on to point out, there is reason to believe that the old attitudes are giving way to "the growth of a new sense of community" in which "[t]he French may come to realise that their mistrust is a defence they do not need anymore, and cooperation a virtue they can no longer do without." Id. at 445. This observation is of course grounds for hope that the secretiveness that has surrounded postwar French practice in the past will not—or at least need not—endure.

[7] Interview with Branche, in Paris, July 10, 1969.

than 8 years later in November 1968, the 1955 Bulgarian claims program involved consideration of only about 190 petitions.[8] That is, the prolongation of commission functioning really has been due to a number of organizational and procedural conditions which, exclusive of the amount and variety of petitions involved, have been conducive to inefficiencies which the French Government might and could profitably avoid: *e.g.*, multiple rather than single commission distribution; use of part-time rather than full-time commission members; understaffing of the commission secretariats; overemployment of older rather than younger, more energetic personnel; excessive adherence to arbitral procedures when patently faulty petitions have justified no more than summary administrative dispositions; and so forth. Of course, delay is not *ipso facto* bad. In context, however, it creates serious problems. In the first place, claimants die. Obviously, speedier operations would alleviate at least some of the evidentiary difficulties and inequities that commonly arise under such circumstances. Second, prolonged functioning inevitably adds to the cost of lump sum distribution. Recalling that distribution expenses have had to be deducted from the already limited lump sums received,[9] more rapid administration surely would make for larger or more widely available lump sum sharing. Finally, unnecessary delay seems hardly justified or equitable in light of the uniform refusal of the French commissions to add interest payments to their awards. Indeed, considering that the French *Trésor* has invested the lump sums received, apparently to the advantage of the French Government rather than to the benefit of claimants,[10] such delays, if not the non-interest payment policy itself, border on the scandalous.[11]

One final major criticism, akin to the first mentioned, concerns what appears to be a heavy concentration on the arbitral phase of French distributive practice to the neglect of pre-arbitral procedures that could ensure smoother commission functioning and a more

[8] *Id.*

[9] *See* text at Part II, preceding note 180. *See also* Part II, note 179.

[10] *See* Part II, note 179.

[11] Soubbotitch has referred to the same policy in the United States as a "misappropriation," a "rapacious practice of the U.S. Treasury." 62 PROCEEDINGS OF THE AMERICAN SOCIETY OF INTERNATIONAL LAW 53 (1968).

efficient safeguarding of claimant interests. That is, one gets the impression that the French commissions or the Quai d'Orsay (or both) have been insufficiently interested in what happens to claimants *before* they come before the commissions, an impression that is gotten not only from the large number of rejected claims that probably would never have been brought were claimants to have had more adequate notice about eligibility prerequisites,[12] but as well from the above-mentioned reluctance to utilize swifter non-arbitral techniques to dispose of patently faulty claims, from the disinclination of the French Government to resort to throughgoing pre-negotiation claims registration programs[13] and, perhaps most importantly, from sentiments expressed by persons who have had opportunity to deal with the French repartition process. Why this seeming disinterest at the pre-arbitral stage has been allowed to exist is a question that cannot be answered with certainty by this writer, although doubtless a partial explanation is to be found in the character of French administration whose military origins have tended to retard the development of bureaucratic sensitivity to the needs of individual well-being. But whatever the reasons and however much French commission practice has itself counterbalanced pre-arbitral deficiencies *a posteriori,* the impression remains that for lack of robust concern for claimant needs before adjudication many claimants have been made to submit to unwarranted inconveniences. One can only speculate whether for the same reason there have been some persons with eligible claims who have been inadvertently excluded from lump sum participation altogether.

For all the criticisms that can be leveled at postwar French commission practice, however, it has to be acknowledged that the commissions have performed most of their basic missions generally with distinction. It appears, for example, that they have succeeded admirably in achieving a wide and on the whole equitable distribution of the lump sums that have been theirs to dispense, exhibiting little discernible favoritism as between different kinds of claimant interests and, with little or no guidance from their Controlling Texts, extending to deprivative creditor claims a protection that

12 *See,* in particular, text at Part III, notes 336–344.
13 *See* Part II, note 235.

customary international and comparative practice has been slow to grant.[14] Also, while not free from a too legalistic or policy-indifferent adherence to their Rules and other Controlling Texts, nonetheless they have adopted more a flexible and pragmatic than a rigid and dogmatic approach to the resolution of the claims that have been brought to them, especially as regards the timeliness of claim, the formalities of application, and matters of proof. Further still, they appear uniformly to have executed the decisions of the *Conseil d'État* and thereby to have assured claimants against inadvertent and potentially malevolent abuses, notwithstanding that under French law the *Conseil d'État* has been powerless to overcome a determined refusal of the commissions to surrender to it. It is, however, in respect of two other distinctive features of French commission practice that special attention must be given. Together they present the basic *mise en scène* against which all judgements, critical and otherwise, should be viewed.

First is the remarkable uniformity of decision that generally has prevailed among the several commissions, remarkable because in the face of a multiple commission system one naturally expects a great deal of decisional variation. As might be supposed, there are a number of explanations for this phenomenon. Most conspicuous, of course, has been the essential similarity of the Settlement Agreements themselves, as earlier mentioned the principal jurisprudential reference points for the French commissions.[15] Indeed, it is the differences that are to be found between the Settlement Agreements that has been mainly responsible for the variation that has emerged among the commission decisions. As indicated, however, still other factors have contributed to this uniformity: the integrative "watchdog function" of the *commissaire du gouvernement*;[16] the administrative overseer role of the *Service des Biens et Intérêts Privés*;[17]

---

[14] As Lillich writes of like reaction to creditor claims in postwar British practice, "Great Britain's settlement of such claims, while lowering the dividends paid under awards to claimants of all classes, has had the benefit of creating new types of claims that may be espousable in the future. In this process the [Foreign Compensation Commission] has made a substantial contribution to the clarification of what may become new rules of international law." LILLICH (G.B.) 142.

[15] *See* text at Part II, notes 137–140.

[16] *See* Part II, note 178.

[17] *See* Part II, notes 148 & 176. This is not to say that the *Service* has dictated the decisions of the French commissions. However, partly because its predecessor,

the responsibility of one *secrétaire* for more than one commission secretariat;[18] the occasional overlap of commission memberships;[19] and, of course, the French legal training of most of the commission members.[20] Yet what matters most is less the reasons for the decisional uniformity than its consequence, or, more precisely, the fact that this uniformity has gone a long way toward building confidence in the national claims commission device, especially among claimants who have had occasion to petition more than one commission, as perhaps the best means for achieving fair dealing in international claims practice.[21] Indeed, it goes a long way toward explaining why the French Government, apparently fearful lest a single and relatively permanent commission might acquire a jurisdiction that would be difficult to control, has thus far been willing to continue with a multiple commission system, however inefficient. It is, in any event, among the principal explanations for French plans to resort to commission distribution when deprivative claims against Algeria and Tunisia are capable of being finally resolved.[22]

Second, and perhaps most praiseworthy, is the generally unparochial perspective that is to be discerned in postwar French practice —at least from the standpoint of Western Judeo-Christian legal tradition. As seen, the decisions of the commissions ordinarily have been consistent with what is said to be customary international law, as well as with comparative American and British practice. To be sure, a major reason for this worldly (or ideological) consistency is to be found in the Settlement Agreements whose prescriptive terms, themselves very much like what is found in the lump sum agreements that have been negotiated among other countries,[23] have conditioned the decisions that the commissions have been obliged to

the *Office des Biens et Intérêts Privés*, was the principal architect of the first French commissions, the *Service* long has enjoyed a special relationship with the commissions which has permitted it to have a significant voice, for example, in the structuring of new commissions and the selection of personnel. Interview with Dervieu, in Paris, June 11, 1969.

18 *See* Part II, note 239.

19 *See* Part II, note 164.

20 *See* Part II, note 165.

21 Interview with Dervieu, in Paris, July 2, 1969; Interview with Henri Glaser, in Paris, July 8, 1969.

22 Interview with Dervieu, in Paris, June 11, 1969.

23 *See* R. LILLICH & B. WESTON, 2 INTERNATIONAL CLAIMS: THEIR SETTLEMENT BY LUMP SUM AGREEMENTS, to be published by the Syracuse University Press.

reach. Still, the Settlement Agreements have not been explicit in every detail. Gaps have had to be filled, contradictions reconciled, and ambiguities clarified. In performing these functions the commissions have succeeded, by and large, like their American and British counterparts, in maintaining a global outlook. Indeed, it is this particular success that causes one to despair at the French commissions' too frequent resort to elliptic explication and their near-total disinterest in exploring, even to the very limited extent attempted in this study, the world order policy implications of what they have decided. Nevertheless, however unsophisticated the French commissions have been about their role in the international legal order, their basically cosmopolitan perspective merits applause.

This study ends, then, where it began—that is, with a profound sense of concern for strengthening and making more enlightened not simply the present or prospective *commissions spéciales de répartition* that the French Government may maintain, but all domestic decision-making institutions which affect "outward" or "upward" the patterns of international authority and control that in turn affect so fundamentally "inward" or "downward" our everyday lives. In a centrifugal international system which is beset on all sides with a tension that permits even the most isolated incident to fan the flames of major and minor destruction, energizing the horizontal possibilities for assuring and expanding world order is an irreducible minimum. International lawyers can assist enormously in this task by shedding the dogmas that traditionally have too often distorted analysis and by undertaking, however tentatively, the pursuit of procedures and policies that can create an effective awareness of the interrelation of law and community process.

Appendix

THE 1955 BULGARIAN ACCORD[1]

The Government of the French Republic and the Government of the Peoples' Republic of Bulgaria, desirous of settling the questions:

Of the indemnification of French natural or juridical persons holding property, rights, or interests affected by the nationalization or other socialist reorganization measures of the Peoples' Republic of Bulgaria;

Of the application, insofar as French interests are concerned, of the terms of the Treaty of Peace of 10 February 1947, signed between the Allied and Associated Powers and Bulgaria;

Of the redemption of Bulgarian foreign public debt obligations belonging to French holders,

have designated for this purpose their plenipotentiaries who, after having exchanged their credentials, recognized in good and due form, have agreed to the following provisions:

Art. 1—The Bulgarian Government shall pay to the French Government a fixed sum of 1,500,000,000 French francs, on the basis of 350 francs per United States dollar, as comprehensive lump sum settlement:

(a) For indemnities due by reason of Bulgarian measures of nationalization, expropriation, confiscation, requisition or other measures of total or partial dispossession which affected the property, rights, and interests of natural or juridical persons having French nationality on the date these measures were taken as well as on the date of the signature of the present Agreement;

(b) For obligations due French natural or juridical persons which devolve upon Bulgaria by virtue of the Treaty of Peace of 10 February 1947 (war damages, restitutions, etc.);

(c) For obligations due French natural or juridical persons on Bulgarian exterior public loans chargeable to former Bulgarian governments, 6% 1892, 5% 1896, 5% 1902, 5% 1904, 4½% 1907, 4½% 1909, 6½% 1923, 7½% 1928, and others.

[1] Decree No. 59–361 of February 27, 1959, [1959] J.O. 2742. "Protocole d'Application" and three "lettres-annexes" omitted.

191

Art. 2—The payment of the sum fixed in Article 1 above shall be carried out as follows:

(a) Within 30 days after the exchange of instruments of ratification of the present Agreement, the National Bank of Bulgaria, acting on behalf of the Bulgarian Government, shall place at the disposal of the French Government, for the latter to pay the equivalent to French holders of Bulgarian obligations, the funds in gold, currency, and francs formerly delivered to French Banks for the payment of Bulgarian external loan coupons;

(b) The difference between the sum fixed in Article 1 and the value of the funds mentioned in the preceding paragraph shall be settled by means of a 7% levy on bank payments made by French purchasers of merchandise of Bulgarian origin. The return from this levy shall be posted to a special account and shall be distributed periodically among the claimants by the French Government, at the rate of 50% to the holders mentioned in Article 1, paragraph (c), and 50% to the other creditors.

Art. 3—At the end of each year, the French Government shall remit to the Bulgarian Government supporting documents corresponding to the permanent settlements as well as to information concerning the temporary settlements that were applied during the course of the year to the profit of the interested parties.

Art. 4—From the signature of the present Agreement, the French Government and the Bulgarian Government shall no longer raise claims concerning the loans, property, rights, and interests mentioned in the preamble of this Agreement.

The French Government shall not support any future claims of its nationals who refuse the benefit of the present Agreement.

Art. 5—The indemnification provided for in the present Agreement should compensate the rights of French natural and juridical persons affected, in their capacity as proprietor, shareholder, creditor, etc., by nationalizations and other similar intervening measures in Bulgaria. On the other hand, these persons shall be released from all obligations against them in such country.

Art. 6—Potential difficulties relating to the interpretation or to the application of the Agreement shall be resolved by common agreement of the two governments.

Art. 7—The present Agreement shall enter into force provisionally on the date of its signature.

It shall be ratified or approved according to the constitutional rules of each of the two countries. The exchange of the instruments of ratification shall take place in Paris.

Done at Sofia, 28 July 1955, in four original copies, two in the French language and two in the Bulgarian language, both texts being equally official.

THE 1967 CUBAN ACCORD[2]

Desiring to settle definitively questions relating to the indemnification of French property, rights, and interests in Cuba which have been affected by the laws and measures promulgated by the Revolutionary Government of the Republic of Cuba since 1 January 1959, and after a bilateral examination of the claims raised by French persons, natural and juridical;

The Government of the French Republic;

The Revolutionary Government of the Republic of Cuba, have agreed as follows:

Article 1

The Revolutionary Government of the Republic of Cuba pays to the French Government by way of indemnification the sum of 10,861,532 F which constitutes a final and comprehensive liquidation for all the property, rights, and interests of natural and juridical persons of French nationality, affected by the laws and measures promulgated by the Revolutionary Government of the Republic of Cuba since 1 January 1959.

Article 2

The payment of the sum of 10,861,532 F is made in 11 equal payments of 905,126 F each and a final payment of 905,146 F.

The first of these payments shall take place on 3 June 1967, the second on 4 September 1967, and successive payments on 3 January and 3 June of the years following, the last of these payments taking place on 3 June 1972.

These payments are made by the National Bank of Cuba, by transfers to the credit of the account which shall be opened in the books of the Bank of France and titled "French-Cuban Agreement of 16 March 1967." The debiting of this account is made by the Bank of France by order of the Ministry of Economy and Finance (Department of the Treasury).

Article 3

The complete payment of the sum mentioned in Article 1 releases from all responsibility the Revolutionary Government of the Republic of Cuba as well as Cuban natural and juridical persons insofar as concerns the French property, rights, and interests. Each partial payment dimin-

[2] Decree No. 67–853 of September 20, 1967, [1967] J.O. 9761.

ishes in due amount the obligations contracted by the Revolutionary Government of the Republic of Cuba in the present Agreement. The final payment completely extinguishes the said obligations.

On the other hand, French natural and juridical persons who are indemnified under the present Agreement are exonerated of all obligations toward the Cuban Government and Cuban natural and juridical persons for the property, rights, and interests for which they have been indemnified.

Article 4

The Government of the French Republic, acting in the name of its nationals, guarantees the Revolutionary Government of the Republic of Cuba and Cuban natural and juridical persons against all claims of French natural and juridical persons who have been affected by the laws and measures promulgated by the Revolutionary Government of the Republic of Cuba up to the date of the present Agreement.

Article 5

The terms of the present Agreement are not applicable to the commercial debts contracted by importers in Cuba in favor of French creditors, which are liquidated in accordance with the procedure set forth in the exchange of correspondence of December, 1963, nor to claims which might be made subsequent to laws and measures which might have been promulgated by the Revolutionary Government of the Republic of Cuba after the signature of the present Agreement.

Article 6

The distribution of the sum corresponding to the indemnification attributed to French natural and juridical persons is the sole responsibility of the Government of the French Republic. It does not engage the responsibility of the Revolutionary Government of the Republic of Cuba or of Cuban natural or juridical persons.

Article 7

With regard to the execution of the present Agreement, the two governments shall reciprocally furnish, as much as possible, all necessary information.

Article 8

All disagreement relating to the interpretation or the application of the present Agreement is to be settled by common agreement between the two governments.

Article 9

The present Agreement shall enter into force beginning on the date of its signature.

In witness whereof the signatories, duly authorized by their respective governments, have signed the present Agreement and have affixed their seals to it.

Done at Havana, 16 March 1967, in two copies, in the French and Spanish languages, the two texts being equally official.

THE 1950 CZECH ACCORD[3]

The President of the French Republic and the President of the Czechoslovak Republic, wishing to bring to a final solution the question of indemnification for French property, rights, and interests in Czechoslovakia affected by Czechoslovak measures of nationalization, expropriation and other restrictive measures of similar character, have designated as their plenipotentiaries for that purpose:

The President of the French Republic;

The President of the Czechoslovak Republic;

Who, after having exchanged their full powers, which are recognized to be in good and due form, are agreed to the following provisions:

Article 1

The Czechoslovak Government shall pay to the French Government the sum of 4,200,000,000 French francs as a comprehensive lump sum indemnity for:

(a) The French interests which are the object of the French-Czechoslovak agreements of 6 August 1948;

(b) All other French interests affected, on the date of the entry into force of the present Agreement, by a Czechoslovak measure of nationalization, expropriation or any other restrictive measure bearing upon reforms directed at the Czech economic structure;

(c) The French interests which are now the object of restitution procedures in Czechoslovakia.

The sum fixed in the present Article shall be paid according to the procedures defined in Additional Protocol No. II.

Article 2

Considered as French interests for the purposes of the present Agreement are interests belonging to natural or juridical persons of French nationality on the date of the Czechoslovak measures mentioned in the preceding Article and on the date the present Agreement enters into force.

Article 3

The complete payments of the sum mentioned in the above Article shall, insofar as concerns the holders of the French interests defined in

[3] Decree No. 51-1286 of November 7, 1951, [1951] J.O. 11188.

Articles 1 and 2, hereinbelow called interested parties, discharge the Czechoslovak State as well as all Czechoslovak institutions and natural or juridical persons considered as the successors-in-interest to the original owners under Czechoslovak law.

From the date of the entry into force of the present Agreement and subject to its execution, the Czechoslovak State as well as all Czechoslovak institutions and natural or juridical persons shall be freed from all claims on the part of the French interested parties.

The French Government agrees to present or espouse no claim emanating from other natural or juridical persons based on the Czechoslovak measures mentioned in Article 1.

Article 4

The French Government shall obtain from the interested parties all supporting documents, title-deeds, and certificates relating to the property, rights, and interests indemnified under the terms of the present Agreement.

It agrees to keep these documents and to transmit them to the Czechoslovak Government after the settlement of the claims to which they refer and, at the very latest, after the complete payment of the sum mentioned in Article 1 above.

Article 5

Interested parties, formerly owners in Czechoslovakia of enterprises or properties affected by measures of nationalization, expropriation or other restrictive measures, are discharged of all obligations incurred by these enterprises or amounting to a charge on the properties incurred before the occurrence of these measures and which appear on the books of the enterprises or on the public land records.

Article 6

The lump sum of 4,200,000,000 French francs mentioned in Article 1 above, has been fixed by taking into account that the interested parties have been discharged of charges and obligations which devolved upon them by virtue of all Czechoslovak taxes.

Article 7

The distribution of the comprehensive lump sum indemnity among the interested parties falls within the sole competence of the French Government and does not involve the liability of the Czechoslovak State, nor of Czechoslovak institutions and natural or juridical persons.

Article 8

For the purpose of the execution of the present Agreement the two governments shall supply each other with all necessary aid and information.

Article 9

French claims resulting from Czechoslovak measures which might be taken after the entry into force of the present Agreement are excluded from the provisions of the said Agreement.

Article 10

Any difficulties relating to the interpretation or application of the present Agreement shall be settled by agreement between the two governments.

Article 11

The present Agreement shall be ratified or approved according to the constitutional rules in force in each of the two States. Minutes of the exchange of instruments of ratification or approval shall be established.

The date of these Minutes shall be the date of the entry into force of the present Agreement.

Done at Prague, 2 June 1950.

ADDITIONAL PROTOCOL No. I

To the Agreement dated 2 June 1950, between the French Republic and the Czechoslovak Republic on the indemnification of certain French interests in Czechoslovakia.

1. It is determined that the provisions of the Agreement apply:

(a) To the interests of the natural or juridical persons mentioned in Article 2 of the Agreement in successions in Czechoslovakia if the interests come within the framework of Article 1 and if the right of succession has come into being before the occurrence of the measures mentioned in the same Article;

(b) To credits held, for whatever reason, against Czechoslovak companies by natural or juridical persons mentioned in Article 2 of the Agreement who at the same time hold at least a 50% participation in these same companies.

2. It is also determined that the provisions of the Agreement do not apply to credits and assets whose transfer is provided for by the Franco-Czechoslovak monetary regulation which is now in force, and by subsequent regulations, except in the case provided for in subparagraph (b) of paragraph 1 above.

3. From the date of the entry into force of the present Agreement and subject to its execution, no claims against the Czechoslovak State or against Czechoslovak institutions or natural or juridical persons may be presented on account of the goods transferred under duress (spoliations), such as: Apollo, Banska Pro Obchod A Prumysl Drive Landerbank, Banska A Hutni Spolecnost.

4. In order to facilitate the distribution of the comprehensive lump sum indemnity, the Czechoslovak Government shall furnish the French Government, at its request and to the extent possible, with all information and documentation necessary to permit the competent French authorities to settle equitably the claims for indemnity filed by the interested parties.

5. To assure the execution of the Agreement, and especially Articles 3 and 8, the French Government shall make known to the Czechoslovak Government as soon as possible:

(a) The names of all natural and juridical persons who have filed claims for indemnity;

(b) The proportion to which interests which are the object of a claim shall be recognized as being French interests.

Done at Prague, 2 June 1950.

ADDITIONAL PROTOCOL NO. II

To the Agreement dated 2 June 1950, between the French Republic and the Czechoslovak Republic on the indemnification of certain French interests in Czechoslovakia.

In execution of Article 1 of the Agreement, the two contracting parties have agreed to the following provisions, which become an integral part of the Agreement.

Article 1

Taking into account the payment of 200,000,000 francs and 350,000,000 francs effectuated by the Czechoslovak Government in execution of the agreements of 6 August 1948 concerning French interests affected by measures of nationalization and confiscation, the amount which still must be paid is 3,650,000 francs.

This amount shall be paid in 20 biannual installments, the first on 31 December 1950, the last on 30 June 1960.

. . . .

Article 2

By agreement between the two parties, a special list of Czechoslovak merchandise amounting to one and one-half times the yearly installments shall be established for each year the Agreement is in effect.

. . . .

Article 3

Annulled are the provisions of the Special Agreement between France and Czechoslovakia concerning the payment of indemnities to French interests affected by nationalization and confiscation, the Additional Protocol to this Special Agreement, and the annexed letter to the Additional Protocol of 6 August 1948.

Done at Prague, in two copies, 2 June 1950.

EXCHANGE OF LETTERS, ANNEX NO. 1[4]

The President of the
French Delegation

Prague, 2 June 1950
To Mister Siroki
Minister of Foreign Affairs
of Czechoslovakia

Mister Minister,

With reference to the Agreement on the indemnification of certain French interests in Czechoslovakia, signed on this date, I have the honor to inform you as follows:

The expression "shall be freed from all claims," which is found in paragraph 2 of Article 3 of the Agreement, signifies that as soon as the Agreement enters into force, and subject to its execution, the French Government shall take all the measures in its power to ensure that the Czechoslovak State as well as Czechoslovak institutions and natural or juridical persons are not, with respect to the interests mentioned in Articles 1 and 2 of the Agreement, held liable for any charge or obligation other than those defined in the Agreement.

I would be grateful if you would confirm to me the agreement of the Czechoslovak Government on what precedes.

Please accept, Mister Minister, the assurance of my high consideration.

J. RIVIÈRE

[4] Decree No. 63–735 of July 10, 1963, [1963] J.O. 6811. Confirmatory reply omitted.

EXCHANGE OF LETTERS, ANNEX No. 2[5]

The President of the
French Delegation

Prague, 2 June 1950
To Mister Siroki
Minister of Foreign Affairs
of Czechoslovakia

Mister Minister,

With reference to Additional Protocol No. I to the Agreement on the indemnification of certain French interests in Czechoslovakia, signed on this date, I have the honor to inform you as follows:

1. The interests mentioned in subparagraph (a) of paragraph 1 of the Protocol include notably the interests of Madame Engel Fuchs in the enterprises Hyneck Fuchs and the Palais Fuchs, at Prague;

2. The provisions of subparagraph (b) of paragraph 1 of the Protocol apply notably to the credits enumerated in the list below, established according to the declarations of the parties:

Manufacture de caoutchouc Michelin, kcs. 25,657,441.47

Lainière de Roubaix, kcs. 21,970,988

Société anonyme des papiers abadie, kcs. 1,217,841.75

Comptoir textile et industriel du Nord (MM. Tiberghien), kcs. 1,143,000

Compagnie française industrielle et commerciale des pétroles, kcs. 1,999,999.50

Compagnie pour la fabrication des compteurs et matériel d'usines à gaz, kcs. 11,464,000.

3. It is specified that the provisions of the Agreement apply to certain participations in Czechoslovak enterprises held indirectly by French parties, which are: participations in the enterprise Tiberghien-Synovia, all considered as French, participations in the premiere fabrique tcheque de soie artificielle held by the Société Viscose Suisse S.A., the Société privée de gestion S.A., the Société Holva S.A., equally considered as French.

I would be grateful if you would confirm to me the agreement of the Czechoslovak Government on what precedes.

Please accept, Mister Minister, the assurance of my high consideration.

J. RIVIÈRE

---

[5] *Id.* Confirmatory reply omitted.

THE 1966 EGYPTIAN ACCORD[6]

The Government of the French Republic and the Government of the United Arab Republic, wishing to come to a rapid and definitive settlement of the problems brought about by the measures which have affected the estates of French nationals situated on the territory of the United Arab Republic, have agreed as follows:

TITLE I

FRENCH PROPERTY, RIGHTS AND INTERESTS AFFECTED BY THE MEASURES TAKEN PRIOR TO 22 AUGUST 1958

Article 1

The two governments observe that the terms of the general agreement of 22 August 1958, and of decree No. 36 of 1958 promulgated 18 September 1958 by the Government of the United Arab Republic have legally terminated the measures of sequestration of French estates arising from Proclamation No. 5 of 1 November 1956.

Consequently, all French property, rights, and interests which were affected by these measures have been liberated under the conditions set down in this general agreement, by decree No. 36, by the agreement of 5 November 1964, and by the stipulations of Title I to this Agreement.

Article 2

The property, rights, and interests for which French owners have demanded restoration, in accordance with the general agreement of 22 August 1958, and with the agreements concluded or having texts promulgated for application, and have completed the necessary procedures and formalities with the appropriate offices of the United Arab Republic, within the allotted time, will be remitted to the claimants within six months of the date on which this Agreement enters into force.

Article 3

When the property, rights, and interests mentioned in Article 2 above have been the object of measures of transfer prior to 22 August 1958, and when the corresponding indemnities have not been entirely paid to the sequestration accounts or to the owner, the debtor will pay, at each due date after the remittance mentioned in Article 2 above, 90% of the amount to the creditor and 10% to the Government of the United Arab Republic.

[6] Decree No. 67–874 of October 4, 1967, [1967] J.O. 9939. Two "lettres-annexes" omitted.

Article 4

Reserving the right of contestation mentioned in Article 2 of the protocol annexed to this Agreement and constituting an integral part of it, the authorities of the United Arab Republic will proceed to the liquidation of estates of French nationals who do not fulfill the conditions mentioned in Article 2 above.

This liquidation will begin six months after the coming into effect of this Agreement.

The proceeds of this liquidation, fixed at the lump sum of 300,000 Egyptian pounds, will be paid, within six months from the date of the entry into force of this Agreement, to an account opened in the name of the Government of the French Republic, which will proceed by its own authority to the distribution of this amount among the claimants residing in France whom it will designate.

As counterpart of this payment, the ownership of the property, rights, and interests liquidated by the application of this Article is transferred to the Government of the United Arab Republic.

Article 5

The indemnities due to French companies whose property, rights, and interests have been the object of measures of disposition before 22 August 1958, will be settled in accordance with the terms of the Zurich agreements and the special agreements which have been concluded with the interested parties.

Article 6

The French diplomatic representatives in the United Arab Republic are authorized, in order to finance their local expenses, to acquire pounds in a capital account registered in the name of French holders to the maximum amount of 500,000 Egyptian pounds per year.

Article 7

Travel agencies are authorized to buy Egyptian pounds in a capital account, within an annual limit of 20 percent of the amount of each account, for the settlement of vacation expenses of French travelers to the United Arab Republic, within the maximum limit of 1,000 Egyptian pounds per year and per traveler.

TITLE II

FRENCH PROPERTY, RIGHTS, AND INTERESTS AFFECTED BY MEASURES AFTER 22 AUGUST 1958

Article 8

This document will consider as French property, rights, and interests, the property, rights, and interests belonging to natural persons of French nationality, as well as juridical persons having their registered office in France and the majority of whose capital belongs to persons of French nationality.

The conditions of nationality required of natural persons and the conditions for registered office and majority required of juridical persons according to the terms of the preceding paragraph must have been met from the date of the measure affecting their property, rights, and interests until the day of the entry into force of the present Agreement.

Article 9

The Government of the United Arab Republic will pay an indemnity to persons fulfilling the conditions stated in Article 8 above, whose property, rights, and interests have been affected by nationalization measures, or by other measures of legal confiscation, of whatever nature they might be, which were taken by the United Arab Republic between 22 August 1958, and the date of the entry into force of this Agreement.

. . . .

TITLE III

GENERAL TERMS

Article 17

A mixed commission is responsible for applying this Agreement. It will take the measures necessary for assuring a satisfactory application of the terms of the Agreement and of the agreements of 22 August 1958. It may, notably, should the need arise, recommend to the two governments other means of utilizing the accounts set forth in this Agreement.

It will meet upon the request of one or the other of the two governments.

Article 18

The application of terms set forth in this Agreement constitutes a definitive settlement of the problems caused by all the confiscatory measures of law mentioned in this Agreement. Consequently, the French Government will not intervene in behalf of its nationals who shall have benefited from it.

Article 19

This Agreement, the protocol and the letters which are annexed to it and which are an integral part of it, are ratified or approved according to the constitutional procedures in effect in each of the two countries. They will go into effect on the date of the exchange of notes attesting to the execution of the required formalities in each of the two countries.

Done in two copies at Paris, 28 July 1966.

PROTOCOL
ANNEX TO THE AGREEMENT

Article 1

The authorities of the United Arab Republic will allow to benefit from the terms of the agreements of 22 August 1958, and of 5 November 1964, as well as those of the 28 July 1966 agreement and of this Protocol, the French nationals who have made demands for restoration of sequestration at a date after that fixed by the effective texts, with the reservation that:

(a) The same demands have been presented before 1 January 1966;

(b) If the property owner cannot go through the necessary procedures and formalities himself, a proxy has been designated within 30 days after the entry into force of the agreement of 28 July 1966.[7]

(c) All documents necessary under the rules currently in effect have been handed over to the general sequestration authority within 90 days following the date on which the sequestration authority has requested them.

As far as the simplified procedure applicable to transferable securities is concerned, only the conditions mentioned in paragraphs (a) and (c) above are required.

Consequently, the property, rights, and interests of persons mentioned above will be liquidated according to Article 4 of the agreement of 28 July 1966.

Article 2

French nationals who have presented, in good order, a demand for restoration of sequestration, but whose estates must be liquidated in accordance with the terms of Article 4 of the agreement of 28 July 1966, for having failed to carry out the necessary procedures and formalities with the proper offices of the United Arab Republic, have the right to contest the decision of liquidation concerning them according to the procedures below:

The general sequestration authority will notify the French diplomatic representatives in the United Arab Republic, as soon as the above-mentioned agreement enters into force, of the lists of French nationals whose estates he intends to liquidate, as well as of all the means he has of identifying and locating these persons. The competent French offices will transmit this notification to the interested parties. Within 30 days following the receipt of this notification by the addressees, the owners or

---

[7] The official French text includes the following footnote: "Persons with French nationality on 28 July 1966, fulfilling the conditions set forth in the present Convention and not having a proxy in Egypt, are invited to contact the *Service des Biens et Intérêts Privés*, Ministry of Foreign Affairs, 80, Rue de Lille, Paris (7e)."

their proxies must address to the general sequestration authority a request for exemption from liquidation accompanied by all justifications. Requests refused by the sequestration authority or upon which it makes no decision within 30 days after the receipt of the request are submitted to the mixed commission mentioned in Article 19 of the said agreement, which will make decisions without appeal during the 2 months of its seisin.

In any case, the estates whose liquidation is not contested by the interested parties within 6 months after the effective date of the said agreement will be subject to the terms of Article 4.

.   .   .   .

Article 5

The competent authorities of the United Arab Republic will deliver, within 30 days of the presentation of the request, the certificate of non-residence requested by a French national, or, in the name of this latter, by a proxy.

The same will hold true if the claimant, having left the territory of the United Arab Republic without having obtained a definite exit visa, declares his intention to give up his residence and asks for the drawing up of a non-residence certificate, even before the expiration of the six-month time limit at the end of which his residence automatically expires.

.   .   .   .

Article 9

The total of annuities due to French nationals by right of the transfer of farmland will be paid before 1 October 1967.

The value of buildings, livestock, machinery, and crops existing on the farmland thus transferred will be estimated in the shortest possible time. The settlement of indemnities due by right of the transfer of these items will be carried out before 1 October 1968.

In the event the French nationals would not be able to remit to the general sequestration authority the property titles themselves, they will furnish to the former, so as to substantiate their claim, all details they can provide to help specify the location and the boundaries of the lands they owned, and notably all useful information about the conditions under which they acquired them. To do this, they will have a six-month period beginning with the entry into force of the agreement of 28 July 1966.

Article 10

For the application of the terms in Article 3 of the 28 July 1966 agreement, the general sequestration authority will notify the interested creditor parties of the indemnities still due them, with the precise indication, for each beneficiary, of the amount with which he must be credited at each due date, and, if necessary, of the proxy authorized to receive the payments.

This notification will be communicated as well to the interested parties or to their proxies. These latter will receive their payments, on the due dates, upon sight of the notification of liberation, in accordance with the contract of transfer concluded between the sequestration authority and the creditor, and without having to furnish new justification.

Article 11

French nationals who, at the date of the entry into force of the agreement of 28 July 1966, did not have this status on 22 August 1958, can benefit from the terms in the general agreement of 22 August 1958, to the extent their property, rights, and interests were placed under sequestration by applying Proclamation No. 5 of 1 November 1956, by nature of their special protected relationship with France.

The terms of the agreement on transfers of the same date apply to them only if they have established permanent residence in France since their departure from the United Arab Republic and until the entry into force of the agreement of 28 July 1966.

The competent French authorities will deliver, if necessary, the necessary attestations to the interested parties.

Article 12

Financial establishments other than Egyptian or French will be permitted to utilize the so-called simplified procedure to obtain restoration of sequestration for their clients who are French nationals and to benefit from the terms of the agreement of 5 November 1964 and of the agreement of 28 July 1966.

They must have addressed their requests to their correspondents in the United Arab Republic no more than 90 days after the date of the entry into force of the said agreement.

Article 13

Companies which are legally neither French nor Egyptian, but the majority of whose capital is held by French nationals, can benefit, with respect to their property, rights, and interests on United Arab Republic territory and put under sequestration by Proclamation No. 5 of 1 November 1956, from the terms of the agreements of 22 August 1958, and of 5 November 1964, and of the agreement of 28 July 1966.

They must have addressed their necessary requests to the competent

authorities of the United Arab Republic no more than 90 days after the
date of the entry into force of the agreement of 28 July 1966.

. . . .

Done in two copies, at Paris, 28 July 1966.

THE 1950 HUNGARIAN ACCORD[8]

The French Government and the Hungarian Government, desirous of
settling definitively the question of the indemnification of French nationals whose property, rights, and interests in Hungary have been
affected by nationalization, expropriation, or other restrictive measures
of a similar character taken by the Hungarian Government, and that of
obligations incumbent upon Hungary by virtue of the stipulations of
Articles 24 and 26 of the Treaty of Peace, taking into account the principles of the protocol of 19 February 1948 relating to these matters, have
agreed to the following provisions:

Article 1

The Hungarian Government shall pay to the French Government, as
a comprehensive lump sum indemnity and without detailed examinations
of particular instances:

On the one hand, the equivalent in French francs of the sum of U.S.
$914,285.

On the other hand, the sum of 2,000,000 forints.

Article 2

The equivalent in French francs of the sum of U.S. $914,285, provided
in the preceding article, shall be paid by the Hungarian Government to
the French Government into an account which the latter shall have
established at the Bank of France, in five annual instalments, the first
to be paid within a period of three months from the date of the signing
of the present Agreement, and according to the following table:

> 1st annuity: U.S. $211,428
> 2nd annuity: U.S. $182,857
> 3rd annuity: U.S. $182,857
> 4th annuity: U.S. $182,857
> 5th annuity: U.S. $154,286

The sum of 2,000,000 forints shall be paid by the Hungarian Govern-

8 Decree No. 52–1079 of September 23, 1952, [1952] J.O. 9260.

ment to the French Legation in Budapest upon the signing of the present Agreement.

Article 3

Considered as French claims, for the purposes of the present Agreement, shall be claims due to the measures or based upon the provisions set forth in the preamble, whether emanating from the French State or directly or indirectly from French natural or juridical persons who possessed French nationality at the moment their rights to indemnification arose, without distinction whether the claims were presented to the French Government, the Hungarian Government, or to an auxiliary agency of those governments, or whether the claims have not yet been presented.

Article 4

The full payment of the sums mentioned in Article 1 above shall discharge, insofar as French claimants are concerned, both the Hungarian State and all Hungarian natural and juridical persons.

Conditional upon this payment and subject to the provisions of Article 5, the French Government, acting in the name of its nationals, guarantees the Hungarian Government and all Hungarian natural and juridical persons against any claims defined in Article 3 above.

Article 5

The present Agreement does not apply to the financial questions referred to in the agreements of 29 December 1949, nor to claims which may arise subsequent to its signature.

Article 6

The sums mentioned in Article 1 above are free and clear of all liens and obligations whatever, which, for whatever reason, are a charge upon the above-mentioned properties and interests.

Article 7

The distribution of the comprehensive lump sum indemnity among the interested parties lies within the sole competence of the French Government and does not engage the responsibility of the Hungarian State, nor of Hungarian natural or juridical persons.

Article 8

The return of loans and advances of whatever kind, of movable or immovable property, previously granted by Hungary on account of the above-mentioned claims, cannot under any circumstance be demanded, and they shall become the property of their holders upon the signing of the present Agreement. Interests or other charges to which these loans or advances may be subject shall be annulled upon the signing of the present Agreement.

Article 9

If the commercial treaty between the two countries should not be renewed, the two governments shall draw up, by mutual consent, a list of commodities to be exported by Hungary to France, in order to settle still outstanding accounts.

Article 10

The present Agreement shall enter into force upon a date fixed by mutual agreement between the two governments.

Done at Paris, in two copies, 12 June 1950.

ANNEX LETTER No. I[9]

Mister Lajor Kadar,
President of the Hungarian Delegation

Mister President,

With reference to the agreement signed this day, relative to certain French interests in Hungary and to the execution of certain clauses of the Treaty of Peace of 1947, I have the honor to inform you of the following:

The French Government does not consider as French claims, for the purposes of the present Agreement, claims of the same nature as those defined in Article 3 of the agreement preceding which might be formulated by French nationals other than those designated in the same article, and agrees not to present or maintain any claim of this nature.

Please accept, Mister President, the assurances of my high consideration.

Done at Paris, 12 June 1950.

HERVÉ ALPHAND

ANNEX LETTER No. II[10]

Mister Lajor Kadar
President of the Hungarian Delegation

Mister President,

With reference to the agreement signed this day relative to certain French interests in Hungary and to the execution of certain clauses of the Treaty of Peace, and notably Article X of said Treaty, I have the honor to inform you as follows:

The date of the entry into force of the agreement preceding established by mutual consent by the two governments, shall be the date of approval of the agreement by the French Government.

[9] Confirmatory reply omitted.
[10] Confirmatory reply omitted.

The first payment should be effectuated within the time limits set forth in Article 2 of the Agreement if the Agreement has entered into force before the expiration of the time limits, and otherwise it should be effectuated within 15 days after the date of the entry into force.

I would be very grateful if you would confirm the agreement of your government with the above.

Please accept, Mister President, the assurances of my high consideration. Done at Paris, 12 June 1950.

HERVÉ ALPHAND

ANNEX LETTER No. III[11]

Mister Lajor Kadar
President of the Hungarian Delegation

Mister President,

You have asked me to stipulate that Article 8 of the agreement signed this day should be interpreted as designating notably movables and immovables actually at the disposition of the French Legation in Hungary (Landway utca 27 and Csaba utca 6).

I have the honor to accept this stipulation.

Please accept, Mister President, the assurances of my high consideration.

HERVÉ ALPHAND

THE 1965 HUNGARIAN ACCORD[12]

The French Government and the Hungarian Government, desirous of settling the financial claims outstanding between the two countries and relating to French property, rights, and interests affected by measures of nationalization, expropriation, or of restriction of a similar character taken by the Hungarian Government and not covered by the Franco-Hungarian Agreement of 12 June 1950, have agreed as follows:

Art. 1—Considered as settled by the terms of the present Agreement are all claims not covered by the Franco-Hungarian Agreement of 12 June 1950 and resulting from Hungarian measures of nationalization, expropriation, and other measures of similarly restrictive character having affected, until the date of the present Agreement, the property, rights, and interests in Hungary of the French State and of natural or juridical persons having French nationality on the date that these measures have been taken and on the date of the signature of the present Agreement.

[11] Confirmatory reply omitted.
[12] Decree No. 65–589 of July 15, 1965, [1965] J.O. 6308.

Art. 2—The Hungarian Government shall pay to the French Government as a comprehensive lump sum indemnity, the sum of 1,150,000 francs. It shall acquit itself of this amount to the French Government in three instalments which shall be effected commencing from the signature of the present Agreement;

The first, of 350,000 francs, two months after this signature;

The second and third, of 400,000 francs each, respectively, 8 months and 14 months after this signature.

Art. 3—The complete payment to the French Government of the sum quoted in Article 2 hereinabove, shall discharge the Hungarian Government as well as, to the extent pertinent, all Hungarian natural and juridical persons from their obligations toward the French State or French natural or juridical persons connected with the French property, rights, and interests referred to in the present Agreement.

The French Government undertakes neither to espouse nor support against the Hungarian Government nor, to the extent pertinent, against any Hungarian natural or juridical person from the date of the signature of the present Agreement, any demand relating to claims or debts covered by the provisions of Article 1 hereinabove.

Art. 4—The distribution of the indemnity referred to in Article 2 hereinabove among the various interested French claimants falls within the sole competence of the French Government and shall in no way engage the responsibility of the Hungarian State nor that of Hungarian natural or juridical persons.

Art. 5—The present Agreement enters into force on the date of its signature.

Done at Budapest, 14 May 1965, in two copies, in the French and Hungarian languages, the two texts being equally official.

THE 1948 POLISH ACCORD[13]

The Government of the Polish Republic and the Government of the French Republic, in order to fix the terms of a comprehensive lump sum indemnification of French interests affected by the Polish law of 3 January 1946 on nationalizations, have agreed to the following provisions:

Article 1

The French Government acts in the name of the French nationals, whether natural or persons designated in Article 4 below.

[13] Decree No. 51–1288 of November 7, 1951, [1951] J.O. 11190. Attached "Annexe" omitted.

Article 2

The present Agreement establishes a comprehensive lump sum indemnity due from Poland on account of the nationalization of enterprises situated within its present frontiers, all French interests in said enterprises being thereby extinguished.

It is understood that the nationalization of these enterprises refers exclusively to property situated within the actual limits of Poland and in no way affects the existence of juridical persons to whom these properties belong, in accordance with the law of 3 January 1946.

Article 3

The indemnification of interests affected by the nationalization law of 3 January 1946 and designated in Article 4 below shall be carried out by the delivery of a quantity of coal by the Polish Government into the hands of the French Government or any French organism designated by it, according to the terms fixed in Article 7.

This delivery shall release the Polish Government insofar as the interested parties are concerned, and subject to this delivery the French Government, acting in the name of French nationals, guarantees the Polish Government against any further claims on the part of these latter.

The French Government declares that the creditors of the natural and juridical persons enumerated in Article 4 shall be indemnified according to the terms of the respective laws now in force. But this undertaking of the French Government as well as the obligations of the debtors does not extend to debts arising after the dispossession of their enterprises.

These same natural and juridical persons may pursue the recovery of their debt claims in Poland, according to law currently in force, against private individuals, except for establishments and enterprises of all sorts belonging to the State and to municipalities.

Article 4

The payment of this comprehensive lump sum shall be deemed to settle all indemnities for nationalization due:

(a) to natural persons of French nationality;

(b) to French companies;

(c) to companies under French control;

(d) to French natural or juridical persons having an interest, even a minority interest, in all other companies or companies under other control.

However, the French Government shall under no circumstances be required to indemnify Polish shareholders of French companies or of companies under French control.

Also considered as settled are the indemnities due:

1. to the Compagnie franco-polonaise des chemins de fer for the withdrawal of its concession as well as for the nationalized assets, but exclusive of the debts of this company guaranteed by the Polish State;

2. to the International Ship-Building Company de Gdansk for the French share in this company and concession;

3. to the Société Skarboferm for the final termination of its concession;

4. to the Société Hohenlohe (Zaklady Hohenlohe Sp. Akc.) for the French share in this company and all other French rights.

Article 5

The distribution of the comprehensive lump sum indemnity among the interested parties shall be within the sole competence of the French Government.

Article 6

The comprehensive lump sum indemnity is fixed at 3,800,000 tons of high-grade coal f.o.b. Polish ports, of which 72% shall be high-grade coal larger than 30 mm, and 28% from 10 to 33 mm.

The quantities to be supplied and the conditions of delivery may be altered from year to year with the agreement of the two parties, providing that the coal delivered each year, f.o.b. Polish ports, represents the equivalent in value of the coal to be delivered during the year in question and mentioned below.

The total quantity representing the entire indemnity to be paid by the Polish Government shall be delivered as follows:

(a) Assuming the opening by France in 1948, of credits provided in the agreements and protocols signed concurrently with the present Agreement usable by Poland for a sum actually corresponding to the value of a million tons, the delivery of two million tons will take place according to the table on page 214:

(b) New negotiations shall take place as soon as possible between the two governments to enable delivery of the remaining 1.8 million tons.

All annual deliveries must be taken into account in future plans for importing Polish coal into France.

Article 7

In order to facilitate the indemnity due to the interested parties, the Polish Government will issue, within three months following the entry into force of this Agreement, bonds made out for amounts of coal corresponding to the amounts shown in Article 6.

These bonds shall be handed over to the organism designated by the French Government at the time of their issue, and shall be restored to the Polish Government when the equivalent deliveries are made under the present Agreement.

| | THOUSANDS OF TONS OF COAL | |
YEARS	Over 30 mm	From 10 to 30 mm
1951	96	37
1952	96	37
1953	96	37
1954	96	37
1955	96	37
1956	144	56
1957	144	56
1958	144	56
1959	144	56
1960	144	56
1961	48	19
1962	48	19
1963	48	19
1964	48	19
1965	48	19
	1,440	560

Article 8

A table annexed to the present Agreement enumerates the enterprises presently known and referred to in Article 4, paragraph 1 of the present Agreement.

This enumeration is suggestive only and in no way modifies the principles set forth in Article 2 and Article 4, paragraphs 1 and 3.

Article 9

Differences concerning the interpretation or application of the present Agreement shall be submitted by either party to a conciliation body composed of an equal number of one or more Polish members, and one or more French members.

If the conciliation body does not reach an agreement, the two governments shall examine the dispute with a view to finding a solution satisfactory to both parties. The two governments shall designate, if such solution cannot be found, an arbitration commission composed of a delegate from each party and a chairman. The chairman, who must be neither a Polish subject nor a French subject, shall be coopted by mutual agreement of the two delegates.

Article 10

The date of the entry into force of the present Agreement shall be the date of signature of the contract detailing the protocol concerning the delivery of French investment goods against Polish coal.

Paris, 19 March 1948.

PROTOCOL OF APPLICATION OF THE AGREEMENT OF 19 MARCH 1948
ON THE INDEMNIFICATION BY POLAND OF FRENCH INTERESTS
AFFECTED BY THE POLISH LAW OF 3 JANUARY 1946
ON NATIONALIZATIONS[14]

The Government of the French Republic and the Government of the Polish Republic are in agreement that the Agreement of 19 March 1948 on the indemnification by Poland of French interests affected by the Polish Law of 3 January 1946 on nationalizations includes the indemnification of French interests affected as of 19 March 1948 by:

1. agrarian and forestry reform;
2. the municipalization of Warsaw terrains;
3. all other measures restrictive of the right of property.

Paris, 7 September 1951.

THE 1959 ROMANIAN ACCORD[15]

The Government of the French Republic and the Government of the Romanian Peoples' Republic, desiring to settle definitively the financial problems described in the present Agreement and pending between the two countries, and to favor the development of economic relations, have agreed as follows:

Article 1

The Romanian Government shall pay to the French Government the equivalent in French francs of U.S. $21,000,000 as comprehensive lump sum indemnification for:

(a) The property, rights, and interests of the French State and of French natural and juridical persons affected by Romanian measures of nationalization, expropriation, requisition, and other similarly restrictive measures;

---

[14] Decree No. 57–892 of July 26, 1957, [1957] J.O. 7779, at 7780 (the 1951 Polish Protocol).

[15] Decree No. 59–439 of March 11, 1959, [1959] J.O. 3287. Two "Protocoles d'Application" and Exchange of Letters No. 2 omitted.

(b) The obligations due the French State and French natural and juridical persons which devolve upon the Romanian State pursuant to Articles 23 and 24 of the Treaty of Peace of 10 February 1947 between Romania and the Allied and Associated Powers;

(c) The obligations of the loans described in Article 1 of the Protocol of Application No. 1 which forms an integral part of the present Agreement;

(d) The petroleum bonds issued by the Romanian State pursuant to the agreements of 30 September and 4 March 1943.

Article 2

The complete payment of the sum mentioned in Article 1 shall have, with respect to the holders of the French interests defined in the same article, a liberating effect for the Romanian State as well as for all Romanian natural or juridical persons considered as successors to the original owners according to Romanian legislation.

Upon the application of the present Agreement, the Romanian State and Romanian natural or juridical persons shall be released of all obligations vis-à-vis the French interests for the claims described in Article 1 hereinabove.

Article 3

The indemnification provided for in the present Agreement shall constitute compensation for the rights of the French State and for French natural or juridical persons, indemnified as owners, shareholders, creditors, etc., for their property, rights, and interests, in accordance with Article 1 hereinabove.

On the other hand, the French State and these same French natural or juridical persons shall be released vis-à-vis the Romanian State and Romanian natural or juridical persons who have succeeded to all their obligations concerning the property, rights, and interests for which they shall be indemnified.

Article 4

All rights pertaining to the loan obligations set forth in Article 1, paragraph (c), hereinabove, and defined in Article 1 of the Protocol of Application No. I shall be considered as liquidated by the payment of the redemption indemnity provided for in Article 1 of the present Agreement.

The collection by a French holder of all or part of the sums due him as indemnity pursuant to Article 1 hereinabove constitutes acceptance of the present Agreement.

The French Government shall support no possible claims of French holders who refuse the benefit of the present Agreement.

Article 5

The two governments, taking into account the proceeds of the levy effectuated by the application of the Franco-Romanian financial protocol of 21 December 1954 and amounting as of 31 December 1958 to U.S. $2,853,598, note that the indemnity provided for in Article 1 of the present Agreement still to be placed at the disposal of the French Government is equal to the equivalent in francs of U.S. $18,146,402.

Article 6

The French Government shall proceed, upon the entry into force of the present Agreement, to the freeing of all Romanian assets in France which have been previously affected, at the demand of the French Government, by protective measures and which continue to be so affected.

Article 7

The Romanian Government, in order to cover the balance set forth in Article 5 hereinabove, shall place at the disposal of the French Government, after the entry into force of the present Agreement, by way of a first settlement, according to the measures provided for in the Protocol of Application No. II, which forms an integral part of the Agreement:

1. Funds in gold, currency and francs deposited in French banks to service the Romanian exterior public debt, on condition that the French Government pay the equivalent in francs to French holders of the title-deeds mentioned in Article 1, paragraph (c), of the present Agreement;

2. Other deposits of the Romanian State and of the former National Bank of Romania in French banks and previously blocked at the demand of the French Government, so that they be utilized, under the present Agreement, for purposes of indemnification of the claimants enumerated in Article 1 hereinabove;

3. The equivalent in French francs of the sum of U.S. $1,000,000.

Article 8

For the execution of the present Agreement, the Bank of France shall open in the name of the State Bank of the Romanian Peoples' Republic, on 1 April 1959, a non-interest-bearing special account in French francs entitled "French financial credits—Franco-Romanian Agreement of 9 February 1959."

Article 9

The account mentioned in Article 8 hereinabove shall be maintained to the amount of the balance of the indemnity provided for in Article 1 of the present Agreement remaining unpaid on 1 April 1959:

1. By the proceeds from an 8% levy on payment received for merchandise exported by the Romanian Peoples' Republic within the framework of the Franco-Romanian payment agreement in force;

2. By the excess of funds and deposits in currency and francs in Article 7, paragraphs 1 and 2 hereinabove, which might be established by a possible common agreement after 31 March 1959.

Article 10

The available funds from the account "French financial credits— Franco-Romanian Agreement of 9 February 1959" shall be placed quarterly at the disposal of the French Government on 31 March, 30 June, 30 September, and 31 December of each year up to the amount of the settlement of the indemnity provided for in Article 1.

Article 11

The sum mentioned in Article 1 of the present Agreement shall be distributed by the French Government as follows:

(a) French Public Treasury, by way of its participation in former Romanian businesses and for ownership of the petroleum bonds: 3%;

(b) French natural or juridical persons affected by measures of nationalization, expropriation, requisition or other similar restrictive measures and claimants of war damages or restitution: 37%;

(c) French holders of the loans mentioned in Article 1, paragraph (c), and defined in Article 1 of the Protocol of Application No. I: 60%.

The distribution among the different claimants shall fall within the sole competence of the French Government and engages in no way the responsibility of the Romanian Government.

Article 12

The present Agreement is not applicable to cases of the same nature as those mentioned in Article 1 of the present Agreement which might arise after its signature.

Article 13

For purposes of executing the present Agreement, the two governments shall provide each other, to the extent possible, with all necessary information.

Article 14

All disputes relating to the interpretation or the application of the present Agreement shall be settled by common agreement between the two governments.

Article 15

The present Agreement shall enter into force on the date of its signature.

In witness whereof, the undersigned, duly authorized by their respective governments, have signed the present Agreement and have affixed their seals to it.

Done at Bucharest, 9 February 1959, in two copies in the French language and in the Romanian language, the two texts being official.

EXCHANGE OF LETTERS NO. 1[16]

The President
of the French Delegation

Bucharest, 9 February 1959
To the President of the Romanian
Delegation, Bucharest

Mister President,

The intention of the French Government is to consider as having the right to lay claim to the benefit of the provisions of Article 1, paragraph (a) of the agreement signed this day only natural and juridical persons having enjoyed and enjoying French nationality at the date the measures restrictive of their rights were taken as well as at the date of signature of the Agreement.

I would be much obliged to you if you would advise me that the Romanian Government has taken note of this interpretation.

Please accept, Mister President, the assurances of my high consideration.

JEAN DECIRY

EXCHANGE OF LETTERS NO. 3[17]

The President
of the French Delegation

Bucharest, 9 February 1959
To the President of the Romanian
Delegation, Bucharest

Mister President,

I have the honor to inform you of the manner in which the French Government intends to avail itself of the provisions of Article 13 of the agreement signed this day.

16 Confirmatory reply omitted.
17 Confirmatory reply omitted.

A French commission to distribute the indemnity provided for in Article 1 shall be instituted by the French Government. This commission shall receive the claims of the claimants. In order to evaluate these, often the commission shall have to ask the French Legation in Bucharest to furnish it with information on the physical and juridical situation of the property and interests for which indemnification shall be sought as well as possibly documentation permitting evaluation of them.

It is this information and this documentation that the French Legation in Bucharest shall thus be called upon to request of the Romanian authorities, through the intermediary of the Minister of Foreign Affairs.

I would be obliged to you to confirm to me that this information and this documentation shall be furnished to the French Legation in Bucharest to the fullest extent possible.

Please accept, Mister President, the assurances of my high consideration.

JEAN DECIRY

THE 1951 YUGOSLAV ACCORD[18]

The Government of the French Republic and the Government of the Federal Peoples' Republic of Yugoslavia, in order to establish procedures for a comprehensive lump sum indemnification for French property, rights, and interests in Yugoslavia which were affected by Yugoslav measures of nationalization, or expropriation, or other restrictive measures of a similar nature, have agreed as follows:

Article 1

As a comprehensive lump sum indemnity on account of Yugoslav measures of nationalization, expropriation, or of any other restrictive measure of similar character having affected French property, rights, and interests in Yugoslavia, the Yugoslav Government shall pay to the French Government the countervalue in [French] francs of U.S. $15,000,000.

The sum mentioned in the preceding paragraph shall be paid within ten years in accordance with the procedures established in the additional protocol annexed to the present Agreement, of which it is an integral part.

Article 2

Considered as settled under the terms of the present Agreement are all those claims which have arisen from Yugoslav measures of nationalization or expropriation or from other restrictive measures of similar charac-

---

[18] Decree No. 53–653 of July 24, 1953, [1953] J.O. 6723. "Protocole Additionnel," "Tableau Annexe," "Protocole Financier," "Procès-Verbal," and three special agreements omitted.

ter having affected the property, rights, and interests in Yugoslavia of French natural or juridical persons, having that status at the time when those measures were taken and at the time of the signing of the present Agreement, including all French interests in Yugoslav enterprises.

Moreover, the French Government shall under no circumstance have to indemnify Yugoslav stockholders of French companies.

A table annexed to the present Agreement, being only informational in character, enumerates the claims known at this time and referred to by the present Article.

The French Government agrees not to espouse or support any claim emanating from other natural or juridical persons and based on Yugoslav measures referred to in the present Article.

Article 3

The complete payment of the sum mentioned in Article 1 above shall, insofar as the holders of the French interests defined in Article 2 are concerned, discharge the Yugoslav State as well as all Yugoslav institutions or natural and juridical persons considered as successors-in-interest of the original owners under Yugoslav law.

From the entry into force of the present Agreement and subject to its execution in accordance with the procedures established between the parties, the Yugoslav State, as well as all Yugoslav institutions and natural or juridical persons, shall be free from any claim on the part of any interested French party.

Article 4

The French Government shall obtain from the interested parties all documents, deeds and certificates relating to the property, rights, and interests indemnified under the terms of the present Agreement.

It agrees to keep these documents and to turn them over to the Yugoslav Government after the settlement of the claims to which they refer and, at the latest, after the complete payment of the sum mentioned in Article 2 above.

Article 5

Under the conditions mentioned in Article 3:

1. French natural and juridical persons subject to French law which have been affected by measures of nationalization, expropriation, or other restrictive measures of similar character in Yugoslavia, shall be compensated for the debts they hold in Yugoslavia and shall be discharged from all debts which they owe in that country. The debts they own and owe concerning natural and juridical persons having their residence outside Yugoslavia shall remain uneffected;

2. French natural or juridical persons holding majority participation in companies subject to Yugoslav law having been affected by measures of nationalization, expropriation, or other restrictive measures of similar character shall be compensated for the debt claims they hold against these companies, and are discharged from all obligations concerning them;

3. French natural or juridical persons holding credits against companies subject to Yugoslav law with French majority participation having been affected by measures of nationalization, expropriation, or other restrictive measures of similar character shall be indemnified by sharing in the comprehensive lump sum indemnity mentioned in Article 1 and under the same conditions as the other beneficiaries of this indemnity;

4. French natural or juridical persons owning participating interests in companies subject to Yugoslav law which have been affected by measures of nationalization, expropriation, or other restrictive measures of similar character have no rights over creditor claims that these companies may own outside France and cannot be held liable for obligations that these companies may have outside France.

Companies subject to Yugoslav law and having French majority participation waive all rights concerning claims that they may hold against natural or juridical persons residing in France. These creditor claims shall be recovered for the accounts of the beneficiaries mentioned in Article 2.

Article 6

The distribution of the comprehensive lump sum indemnity among the interested parties falls within the sole competence of the French Government and imposes no liability either on the Yugoslav State or on Yugoslav institutions or natural or juridical persons.

Article 7

French claims resulting from Yugoslav measures taken after the signing of the present Agreement are not covered by the provisions of said Agreement.

Article 8

For the purpose of the execution of the present Agreement the two governments shall furnish each other with all necessary aid and information.

Article 9

Any difficulty relating to the interpretation or the application of the present Agreement shall be settled by agreement between the two governments.

Article 10

The present Agreement shall be ratified or approved in accordance with the constitutional rules in force in each country.

Minutes of the exchange of the instruments of ratification or approval shall be established.

The date of these minutes shall be the date the present Agreement enters into force.

Done at Paris, in two copies, 14 April 1951.

THE 1963 YUGOSLAV ACCORD[19]

The Government of the French Republic and the Government of the Federal Peoples' Republic of Yugoslavia, in order to fix the terms of a comprehensive lump sum indemnification for French property, rights, and interests nationalized in Yugoslavia, not covered by the agreement between France and Yugoslavia of 14 April 1951 on the indemnification of French interests nationalized in Yugoslavia, have agreed to the following provisions:

Article 1

As comprehensive lump sum indemnity, the Yugoslav Government shall pay to the French Government the equivalent in French francs of the sum of 200,000 dollars.

The sum mentioned in the paragraph hereinabove shall be paid in two installments; the payment of the first installment shall take place on 15 July 1963 and the second on 15 July 1964.

Article 2

Considered as settled by the terms of the present Agreement are all claims not covered by the agreement of 14 April 1951 and resulting from Yugoslav measures of nationalization, expropriation, and other measures of similar restrictive character having affected, up to the date of the present Agreement, property, rights, and interests in Yugoslavia or French participation in enterprises in Yugoslavia, properties of French natural or juridical persons, having this status at the date when these measures were taken and at the date of the signature of the present Agreement.

Also considered as settled by the terms of the present Agreement are all creditor claims prior to 15 May 1945 against Yugoslav natural or juridical persons or the Yugoslav State held by French natural or juridical persons having this status at that date and at the date of the signature of the present Agreement.

Article 3

The French Government undertakes neither to present nor to maintain against the Yugoslav Government as well as against all Yugoslav natural or juridical persons, after the date of the signature of the present Agree-

[19] Decree No. 64–239 of March 13, 1964, [1964] J.O.

ment, any demand relating to the claims or debts covered by the provisions of the two paragraphs of Article 2 hereinabove which might be presented after that date by French nationals.

This undertaking of the French Government applies likewise to claims which might be presented by nationals who did not have the status of French citizenship at the date the Yugoslav measures mentioned in Article 2 (paragraph 1) of the present Agreement took place or to those to which this status shall be accorded after the date of the signature of the present Agreement. The same undertaking applies to claims which might be presented as creditor claims under Article 2 (paragraph 2) of the present Agreement by persons who did not have the status of French citizenship on 15 May 1945.

Article 4

Also applicable to the present Agreement *mutatis mutandis* and as needed are the provisions of Articles 3 to 9 inclusive of the French-Yugoslav Agreement of 14 April 1951.

In any event, insofar as concerns the application of paragraph 1 of Article 5 of the said agreement, the debts from which the beneficiaries of the present Agreement are released are exclusively those which have a direct connection with the property, rights, and interests mentioned in the present Agreement.

Article 5

The present Agreement shall enter into force as soon as it is approved according to the constitutional rules in force in each of the two countries.

Done at Paris, 12 July 1963, in two copies.

Index

Accords. *See* Lump sum settlements; "Settlement Agreements"

"Acquired rights" doctrine, 98

Administrative distribution: French repugnance for, 18; as means for paying "ordinary" debt claims, 21, 24–25, 43, 152–54 *passim*, 172; inoperative in British practice, 21; as means for paying stockholder claims, 25, 167–68

Administrators. *See* Claimants, eligibility of

Affiliated nationals. *See* Claimants, eligibility of; Nationality

Algeria, 28, 107n, 118n, 189

Analytical positivism. *See* Jurisprudence

Anti-Semitic legislation: decisions concerning, 132, 136, 150

Anton, A.E., 52n, 53n, 165n

Antonescu, Ion, 100n

"Application Laws": defined, 45n. *See also* "Statutory Instruments"

Arbitral tribunals, *ad hoc. See* Mixed claims commissions

Ardagh, John, 6n, 33n, 185n

Assemblée Nationale: debate on German (French-owned) property transfer, 54n. *See also* German (French-owned) property; Parliament

Assignees. *See* Claimants, eligibility of; Nationality

Association Nationale des Porteurs Français de Valeurs Mobilières: described, 14n; similar to British Council of Foreign Bondholders, 14n, 24; responsible for certain debt claims distributions, 43n; authorized to represent claimants, 66; mentioned, 183n

Association Nationale des Sinistrés Français de Pologne, 66

Association Pour la Sauvegarde et l'Expansion des Biens et Intérêts Français à l'Étranger: described, 13n; periodical of, 20n; participation in negotiation of 1948 Polish Accord, 35n; authorized to represent claimants, 66; mentioned, 17n, 183n

Associations: compensability of non-stock interests in, 167–71; mentioned, 169. *See also* Claimants, eligibility of

Assumption of risk, 118

Attribution of State responsibility: for losses caused by third countries, 99–100; for losses caused by minor officials, 100–01; for losses caused by private persons, 101–02; policy considerations concerning, 102

Australia, 21n

Austria, 22n

Austro-Hungary, 11n

Axis Powers: responsibility for war damage claims, 36, 96–100 *passim*, 106–16. *See also* Peace Treaties (1947); War damage claims

Baldus, David C., 114n

Barcelona Traction Case (I.C.J.), 92n, 170

225

228   INTERNATIONAL CLAIMS

Commission spéciale pour l'indemnisa-tion des dommages de guerre fran-çais à l'étranger, 4n
Community property (*communauté de biens*). *See* Property
Compagnie Universale du Canal Mari-time de Suez: nationalization of, 15, 28; as co-negotiator, 15n
Companies (*sociétés*). *See* individual headings
Compensation: mere promise of, in 1948 Czech Accord, 19–20; "prompt, adequate, and effective" rule of, diplomatically challenged, 30–33; as non-interest-bearing installments, 31; in kind, 32–33; not supple-mented by French appropriations, 35; percentage of, received by claim-ants, 178–79; criteria for measur-ing, 180–81; nonpayment of, for *de minimis* claims, 181; same for "peacetime" and "wartime" depriva-tions, 181; payment of, without in-terest, 182
—principle of: confirmed in French practice, 22–23 *passim*, 178–79; un-affected by revolutionary upheaval, 117; qualified by capacity to pay, 119
Concession agreements, revocation of: permissibility, 112–13; legal con-sequences, 113–14; policy consi-derations concerning, 114
Concessionaires. *See* Claimants, eligi-bility of; Concession agreements, revocation of
Confiscation. *See* Deprivation, strate-gies of; Wealth deprivations
Conflict of laws: and horizontal legal order, 4; as source of law for French commissions, 91; Draft Convention on, 92n; and escape devices for dis-honoring deprivative competence, 107n; as affecting the nationality of co-ownership interests, 166–67

Conseil d'État: judicial review by, 51–53, 52n, 53n, 59, 69, 184, 188; functions of, 51–53, 52n, 53n, 56, 184; described, 52n; publication and non-publication of decisions, 76n; decisions executed by French com-missions, 115n, 188; role of, in measuring damages, 180n; as check on governmental power, 184, 188. *See also* Judicial review; Decisions, non-publication of
Conseil de la République: debate on ratification of 1951 Polish Protocol, 34–35. *See also* Parliament
Constitution, 1958 French: making international agreements superior to municipal law, 39n
"Constitutive Laws": defined, 45n. *See also* "Statutory Instruments"
Contextual analysis: need for, 9
Continuity of nationality. *See* Nation-ality
Contract claims. *See* Creditor claims
Contracts, State. *See* Concession a-greements, revocation of
"Controlling Texts": defined, 40
Convention on Recognition of the Le-gal Personality of Foreign Compan-ies (*Sociétés*), Associations and Foundations, 92n
Conventions. *See* Lump sum settle-ments; "Settlement Agreements"
Corbett, Percy, 2
Cour de Cassation: as contributor to French commission membership, 46, 54; described 53n; recent pertinent decisions of, 107n, 118n. *See also* Claims commissions, French
Cour des comptes: as contributor to French commission membership, 46, 58. *See also* Claims commissions, French
Creditor claims: payable via adminis-trative distribution if "ordinary" in character, 21, 24–25, 43, 152–54

234   INTERNATIONAL CLAIMS

Policy-oriented jurisprudence. *See* Jurisprudence
Policy-oriented thinking: need for, 74–75, 190; disinterest of French commissions in, 190
Polish Accord (1948). *See* "Settlement Agreements"
Polish Protocol (1951). *See* "Settlement Agreements"
Post-settlement claims: not compensable, 153
Pre-adjudication of claims: non-existent in French practice, 61n. *See also* French practice
Pre-adjudication recoupments. *See* Deductions from awards
Preliminary examination of claims; rules governing, 63–65
Pre-registration procedures: unique to Egyptian Commission, 158–59. *See also* Egyptian Commission
Prerogative powers. *See* French Government, prerogative powers of
Presentation of claims: rules governing, 61–62
Private international law. *See* Conflict of laws
Private law, issues of: French commissions incompetent to decide, 68, 79
Procedural norms: as source of law for French commissions, 39–40; compared to substantive norms, 40
Procedure, rules of. *See* "Commission Rules"
Property: as "wealth," 12n; as referred to in the "Settlement Agreements," 160–61; as construed by the French commissions, 162; as defined in international usage, 162n
—compensation for loss of: policy considerations concerning, 160; relative to other values (including goodwill), 161–62; as corporeal wealth, 163; as incorporeal wealth, 163–78; as aleatory, 164; as *fonds de com-*

merce, 164–65; as co-ownership interests, 165–67; as community property, 166–67; as shareholder interests, 167–71; as creditor interests, 171–77; as third-party beneficial interests, 178; as usufructuary interests, 178. *See also* Claimants, eligibility of
Protected nationals. *See* Claimants, eligibility of; Nationality
Public ownership: postwar French acceptance of, 12
"Public purpose" doctrine, 103
Purpose of deprivation: as determinant of compensatory liability, 102–06

Quai d'Orsay. *See* Foreign Ministry

Racial laws. *See* Anti-Semitic legislation
Rapporteurs: reports of, 6n, 63–65; functions of, 63–64, 65–68; qualifications of, 63n; fees of, 50
Re, Edward D., 16n
Réglements de procedure. See "Commission Rules"
Reparations for Injuries Suffered in the Service of the United Nations Case (I.C.J.), 83
Répartition administrative. See Administrative distribution
Representative authority: as prerequisite for relief, 77–79. *See also* Claimants, eligibility of
Requisitions. *See* Deprivation, strategies of; Wealth deprivations
Residence (French): as exceptional prerequisite for relief, 92–94; narrowly construed by Egyptian Commission, 93–94. *See also* Claimants, eligibility of
Revolutionary change: as basis for mitigating responsibility for deprivations concurrently imposed, 117–18